T0133890

New Developments in

Biological and Chemical Terrorism Countermeasures

New Developments in
Biological and Chemical Terrorism Countermeasures

Edited by
Ronald J. Kendall
Texas Tech University
Lubbock, Texas, USA

Steven M. Presley
Texas Tech University
Lubbock, Texas, USA

Seshadri S. Ramkumar
Texas Tech University
Lubbock, Texas, USA

CRC Press
Taylor & Francis Group
Boca Raton London New York

CRC Press is an imprint of the
Taylor & Francis Group, an **informa** business

CRC Press
Taylor & Francis Group
6000 Broken Sound Parkway NW, Suite 300
Boca Raton, FL 33487-2742

First issued in paperback 2020

© 2016 by Taylor & Francis Group, LLC
CRC Press is an imprint of Taylor & Francis Group, an Informa business

No claim to original U.S. Government works

ISBN-13: 978-1-4987-4756-1 (hbk)
ISBN-13: 978-0-367-77885-9 (pbk)

This book contains information obtained from authentic and highly regarded sources. Reasonable efforts have been made to publish reliable data and information, but the author and publisher cannot assume responsibility for the validity of all materials or the consequences of their use. The authors and publishers have attempted to trace the copyright holders of all material reproduced in this publication and apologize to copyright holders if permission to publish in this form has not been obtained. If any copyright material has not been acknowledged please write and let us know so we may rectify in any future reprint.

Except as permitted under U.S. Copyright Law, no part of this book may be reprinted, reproduced, transmitted, or utilized in any form by any electronic, mechanical, or other means, now known or hereafter invented, including photocopying, microfilming, and recording, or in any information storage or retrieval system, without written permission from the publishers.

For permission to photocopy or use material electronically from this work, please access www.copyright.com (http://www.copyright.com/) or contact the Copyright Clearance Center, Inc. (CCC), 222 Rosewood Drive, Danvers, MA 01923, 978-750-8400. CCC is a not-for-profit organization that provides licenses and registration for a variety of users. For organizations that have been granted a photocopy license by the CCC, a separate system of payment has been arranged.

Trademark Notice: Product or corporate names may be trademarks or registered trademarks, and are used only for identification and explanation without intent to infringe.

Library of Congress Cataloging-in-Publication Data

New developments in biological and chemical terrorism countermeasures / editors, Ronald J. Kendall, Steven M. Presley, and Seshadri S. Ramkumar.
    pages cm
Includes bibliographical references and index.
ISBN 978-1-4987-4756-1 (alk. paper)
  1. Bioterrorism--Prevention. 2. Chemical terrorism--Prevention. 3. Emergency management. 4. Biological warfare. 5. Chemical warfare. I. Kendall, Ronald J., editor of compilation. II. Presley, Steven M., editor of compilation. III. Ramkumar, Seshadri S., editor of compilation.

HV6433.3.N49 2016
363.325'36   2015033835

Visit the Taylor & Francis Web site at
http://www.taylorandfrancis.com

and the CRC Press Web site at
http://www.crcpress.com

Contents

Preface

New Developments in Biological and Chemical Terrorism Countermeasures is offered as a new contribution advancing the state of the science of research in countermeasures to biological and chemical threats. Although the context of this book continues to be heavily focused on the United States as was done in our previous book, *Advances in Biological and Chemical Terrorism Countermeasures*, its application should be considered global in nature since we deal with global threats of terrorism daily. Biological and chemical terrorism continues to grow in the form of threats to the United States and other nations. Nowadays, there is not a day that goes by when we do not consider terrorist threats either to the United States or internationally, and we do not see this problem going away in the foreseeable future. Therefore, we believe that this book is timely and will continue to offer strategies and perspectives to assist the United States and other nations to defend themselves from terroristic threats.

Research began in 1998 at Texas Tech University to develop countermeasures against biological and chemical threat agents. Subsequently, through The Institute of Environmental and Human Health (TIEHH) at Texas Tech University, the Admiral Elmo R. Zumwalt, Jr. National Program for Countermeasures to Biological and Chemical Threats (Zumwalt Program) was commissioned to further advance the university's and its collaborators' research and development of countermeasures to biological and chemical threats. In addition to the many scientific publications and patents that the program has produced, we offered, in 2008, the book *Advances in Biological and Chemical Terrorism Countermeasures*. The current book emerged from the new information obtained through our continuous research and development in this field.

Support for this research program primarily came from the U.S. Army and particularly from the Research, Development and Engineering Command, which challenged us to develop a multidisciplinary toxicology research program to address countermeasures to biological and chemical threat agents. Indeed, *New Developments in Biological and Chemical Terrorism Countermeasures* continues to draw heavily from the funding received through the U.S. Army and incorporates other leading scientists' research and their involvement with countermeasures against biological and chemical threat agents over the past few years.

Drawing upon the research data developed on countermeasures to biological and chemical threats and literature review, this book involved many months of planning and coordination by its authors and a meeting in May 2014, in Mescalero, New Mexico, to bring all the chapters together for the book. Following the months of planning, the authors met and discussed these issues for several days to coordinate this book as it relates to new developments in countermeasures to both types of threats. Although the book does not attempt to completely implement all aspects of countermeasures to biological and chemical threats, it particularly addresses the continued research and development on this topic that has occurred through the Zumwalt Program at Texas Tech University.

The main authors (Galen P. Austin, Joe A. Fralick, Ronald J. Kendall, Steven M. Presley, Christopher J. Salice, Ernest Smith, Jia-Sheng Wang, and Richard E. Zartman) of this book participated fully, with a collegial and multidisciplinary perspective in the New Mexico meeting. Others who offered input to individual chapters are also noted as contributors, along with the main authors, even if they did not participate in the New Mexico meeting. The authors who participated in the meeting fully support the conclusions reached by the group, particularly those related to Chapter 8.

New Developments in Biological and Chemical Terrorism Countermeasures continues to evolve as a national priority issue and we envision this issue will remain before us for many years to come. This book is offered as a science-based text to improve our ability to implement countermeasures to biological and chemical terrorism.

The authors believe that this book will contribute to new developments in the science of addressing countermeasures to biological and chemical terrorism that oftentimes challenges environmental toxicologists by virtue of the potential threats that are continuing to emerge with biological and chemical threat agents and that may require more complex experimental designs to evaluate. We appreciate the opportunity to work together as a team in writing this book. The manuscript was peer-reviewed and subsequently the editors met, then approved the text, and submitted the current format for publication. We appreciate the Research, Development and Engineering Command of the U.S. Army for supporting our research and the ultimate development of this book.

Ronald J. Kendall, PhD
Editor

Acknowledgments

We gratefully acknowledge and appreciate the financial support from the U.S. Army Research, Development and Engineering Command (RDECOM) for the development of this book. In particular, we appreciate the encouragement and support from RDECOM throughout the many years of our association. They have been major supporters of our program and research efforts and have encouraged the production of this new book. A major part of the research was ultimately integrated into the context of this new book resulting from research conducted through the Admiral Elmo R. Zumwalt, Jr. National Program for Countermeasures to Biological and Chemical Threats (Zumwalt Program), which is operated through The Institute of Environmental and Human Health (TIEHH), an institute with the Texas Tech University System. The Zumwalt Program comprises and is supported by many individual investigators throughout the Texas Tech University System, whose research and written contributions to this book are greatly appreciated. We also express our sincere appreciation to the administration and support personnel at Texas Tech University, in particular Tammy Henricks and Lori Gibler, for their professionalism and dedication toward the completion of this book.

Editors

Dr. Ronald J. Kendall is a professor in the Department of Environmental Toxicology at Texas Tech University (TTU), Lubbock, Texas. He is director emeritus and founding director of The Institute of Environmental and Human Health (TIEHH), a joint venture between TTU and TTU Health Sciences Center. He is also the founding department chair of the Department of Environmental Toxicology at TTU. He graduated from the University of South Carolina with a BS. He received his MS from Clemson University and PhD from Virginia Polytechnic Institute and State University. He received a U.S. Environmental Protection Agency (USEPA) postdoctoral traineeship at the Massachusetts Institute of Technology. Dr. Kendall served on USEPA's Federal Insecticide, Fungicide, and Rodenticide Act (FIFRA) Science Advisory Panel from June 1995 to December 2002 and was appointed chairman for the period January 1999–December 2002. He also served as a member of the Endocrine Disruptor Screening and Testing Advisory Committee, USEPA. He is past-president of the Society of Environmental Toxicology and Chemistry and has been serving as an editor of the scientific journal *Environmental Toxicology and Chemistry* since 1986. He has received numerous awards, addressed the United Nations Committee on Sustainable Development, and consulted with many foreign countries on environmental issues. Dr. Kendall was awarded a Fulbright fellowship in 1991. He has published extensively, including more than 200 publications and technical articles in wildlife toxicology, and his latest book, *Wildlife Toxicology: Emerging Contaminant and Biodiversity Issues*, has been very successful. He is the recipient of a 2013 Texas Environmental Excellence Award given through the Texas Commission on Environmental Quality and Governor Rick Perry. He has received millions of dollars of research support from local, state, and federal sponsors, as well as private industries, and continues to maintain an active and well-funded research program.

Dr. Steven M. Presley's research and teaching focus on risks and threats associated with and the potential impact of biological pathogens naturally or intentionally introduced into military and civilian populations and the agricultural industry. The overarching goal of his research is the development and fielding of preventative measures against vector-borne infectious and zoonotic diseases, and biological weapon agents, and the possible utilization of arthropod vector and nonvector species for prediction and forensic validation of such occurrences. Dr. Presley offers an advanced graduate-level course in biological threats in the environment in the Department of Environmental Toxicology at Texas Tech University (TTU). Additionally, he serves as the research coordinator for the Admiral Elmo R. Zumwalt, Jr. National Program for Countermeasures to Biological and Chemical Threats at TTU. Dr. Presley earned his BS in animal science from TTU in 1982 and his MS (1985) and PhD (1987) from Oklahoma State University, studying medical/veterinary entomology, and then completed a postdoctoral fellowship at the University of Kentucky. He served in the U.S. Navy as a medical service corps officer for more than 12 years before joining the faculty at TTU in 2002. He is a graduate of the U.S. Marine Corps Command and Staff College, where he earned a master's degree in military studies focused on domestic terrorism and has completed various aspects of chemical, biological, radiological, and environmental-related response and control training and practical experience. His operational and research experience has focused on the surveillance, prevention, and control of biological threats in the environment, specifically vector-borne infectious diseases in tropical and semi-tropical environments. He has led malaria control operations and research efforts in Africa, Asia, and South America, as well as Rift Valley fever, Crimean Congo hemorrhagic fever, and cutaneous leishmaniasis studies in Africa and Asia. He has published more than 35 scientific and technical manuscripts and has made numerous professional and technical oral presentations. Dr. Presley was awarded the Rear Admiral Charles S. Stephenson Award for Excellence in Preventive Medicine for the year 2000–2001 (U.S. Navy Medical Department worldwide competitive award). He serves as a chairperson of the Publications Committee and on the Science and Technology Committee of the American Mosquito Control Association. Additionally, he is a member of many local, regional, and state professional boards and committees related to emergency preparedness and public health response to human and animal diseases and catastrophic events.

**Dr. Seshadri S. Ramkumar** is a full professor in the Department of Environmental Toxicology at Texas Tech University (TTU), Lubbock, Texas. His research focuses on developing value-added materials using nonwoven and nanotechnology. He supervises the Nonwoven and Advanced Materials Laboratory at The Institute of Environmental and Human Health, TTU. He currently holds two U.S. patents and two U.S. pending applications. He is the editor of a comprehensive magazine on technical textiles, *Nonwoven and Technical Textiles*. In addition, he serves on the editorial boards of three international peer-reviewed journals. He is the co-chairman of The Association of Nonwoven Industry's India committee. Dr. Ramkumar has successfully organized four international conferences on advances in fibrous materials. To date, he has guided 13 MS and PhD students at TTU. His research on nonwoven decontamination wipes resulted in a technology transfer that is being commercialized.

Contributors

Galen P. Austin
Department of Environmental
  Toxicology
The Institute of Environmental
  and Human Health
Texas Tech University
Lubbock, Texas

Daniel E. Dawson
Department of Environmental
  Toxicology
The Institute of Environmental
  and Human Health
Texas Tech University
Lubbock, Texas

Joe A. Fralick
Health Sciences Center
Texas Tech University
Lubbock, Texas

Angella Gentles
Department of Environmental
  Toxicology
The Institute of Environmental
  and Human Health
Texas Tech University
Lubbock, Texas

Anna G. Gibson
Department of Environmental
  Toxicology
The Institute of Environmental
  and Human Health
Texas Tech University
Lubbock, Texas

William F. Jaynes
Department of Plant and Soil
  Science
Texas Tech University
Lubbock, Texas

Mathew Kay
Health Sciences Center
Texas Tech University
Lubbock, Texas

Ronald J. Kendall
Wildlife Toxicology Laboratory
Texas Tech University
Lubbock, Texas

Steven M. Presley
Department of Environmental
  Toxicology
The Institute of Environmental
  and Human Health
Texas Tech University
Lubbock, Texas

Seshadri S. Ramkumar
Department of Environmental
   Toxicology
The Institute of Environmental
   and Human Health
Texas Tech University
Lubbock, Texas

Christopher J. Salice
Department of Biological Sciences
The Jess & Mildred Fisher College
   of Science & Mathematics
Towson University
Towson, Maryland

Vinitkumar Singh
Department of Environmental
   Toxicology
The Institute of Environmental
   and Human Health
Texas Tech University
Lubbock, Texas

Ernest E. Smith
Department of Environmental
   Toxicology
The Institute of Environmental
   and Human Health
Texas Tech University
Lubbock, Texas

Lili Tang
College of Public Health
The University of Georgia
Athens, Georgia

Uday Turaga
Wildlife Toxicology Laboratory
Texas Tech University
Lubbock, Texas

Kristyn N. Urban
Department of Environmental
   Toxicology
The Institute of Environmental
   and Human Health
Texas Tech University
Lubbock, Texas

Jia-Sheng Wang
College of Public Health
The University of Georgia
Athens, Georgia

Scott M. Weir
Department of Environmental
   Toxicology
The Institute of Environmental
   and Human Health
Texas Tech University
Lubbock, Texas

Richard E. Zartman
Department of Plant and
   Soil Science
Texas Tech University
Lubbock, Texas

chapter one

State of the science
Background, history, and current threats

Galen P. Austin, Anna G. Gibson, and Steven M. Presley

Contents

1.1 Introduction

The world is at war. This war is not a conventional war where nation-states are warring with each other such that enemies and battle lines are well defined. Rather the nation-states are the collective of free, advanced, modern, self-governed Western nations made up of the United States, Canada, and the European Union, among others. The enemy is not any one nation-state but is an undefined collective of individuals from nation-states the world over bound together by a common radical religious ideology that seeks to control the world a under global, theocratic rule. In this war, there are no standardized rules of engagement such as the Geneva Protocol of

1925 that specifies what weapons and tactics are acceptable so that civilized nations can settle their disputes when diplomatic negotiations fail. Although many of the uniformed militaries of the Western nations are engaged in this world war, the enemy wears no uniform and is not readily recognizable; the enemy could be anyone, anywhere. Although many are, the enemy is not necessarily a faceless individual in a distant battlefield but may be a neighbor, a store clerk, or a colleague—the enemy could be anyone at home or abroad.

Driven by hatred of the West and radical religious fanaticism, the enemy will utilize any tactic necessary to advance their goal of total world dominance but primarily utilize terrorism to achieve their goals. These terrorists employ both conventional and unconventional weapons to terrorize civilian populations in an effort to disrupt national economies, limit freedom, and, ultimately, drive the peoples of the world into submission under their theocratic rule by exploiting the vulnerabilities of free and open societies. Some examples of their tactics are the 1993 and 2001 attacks on the World Trade Center in New York City, the 2004 Madrid commuter train bombings, the 2005 London underground bombings, and the 2013 Boston Marathon bombings, to name but a few. These attacks did not occur in far-off distance battlefields but occurred in civilized population centers to instill the fear in Western society that no one is safe from the terroristic tentacles of the enemy. In many ways, the enemy has succeeded in their attempts to control the world because with each successive attack, driven by the fear of subsequent attacks, the governments of Western society continue to try to limit subsequent attacks by implementing security measures that ultimately limit the freedom of their citizens.

Overt attacks by the enemies and terrorists, utilizing conventional explosives or fuel-laden aircraft, have proven quite successful and are typically what most everyone cites as an example of a terrorist attack. However, the greater terroristic threat to the world lies in the covert use of biological or chemical threat agents—weapons of mass destruction—because such agents are not so readily detected or understood by the general populous. The use of terrorism on civilian populations and militaries to commit crimes, exploit, coerce, extort, or dominate is not a new tactic deployed only in recent history. Since the beginning of the history of mankind, poisons, toxins, and disease pathogens, and later, chemicals and explosives, have been utilized in terroristic tactics.

1.2   Biological threat agents

Biological threat agents are microorganisms and the toxins produced by microorganisms that may cause disease or death in humans, animals, or plants and include bacteria, rickettsiae, viruses, and fungi (U.S. Army, 2005; OSHA, 2014). The U.S. Centers for Disease Control and

Prevention (CDC) further categorizes certain biological threat agents into three distinct categories relative to their potential use as weapons of terror or warfare—A, B, and C. These categories are based on the agent's ease of dissemination and transmissibility, morbidity and mortality rate, and ease of detection and identification. The attributes of each category are listed as follows (CDC, 2014a).

Category A agents are pathogens of highest priority that have the potential to threaten national security because they

- Can be easily disseminated or transmitted from person to person
- Result in high mortality rates and have the potential for major public health impact
- Might cause public panic and social disruption
- Require special action for public health preparedness

Category B agents are pathogens and toxins of the second highest priority and are those agents that

- Are moderately easy to disseminate
- Result in moderate morbidity rates and low mortality rates
- Require specific enhancements of CDC's diagnostic capacity and enhanced disease surveillance

Category C agents are agents of the third highest priority, which includes emerging pathogens that have the potential to be manipulated for mass dissemination because of their

- Availability
- Ease of production and dissemination
- Potential for high morbidity and mortality rates and major health impact

Table 1.1 provides a listing of biological threat agents that have been, or may be potentially, utilized as terroristic or warfare weapons.

1.2.1   History: Biological threats—Warfare

400 BC—Scythian archers contaminate their arrows by dipping the points in blood, manure, or decomposing corpses (Smart, 1997).

190 BC—Hannibal used venomous snakes against King Eumenes of Pergamum by placing them in clay pots and launching them onto enemy ships (Smart, 1997; Martin et al., 2007).

1155—Barbarossa contaminated the enemy's water supply with dead bodies during the battle of Tortona (Smart, 1997).

Table 1.1 Biological agents

Agent	Incubation	Lethality	Persistence	Dissemination
Bacteria				
Anthrax	1–5 days	3–5 days fatal	Very stable	Aerosol
Cholera	12 hours to 6 days	Low with treatment High without treatment	Unstable Stable in saltwater	Aerosol Sabotage of water
Plague	1–3 days	1–6 days fatal	Extremely stable	Aerosol
Tularemia	1–10 days	2 weeks moderate	Very stable	Aerosol
Q fever	14–26 days	Very low	Stable	Aerosol Sabotage
Viruses				
Smallpox	10–12 days	High	Very stable	Aerosol
Venezuelan equine encephalitis	1–6 days	Low	Unstable	Aerosol Vectors
Ebola	4–6 days	7–16 days fatal	Unstable	Aerosol Direct contact
Biological toxins				
Botulinum toxins	Hours to days	High without treatment	Stable	Aerosol Sabotage
Staphylococcal enterotoxin B	1–6 days	Low	Stable	Aerosol Sabotage
Ricin	Hours to days	10–12 days fatal	Stable	Aerosol Sabotage
Trichothecene mycotoxins (T2)	2–4 hours	Moderate	Extremely stable	Aerosol Sabotage

Sources: ECBC, *Biological and Chemical Agent Quick Reference Tables*, Edgewood Chemical Biological Center, U.S. Army Research, Development and Engineering Command, Aberdeen Proving Ground, MD, 2014, http://www.ecbe.army.mil/hld/ip/bce-qr. htm (accessed December 8, 2014); USAMRIID, *Medical Management of Biological Casualties Handbook*, 7th edn., lead editor: Z.F. Dembek, Contributing editors: D.A. Alves, T.J. Cieslak, R.C. Culpepper et al., U.S. Army Medical Research Institute of Infectious Diseases, Washington, DC, 2011, http://www.usamriid.army.mil/ education/bluebookpdf/USAMRIID%20BlueBook%207th%20Edition%20-%20 Sep%202011.pdf (accessed December 8, 2014).

1346—At the siege of Caffa, De Mussis catapulted corpses of plague victims into the city (Smart, 1997).

1495—The Spaniards infused wine with the blood of leprosy patients in an effort to defeat the French (Smart, 1997).

1650—The Polish general Siemienowicz fired cannon balls filled with the saliva of rabid dogs at his enemies (Smart, 1997).

1710—The Russians use the same tactic as De Mussis and catapulted corpses of plague victims into Reval, Estonia, which was occupied by the Swedish (Smart, 1997).

1763—British Colonel Henry Bouquet proposed giving Indians blankets that had been used by smallpox victims (Smart, 1997).

1785—The Tunisians attempted to infect Christians in control of La Calle with plague, by throwing clothing contaminated with plague into the city (Smart, 1997).

1863—Confederate and Union soldiers polluted ponds and wells with the carcasses of dead animals as they retreated in Mississippi (Smart, 1997).

World War I—Throughout World War I German agents attempted, with some success, to infect the horses and cattle of the Allies' with glanders and anthrax, respectively. Approximately 4500 mules in Mesopotamia were successfully infected with glanders (Smart, 1997).

1932—The Japanese military established a biological agent research laboratory under the direction of Major Shiro Ishii in Manchuria where experiments were conducted on human subjects (Martin et al., 2007).

1936—Land was acquired, and subsequently a large-scale research facility was built by the Japanese military in Manchuria under the direction of the newly promoted Lieutenant Colonel Shiro Ishii. This new research facility became known as Unit 731. More than 3000 Chinese prisoners died as a result of the human experiments conducted at Unit 731 (Martin et al., 2007).

1.2.2 History: Biological threats—Terrorism

1984—In an effort to gain control of the government in Wasco County, Oregon, the Rajneesh cult contaminated food in 10 restaurants in The Dalles, OR, with *Salmonella typhimurium*. Their efforts resulted in 751 enteritis cases (Martin et al., 2007).

1990—The Aum Shinrikyo cult targeted Japan's parliament in Tokyo, the city of Yokohama, Narita International Airport, and the U.S. Navy Base at Yosuka with botulinum toxin sprayed from vehicles (Martin et al., 2007).

1993—Aum Shinrikyo cult sprayed anthrax targeting Japan's parliament and the Imperial Palace in Tokyo (Martin et al., 2007).

1995—Aum Shinrikyo cult targeted the Tokyo subway with botulinum toxin (Martin et al., 2008).

1.2.3 History: Biological threats—Criminal

1995—Dr. Debra Green used ricin in an attempt to kill her husband (Martin et al., 2007).

1996—A hospital microbiologist, Diane Thompson, used *Shigella dysenteriae*–laced pastries to infect 12 laboratory coworkers (Martin et al., 2007).

2001—Letters containing anthrax spores were mailed to various locations in the United States, including Florida, New York City, and the Hart Senate Office Building in Washington, DC, and resulted in the contamination of U.S. Postal Service facilities in Washington, DC, and Trenton, NJ. The anthrax spore–laden letters resulted in 22 cases of anthrax, including five deaths (Martin et al., 2007).

2013—James Everett Dutschke sent ricin-laced letters to President Barack Obama, Mississippi Senator Roger Wicker, and Lee County, Mississippi, Judge Sadie Holland in an attempt to frame his rival and Elvis impersonator, Paul Kevin Curtis (Amy, 2014).

2013—Shannon Guess Richardson sent ricin-laced letters to President Barack Obama; former New York City mayor, Michael Bloomberg; and Mark Glaze in an attempt to frame her estranged husband (Queally, 2014).

1.3   Chemical threat agents

Chemical threat agents are any toxic chemical or its precursor that may cause death, injury, temporary incapacitation, or sensory irritation through its chemical action. They are categorized based on how they penetrate the human body and affect humans and include chemicals used in legitimate industry (OPCW, 2014). The CDC (2014b) lists the following chemical threat agent categories:

- *Biotoxins*—Poisons that come from plants or animals
- *Blister agents/vesicants*—Chemicals that severely blister the eyes, respiratory tract, and skin on contact
- *Blood agents*—Poisons that affect the body by being absorbed into the blood
- *Caustics (acids)*—Chemicals that burn or corrode people's skin, eyes, and mucus membranes (lining of the nose, mouth, throat, and lungs) on contact
- *Choking/lung/pulmonary agents*—Chemicals that cause severe irritation or swelling of the respiratory tract (lining of the nose, throat, and lungs)
- *Incapacitating agents*—Drugs that make people unable to think clearly or that cause an altered state of consciousness (possibly unconsciousness)
- *Long-acting anticoagulants*—Poisons that prevent blood from clotting properly, which can lead to uncontrolled bleeding
- *Metals*—Agents that consist of metallic poisons
- *Nerve agents*—Highly poisonous chemicals that work by preventing the nervous system from working properly

- *Organic solvents*—Agents that damage the tissues of living things by dissolving fats and oils
- *Riot control agents/tear gas*—Highly irritating agents normally used by law enforcement for crowd control or by individuals for protection (e.g., mace)
- *Toxic alcohols*—Poisonous alcohols that can damage the heart, kidneys, and nervous system
- *Vomiting agents*—Chemicals that cause nausea and vomiting

Table 1.2 provides a listing of chemical threat agents that have been, or may be potentially, utilized as terroristic or warfare weapons.

1.3.1 History: Chemical threats—Warfare

1000 BC—Smoke containing arsenic was used by the Chinese (Smart, 1997).

600 BC—Plant roots from the genus *Helleborus* were used by Solon of Athens to poison water at the siege of Kirrha (Smart, 1997).

431–404 BC—Spartans utilized smoke from burning pitch and sulfur against their enemies in the Peloponnesian War (Szinicz, 2005).

1861–1865—During the American Civil War, a number of chemical weapons were suggested for use by both the Union and Confederate Armies, but none were implemented (Smart, 1997).

1899–1902—British fired artillery shells containing picric acid (Smart, 1997).

Chemical weapons of various types had been utilized by militaries throughout history to gain an advantage over their adversaries. The use of more "modern"-type chemical warfare agents was suggested and researched in the nineteenth century, but most military leaders were reluctant to deploy them. However, it was not until the outbreak of World War I in 1914 that true "modern" chemical warfare began. Chemical weapon agents were used throughout the war until its end in 1918 (Smart, 1997).

1914—French use ethyl bromoacetate grenades against invading German forces (Smart, 1997).

Germans fire artillery shells filled with dianisidine chlorosulfate on the British (Smart, 1997).

Germans fire artillery shells filled with xylyl bromide against the Russians (Smart, 1997).

1915—Germans release chlorine gas against Allied forces. Later that year, the French and British retaliate by releasing chlorine gas against the Germans (Smart, 1997).

1916—Germans begin using trichloromethyl chloroformate (diphosgene) and the French deploy hydrogen cyanide and cyanogen chloride (Smart, 1997).

Table 1.2 Chemical agents

Agent	Signs and symptoms	Decontamination	Persistence
Nerve agents			
Tabun (GA)	Salivation	Remove contaminated clothing	1–2 days if heavy concentration
Sarin (GB)	Lacrimation	Flush with a soap and water solution for patients	1–2 days will evaporate with water
Soman (GD)	Urination	Flush with large amounts of a 5% bleach and water solution for objects	Moderate, 1–2 days
V agents (VX)	Defecation		High, 1 week if heavy concentration
	Gastric disturbances		As volatile as motor oil
	Emesis		
Vesicants (blister agents)			
Sulfur mustard (H)	Acts first as a cell irritant and then as a cell poison. Conjunctivitis, reddened skin, blisters, nasal irritation, inflammation of the throat and lungs.	Remove contaminated clothing	Very high, days to weeks
Distilled mustard (HD)		Flush with soap and water solution for patients.	
Nitrogen mustard (HN 1,3)		Flush with large amounts of a 5% bleach and water solution for objects	
Mustargen (HN2)			Moderate
Lewisite (L)	Immediate pain with blisters later.		Days, rapid hydrolysis with humidity
Phosgene oxime (CX)	Immediate pain with blisters later—necrosis equivalent to second- and third-degree burns.		Low, 2 hours in soil
Chemical asphyxiants (blood agents)			
Hydrogen cyanide (AC)	Cherry red skin or ~30% cyanosis. Patients may appear to be gasping for air. Seizures prior to death. Effect is similar to asphyxiation but is more sudden.	Remove contaminated clothing	Extremely volatile, 1–2 days
Cyanogen chloride (CK)		Flush with a soap and water solution for patients	Rapidly evaporates and disperses
Arsine (SA)		Flush with large amounts of 5% bleach and water solution for objects	Low

Source: ECBC, *Biological and Chemical Agent Quick Reference Tables*, Edgewood Chemical Biological Center, U.S. Army Research, Development and Engineering Command, Aberdeen Proving Ground, MD, 2014, http://www.ecbc.army.mil/hld/ip/bce-qr.htm (accessed December 8, 2014).

1917—By 1917 most forces had equipped their troops with gas masks for respiratory protection against gas attacks. To circumvent the protection afforded by gas masks, the Germans began using mustard agent because it was effective against unprotected skin (Smart, 1997).

1980–1988—Iraq used mustard agent and tabun against Iranian forces during the Iraq–Iran War and also utilized these agents against its own citizens, the Iraqi Kurds, late in the war (Smart, 1997).

2013—Sarin gas attack on suburbs of Damascus, Syria, kills an estimated 1500 civilians (Notman, 2014).

1.3.2 History: Chemical threats—Terrorism

1994—Aum Shinrikyo cult released the nerve agent sarin in a neighborhood in Matsumoto, Japan, which killed seven people and sent 500 others to local hospitals (Olson, 1999).

1995—Aum Shinrikyo cult released the nerve agent sarin in the Tokyo subway system, injuring approximately 3800 people and killing 12 (Olson, 1999).

1.3.3 History: Chemical threats—Industrial accidents

1984—An industrial accident at the Union Carbide India Limited plant in Bhopal, India, released 30–40 tons of methyl isocyanate gas exposing an estimated 200,000 of the 800,000 residents. It is estimated that 5,000 died within 2 days of the accident, which ultimately killed an estimated 20,000 (Varma and Varma, 2005).

1.4 Biological threat agent detection and identification

Biological threat agents include bacteria, rickettsiae, viruses, fungi, and the toxins produced by microorganisms (U.S. Army, 2005; OSHA, 2014). These agents can infect and cause disease and/or death in humans, animals, or plants and occur naturally in the environment, or for some, weaponized strains have been developed by biological weapons programs. They have been and are likely to continue to be used intentionally and maliciously in warfare or to terrorize a civilian population with the intent to cause disease and/or death, thus causing fear in the population. Biological weapons pose a unique threat over other weapons of mass destruction. Nuclear and chemical weapons, for the most part, result in immediate casualties. Effects are rapidly detected and the impact is contained to the attack foci. Biological agents, however, have extended incubation periods and it may be days to weeks before the biological attack is recognized. An infected individual may travel great distances and be in contact with numerous people before falling seriously ill.

From a psychological perspective, biological threat agents may provide more of a "fear factor" than chemical threat agents because they can be easily disseminated covertly, have a low infective dose, reproduce rapidly in humans, and can quickly cause disease and/or death (Fatah et al., 2007a). All of this can occur before the medical community is aware of the outbreak of a disease they have little or no experience recognizing and treating. Many diseases will be initially misdiagnosed as influenza because of the initial clinical symptoms and because most clinics, emergency rooms, and doctor's offices do not obtain clinical samples from patients for laboratory analyses to identify the causative pathogen. By the time clinical samples are obtained from a patient, the misdiagnosed disease will have progressed in severity to the point where treatment is likely to be too late to prevent the transmission of the pathogen within the population and/or the death of the patient. Additionally, biological threat agents are particularly appealing to terrorists because, with some knowledge, they are easy to obtain from natural sources and can be inexpensive to produce (Fatah et al., 2007a).

The detection and identification of biological threat agents presents a difficult challenge, because the release of an agent will be either overt or covert and occur either in the open environment or in an enclosed building; biological threat agents do not produce a tell-tale odor or have immediate effects, as with many chemical agents, and detection and identification must be rapid and accurate in order to be effective in providing proper protection for a population. Whether the agent release occurs in the open environment or an enclosed building, both environments can present challenges to detection and identification of biological threat agents. Pathogen detection relies on costly, time-, and labor-intensive diagnostic assays that must be performed by trained laboratory clinicians such as polymerase chain reaction (PCR), enzyme-linked immunosorbent assay (ELISA), passive hemagglutination assay (PHA), or immunofluorescence testing (IF). Additionally, the handling of infected patients and/or the manipulation of infectious microorganisms poses an elevated risk of infection to diagnostic laboratory technicians.

Most biological threat agents have a low infective dose and can have a relatively short incubation period, thus quickly causing disease. Therefore, detection of a release event and identification of the pathogen released must be accomplished quickly and accurately and require detection equipment with a high sensitivity that can discriminate between the biological threat agent and nonpathogenic, naturally occurring biological organisms and other nonbiological materials in the ambient environment that can cause detection interference.

It is most likely that a biological threat agent release would be an aerosolized release, which would require a detection system that would have high-throughput air sampling capabilities. However, depending upon the wind, the aerosolized particles would quickly settle onto the soil surface, water surface, and other existing surfaces (i.e., buildings, automobiles), thus requiring detection equipment specific to sampling these other surfaces and substrates (Fatah et al., 2007a).

Biological threat agent detection systems are commercially available; however, these systems are actually environmental sampling systems that require fixed-base or mobile laboratory analyses of the samples collected in order to identify any biological threat agents that may have been intentionally released into the environment. While some biological threat agent detection systems exist that have the ability to sample the environment and display the detection results in the field, few of these detection systems are commercially available, and all are limited to the detection of a specific pathogen. They do not have the capability of detecting multiple pathogens simultaneously and do not operate autonomously. Biological threat agent detection systems developed for the U.S. military have the ability to detect multiple pathogens, but these systems can only detect a limited number of different pathogens and are cost prohibitive for use in public health protection (Fatah et al., 2007a).

After the anthrax-contaminated letter attack in 2001, biohazard detection systems (BDSs) were placed in postal distribution plants across the United States. The U.S. Postal Service BDS continuously collects air samples from mail cancelling equipment in postal distribution plants. Airborne particles are absorbed into sterile water that is injected into a single-use cartridge to be tested. Each test requires 90 minutes for analysis, 60 minutes for air collection, and 30 minutes for testing (NALC, 2008).

In 2003, the Department of Homeland Security (DHS) implemented the BioWatch program and deployed hundreds of air samplers in several metropolitan cities to detect a limited panel of biological threat agents of critical concern. BioWatch is an early warning system for the detection of Category A and B agents that have been intentionally released into the air. The system collects and concentrates air samples for laboratory analysis. Laboratory results are available 10–34 hours after sample collection (IOM/ NRC, 2011). Both of the BDS and BioWatch technologies are DNA-detecting PCR assays.

Biosurveillance efforts such as the BioWatch and BDS technologies allow for detection of biological threat agents in the environment potentially before exposure and human symptom manifestation such that life-saving therapies can be deployed. Both the BioWatch and the BDSs are only useful for identifying intentional release events of aerosolized biological threat agents.

1.5   Chemical threat agent detection and identification

Local first responders are the first line of defense whether chemicals are released in an industrial accident or by a terrorist act. However, they do not have the proper tools to immediately identify when, where, and what chemicals have been released, and this is particularly true for chemical warfare agents. Commercially available chemical detection equipment cannot detect all chemical warfare agents and vary in their selectivity and sensitivity. The DHS considers currently available chemical detection equipment inadequate for detecting chemical warfare agents at less than lethal, but still harmful, levels. The greatest obstacle for any chemical detection equipment is to be able to overcome the ambient chemical environment and determine which threats to human health and life have been released (GAO, 2008).

Of the technologies available to first responders for the detection of chemical threat agents, the most numerous are for the detection of vapors in the air and a limited number are available for the detection of liquid droplets. Technologies available for the detection of chemical threat agents in water are primarily limited to laboratory-based equipment, thus requiring field-collected samples to be brought in to the laboratory for analysis. Regardless of the detection technology available, proper analysis and identification of chemical threat agents is dependent upon proper training on the use of detection equipment, as well as proper sampling and handling techniques in the field prior to analysis. With the exception of laboratory-based detection methods, most field-deployable detection technologies do not have the ability to detect chemical threat agents at low levels or distinguish between chemical threat agents and urban environmental chemicals (e.g., automotive chemicals, personal hygiene chemicals, insecticides, herbicides), thus producing false positives (Fatah et al., 2007b).

As previously noted, the equipment commercially available to first responders for the detection of chemical threat agents is limited and not completely reliable, excepting laboratory-based equipment. Fatah et al. (2007b) categorize detection technologies available to first responders into three categories: point detection technologies, standoff detectors, and analytical instruments. The different technologies that fall under these broad categories are listed as follows.

1.5.1   Point detection technologies

- Ionization/ion mobility spectrometry
- Flame photometry
- Infrared spectroscopy
  - Photoacoustic infrared spectroscopy
  - Filter-based infrared spectrometry

- Electrochemistry
- Colorimetric
- Surface acoustic wave
- Photoionization detection
- Thermal and electrical conductivity
- Flame ionization
- Polymer composite detection materials

1.5.2   Standoff detectors

- Fourier transform infrared
- Forward looking infrared
- Ultraviolet standoff

1.5.3   Analytical instruments

- Gas chromatography
- Mass spectrometry
- High-performance liquid chromatography
- Ion chromatography
- Capillary zone electrophoresis
- Ultraviolet spectroscopy

Of all detection technologies available, mass spectrometry is the most sensitive and reliable method for chemical threat agent detection. However, because this equipment is laboratory-based, it cannot provide the quick response that first responders and the general public need. Standoff detectors are the only technology available that affords long-distance detection of chemical threat agents. Unfortunately, deploying enough of these detectors to protect every population center in the United States would be cost prohibitive (Fatah et al., 2007b) and an unwise use of limited tax dollars. The greatest chemical threat to the general population is more likely to come from an industrial accident rather than from the terroristic deployment of a chemical threat agent.

1.6   Emerging and future threats

Since the terrorist attacks on the World Trade Center in New York City and the Pentagon in Washington, DC, on September 11, 2001, there has been much discussion in the United States and around the world regarding the threat of the use of biological or chemical weapons by nation-states and terrorist organizations. The justification for the invasion of Iraq in 2003 was based, in part, on intelligence that concluded that Iraq continued to produce chemical and biological weapons in defiance of

United Nations (UN) Security Council Resolutions, which called for Iraq to destroy such weapons (CIA, 2002; Bush, 2003a,b). Through deceit, obfuscation, and deception, the UN inspectors were not completely able to verify that the Iraqis destroyed their chemical and biological weapons stocks and manufacturing capabilities. However, the Iraq Survey Group (ISG) lead by Charles Duelfer (2007) concluded that Iraq had destroyed their chemical and biological weapons stocks and had never rebuilt production capabilities for such weapons even though they desired to and maintained their knowledge base to do so (Duelfer, 2007). Even after the Duelfer (2007) report, questions still remained regarding the disposition of Iraq's weapons of mass destruction, thus leading to much discussion as to whether or not different terrorist organizations could possess chemical or biological weapons, or have the capability to develop and produce such weapons, even on a limited scale. Up until October 2014, there had been little evidence suggesting that such weapons existed; however, the New York Times (Chivers, 2014) reported that from 2004 to 2011, the U.S. military and U.S.-trained Iraqi forces found approximately 5000 Iraqi artillery or aviation chemical weapons. On at least six occasions, the discovery of the Iraqi chemical weapons resulted in exposure of U.S. and/or Iraqi forces to nerve or mustard agents. One exposure incident involved two U.S. soldiers investigating the detonation of a roadside bomb where they found a cracked artillery round, which they removed and took back to their base to prevent further use by Iraqi terrorists. Upon detonation, the artillery round only cracked open because it was a chemical round and not a high-explosive round. By the time the two U.S. soldiers arrived back at their base, they had been exposed to the nerve agent sarin. In 2009, at the insistence of the U.S. Government, the Iraqi Government signed on to the Convention of Chemical Weapons and assumed responsibility for the security and destruction of the discovered chemical weapons that remained in Iraq. As of 2013, many of the chemical weapons had not been destroyed and some of those chemical weapons are located in areas of Iraq that are now under the control of the Islamic State (Chivers, 2014).

Most likely the Iraqi terrorist(s) who used the chemical artillery round as a roadside bomb and successfully detonated it in an effort to kill U.S. troops probably thought they were using a high-explosive round that did not provide the intended outcome. Regardless of whether or not the terrorists in Iraq knew specifically whether or not they were using chemical or high-explosive artillery rounds as roadside bombs, they were finding them, and they most likely know now where others are located. This is particularly true now that the New York Times article (Chivers, 2014) on chemical weapons in Iraq has been published. As reported by Chivers (2014) in the New York Times, many of the chemical weapons the Iraqi

Government had not destroyed by 2013 were at the Al Muthanna State Establishment, a major chemical weapon production and storage facility in Saddam Hussein's chemical weapons program, which is located in an area now controlled by the Islamic State.

Although it's unlikely that terrorists would be able to smuggle old 1980s–1990s vintage Iraqi chemical artillery or aviation munitions into the United States and detonate them, they certainly could extract the chemicals, which would be much more easily transportable and smuggled into the United States. Regardless of how difficult it may or may not be for terrorist to obtain chemical weapons and overtly or covertly deploy them, we must always remain ever vigilant because mankind has created and used such weapons in the past and likely will use them again in the future.

While the threat of the use of chemical threat agents by terrorists is ever present, it is likely that the greatest threat, particularly from a biological perspective, is, or will be coming, from the natural environment and mankind's interaction with it. Emerging diseases, those that have never existed in a population, and reemerging diseases, those diseases that were previously eradicated or limited by past control measures and now have an increasing prevalence in a population (Morens et al., 2004), are likely a greater threat. Whitehouse et al. (2007) state that "[e]merging infectious diseases are among the most important future threats facing both military and civilians populations."

One of the first successful disease control programs was implemented at the turn of the twentieth century in 1900 in Cuba to control yellow fever. Many successful vector-borne disease control programs soon followed, which included the control of yellow fever and malaria in Panama (Morens et al., 2004) without which the Panama Canal would not have been completed.

Vaccinations have long been used in developed nations to protect populations against endemic diseases and, in some cases, eradicate diseases, such as smallpox. In the 1950s, childhood vaccinations became routine, and as more vaccines were developed, the vaccination schedules for children were updated. Currently the CDC recommends the following vaccinations for children up to 18 years: varicella (chickenpox), diphtheria, pertussis, tetanus, haemophilus influenza type b, hepatitis A, hepatitis B, influenza, measles, mumps, rubella, polio, pneumococcal, rotavirus, human papilloma virus, and meningococcal conjugate vaccine. These vaccines have proven effective in the prevention and control of disease; however, for adults, the immunity acquired through vaccinations as a child has now waned, and some adults are now acquiring the childhood diseases they once had immunity to. Additionally, some parents are choosing not to vaccinate their children against many childhood diseases, particularly measles, mumps, and rubella, because they fear perceived side effects of the vaccinations. Although some parents are opting out of vaccinating their children, the CDC states that close to 95% of the children in the United States receive the CDC recommended vaccinations—95% is the CDC targeted goal. Unfortunately, for many emerging or reemerging diseases, vaccinations are either few or non-existent (Gubler, 1998).

There are many reasons for the emergence or resurgence of disease-causing pathogens. Many disease control programs and pharmaceuticals were so effective at controlling disease that governments and the general public became complacent and no longer considered disease a threat to public health (Gubler, 1998). As an example, "in 1967, the US Surgeon General stated that 'the war against infectious diseases has been won'" (Morens et al., 2004). Along with this complacency came changes in political policy that deemphasized the focus on and funding for public health and vector surveillance and control programs (Gubler, 1998; Morens et al., 2004). The widespread use of insecticides and pharmaceuticals eventually led to insecticide resistance in insect vectors and drug resistance in pathogens (Gubler, 1998; Morens et al., 2004). Other contributing factors are population growth and increased density, urbanization, pathogen and vector adaptation, immunosuppression (e.g., AIDS, cancer, malnutrition, aging), climatic factors, weather, international travel and commerce, and primarily in developing countries, natural disasters, war, political unrest, and lack of adequate health care, housing, and basic sanitation (i.e., water, sewage, and waste management) (Gubler, 1998; Morens et al., 2004; Whitehouse et al., 2007).

One of the most significant contributing factors is the jet-powered aircraft. With the advent of jet-powered aircraft, the population of the world has become more mobile and international travel has increased significantly in the last 50 years. It is now possible with today's air transportation network for anyone to travel to almost any location on the Earth within 24 hours. Anyone who is knowingly or unknowingly infected with a disease-causing pathogen could travel during the contagious stage of the disease and risk infecting hundreds of people in the enclosed aircraft, thousands more in crowded airports, and even more people once they reach their destination. Taking into consideration that the influenza pandemic of 1918–1919 only took 6 months to spread around the world (Whitehouse et al., 2007), today's air travel infrastructure could easily facilitate a similar pandemic in weeks. As an example, severe acute respiratory syndrome (SARS) emerged in China in 2003 and within weeks, not months, had spread to 25 countries on five continents (Morens et al., 2004; Whitehouse et al., 2007). Table 1.3 presents a list of pathogens noted by Gubler (1998), Morens et al. (2004), Whitehouse et al. (2007), and NIAID (2014) as emerging and resurgent.

Table 1.3 Emerging and/or resurgent pathogens

Bacteria

Acinetobacter baumannii	*Klebsiella pneumoniae*
Anaplasma phagocytophilum	*Legionella pneumophila*
Bacillus anthracis	*Listeria monocytogenes*
Bartonella henselae	*Mycobacterium tuberculosis*
Borrelia afzelii	*Mycobacterium tuberculosis*—MDR
Borrelia burgdorferi	*Leptospira* spp.
Borrelia garinii	*Neisseria gonorrhoeae*
Borrelia hermsii	*Pseudomonas aeruginosa*
Borrelia lonstari	*Salmonella enteritidis*
Borrelia miyamotoi	*Salmonella typhi*
Borrelia recurrentis	*Salmonella typhimurium*
Brucella spp.	*Shigella flexneri*
Burkholderia mallei	*Shigella sonnei*
Burkholderia pseudomallei	*Staphylococcus aureus*
Campylobacter jejuni	*Streptococcus*—Group A
Chlamydia psittaci	*Streptococcus pneumoniae*
Clostridium botulinum	*Trypanosoma brucei*
Clostridium difficile	*Vibrio alginolyticus*
Coccidioides spp.	*Vibrio cholerae*
Coxiella burnetii	*Vibrio cincinnatiensis*
Cryptosporidium parvum	*Vibrio fluvialis*
Cyclospora cayetanensis	*Vibrio furnissii*
Ehrlichia spp.	*Vibrio hollisae*
Ehrlichia chaffeensis	*Vibrio metschnikovii*
Enterobacter cloacae	*Vibrio mimicus*
Enterococcus faecalis	*Vibrio parahaemolyticus*
Enterococcus faecium	*Vibrio vulnificus*
Escherichia coli	*Vibrio damsela*
Escherichia coli O157:H7	*Yersinia enterocolitica*
Francisella tularensis	*Yersinia pestis*

Rickettsia

Anaplasma spp.	*Rickettsia prowazekii*

Viruses

Australian bat lyssavirus	Japanese Encephalitis virus
Alkhurma virus	JC virus
BK virus	Junin virus
Caliciviruses	Kyasanur forest virus
California encephalitis virus	LaCrosse encephalitis virus
Chapare virus	Lassa virus
Chikungunya virus	Lujo virus
Crimean–Congo hemorrhagic fever virus	Machupo virus
	Menangle virus

(Continued)

Table 1.3 (Continued) Emerging and/or resurgent pathogens

Viruses

Dengue virus
Dengue hemorrhagic fever virus
Eastern equine encephalitis virus

Ebola virus
Enterovirus 71
Guanarito virus
Hanta virus
Heartland virus
Hendra virus

Hepatitis A
Hepatitis B
Hepatitis C
Hepatitis E
Human herpesvirus 6
Human herpesvirus 8
Human immunodeficiency virus-1
Human immunodeficiency virus-2
Influenza A virus

Middle East respiratory syndrome
  coronavirus
Mumps virus
Nipah virus
Omsk hemorrhagic fever virus
Rabies virus
Rift Valley fever virus
Rubeola virus
Severe acute respiratory syndrome
  coronavirus
Severe fever with thrombocytopenia
  syndrome virus
St. Louis encephalitis virus
Timan virus
Venezuelan equine encephalitis virus
Variola major virus and related pox viruses
West Nile virus
Western equine encephalitis virus
Yellow fever virus

Protozoa

Acanthamoeba spp.
Babesia spp. *Atypical*
Balamuthia mandrillaris
Cryptosporidium parvum
Cyclospora cayetanensis

Entamoeba histolytica
Naegleria fowleri
Plasmodium falciparum
Toxoplasma gondii

Fungi

Aspergillus spp.
Cryptococcus gattii

Mucoromycotina
Microsporidia

Prions

Bovine spongiform
  encephalopathy
Creutzfeldt–Jakob disease

Chronic wasting disease
Scrapie

Sources: Gubler, D.J., *Emerg. Infect. Dis.*, 4, 442, 1998; Morens, D.M., *Nature*, 430, 242, 2004; Whitehouse, C.A. et al., Emerging infectious diseases and future threats, in: Z.F. Dembek, ed., *Medical Aspects of Biological Warfare*, Office of the Surgeon General, U.S. Army Medical Department Center and School, Borden Institute, Washington, DC, 2007, pp. 579–607; NIAID, Emerging infectious diseases/pathogens, U.S. Department of Health and Human Services, National Institute of Allergies and Infectious Diseases, Bethesda, MD, http://www.niaid.nih.gov/topics/Biodefense Related/Biodefense/Pages/CatA.aspx (accessed October 22, 2014).

MDR, multiple drug resistant.

References

Amy, J. 2014. Sender of ricin letters sentenced on state charges. Associated Press, New York. http://bigstory.ap.org/article/sender-ricin-letters-sentenced-state-charges (accessed July 29, 2014).

Bush, G.W. 2003a. President says Saddam Hussein must leave Iraq within 48 hours. The White House, Washington, DC. http://georgewbush-whitehouse.archives.gov/news/releases/2003/03/print/20030317-7.html (accessed September 15, 2014).

Bush, G.W. 2003b. President Bush addresses the nation. The White House, Washington, DC. http://georgewbush-whitehouse.archives.gov/news/releases/2003/03/print/20030319-17.html (accessed September 15, 2014).

CDC. 2014a. Bioterrorism agents/diseases. U.S. Centers for Disease Control and Prevention, Atlanta, GA. http://www.bt.cdc.gov/agent/agentlist-category.asp (accessed May 20, 2014).

CDC. 2014b. Chemical categories. U.S. Centers for Disease Control and Prevention, Atlanta, GA. http://emergency.cdc.gov/agent/agentlistchem-category.asp (accessed May 20, 2014).

Chivers, C.J. 2014. The secret casualties of Iraq's abandoned chemical weapons. New York Times, New York. http://www.nytimes.com/interactive/2014/10/14/world/middleeast/us-casualties-of-iraq-chemical-weapons.html (accessed October 17, 2014).

CIA. 2002. Iraq's weapons of mass destruction programs. U.S. Central Intelligence Agency. Langley, VA. https://www.cia.gov/library/reports/general-reports-1/iraq_wmd/Iraq_Oct_2002.pdf (accessed September 15, 2014).

Duelfer, C. 2007. Comprehensive report of the special advisor to the DCI on Iraq's WMD—Key findings. U.S. Central Intelligence Agency, Langley, VA. https://www.cia.gov/library/reports/general-reports-1/iraq_wmd_2004/Comp_Report_Key_Findings.pdf (accessed September 15, 2014).

ECBC. 2014. *Biological and Chemical Agent Quick Reference Tables*. Edgewood Chemical Biological Center, U.S. Army Research, Development and Engineering Command, Aberdeen Proving Ground, MD. http://www.ecbc.army.mil/hld/ip/bce-qr.htm (accessed December 8, 2014).

Fatah, A.A., Arcilesi, Jr., R.D., Chekol, T., Lattin, C.H., Sadik, O.W., and Aluoch, A.O. 2007a. Guideline for the selection of biological agent detection equipment for emergency first responders, 2nd edn. U.S. Department of Homeland Security, Washington, DC.

Fatah, A.A., Arcilesi, Jr., R.D., Peterson, J.C., Lattin, C.H., Wells, C.Y., and McClintock, J.A. 2007b. Guide for the selection of chemical detection equipment for emergency first responders. Guide 100-06, 3rd edn. Preparedness Directorate, Office of Grants and Training, U.S. Department of Homeland Security, Washington, DC.

GAO. 2008. First responder's ability to detect and model hazardous releases in urban areas is significantly limited—Report no. GAO-08-180. United States Government Accountability Office, Washington, DC.

Gubler, D.J. 1998. Resurgent vector-borne diseases as a global health problem. *Emerg. Infect. Dis.* 4:442–450.

IOM/NRC. 2011. BioWatch and public health surveillance: Evaluating systems for the early detection of biological threats, abbreviated version. Institute of Medicine and National Research Council, The National Academies Press, Washington, DC.

Martin, J.W., Christopher, G.W., and Eitzen, E.M., Jr. 2007. History of biological weapons: From poisoned darts to intentional epidemics. In *Medical Aspects of Biological Warfare*, ed. Z.F. Dembek, pp. 1–20. Office of the Surgeon General, U.S. Army Medical Department Center and School, Borden Institute, Washington, DC.

Morens, D.M., Folkers, G.K., and Fauci, A.S. 2004. The challenge of emerging and re-emerging infectious diseases. *Nature* 430:242–249.

NALC. 2008. Keeping letter carriers safe on the job: USPS biohazard detection system. National Association of Letter Carriers, Washington, DC. http://216.164.46.16/depart/safety/USPSBDS.html (accessed January 6, 2015).

NIAID. 2014. Emerging infectious diseases/pathogens. U.S. Department of Health and Human Services, National Institute of Allergies and Infectious Diseases, Bethesda, MD. http://www.niaid.nih.gov/topics/BiodefenseRelated/Biodefense/Pages/CatA.aspx (accessed October 22, 2014).

Notman, N. 2014. Eliminating Syria's chemical weapons. Chemistry World, Royal Society of Chemistry, London, U.K. http://www.rsc.org/chemistry-world/2014/05/syrian-chemical-weapons-feature (accessed May 29, 2014).

Olson, K.B. 1999. Aum Shinrikyo: Once and future threat. *Emerg. Infect. Dis.* 5:513–516.

OPCW. 2014. Brief description of chemical weapons. Organisation for the Prohibition of Chemical Weapons, Hague, the Netherlands, http://www.opcw.org/about-chemical-weapons/what-is-a-chemical-weapon/ (accessed May 21, 2014).

OSHA. 2014. Biological agents. U.S. Occupational Health and Safety Administration, Washington, DC. https://www.osha.gov/SLTC/biologicalagents/ (accessed May 21, 2014).

Queally, J. 2014. Texas actress to serve 18 years for sending ricin letter to Obama. Los Angeles Times, Los Angeles, CA. http://www.latimes.com/nation/nationnow/la-na-nn-texas-ricin-20140716-story.html (accessed July 29, 2014).

Smart, J.K. 1997. History of chemical and biological warfare: An American perspective. In *Medical Aspects of Chemical and Biological Warfare*, eds. F.R. Sidell, E.T. Takafuji and D.R. Franz, pp. 9–86. Office of the Surgeon General, Department of the Army, Washington, DC.

Szinicz, L. 2005. History of chemical and biological warfare agents. *Toxicology* 214:167–181.

USAMRIID. 2011. *Medical Management of Biological Casualties Handbook*, 7th edn. Lead editor: Z.F. Dembek, Contributing editors: D.A. Alves, T.J. Cieslak, R.C. Culpepper et al. U.S. Army Medical Research Institute of Infectious Diseases, Washington, DC. http://www.usamriid.army.mil/education/bluebookpdf/USAMRIID%20BlueBook%207th%20Edition%20-%20Sep%202011.pdf (accessed December 8, 2014).

U.S. Army. 2005. Potential military chemical/biological agents and compounds—FM 3-11.9. U.S. Army Chemical School, Ft. Leonard Wood, MO. http://fas.org/irp/doddir/army/fm3-11-9.pdf (accessed May 20, 2014).

Varma, R. and Varma, D.R. 2005. The Bhopal disaster of 1984. *Bull. Sci. Technol. Soc.* 25:37–45.

Whitehouse, C.A., Schmaljohn, A.L., and Dembek, Z.F. 2007. Emerging infectious diseases and future threats. In *Medical Aspects of Biological Warfare*, ed. Z.F. Dembek, pp. 579–607. Office of the Surgeon General, U.S. Army Medical Department Center and School, Borden Institute, Washington, DC.

chapter two

Challenges and paths forward in predicting risk of vector-borne diseases

From mechanistic to rule-based modeling frameworks

Christopher J. Salice, Daniel E. Dawson, and Scott M. Weir

Contents

2.1   Introduction

Vector-borne diseases have been and are currently a considerable concern for the public and the military as they have significant health and
economic impacts. The ease of global travel and trade serve as means by
which vectors can be introduced into novel areas, increasing disease risk.
Predictive tools including mathematical models are essential in managing vector-borne disease risk but vary in their predictive power, ease of
use, and the extent to which they have been compared to field data. To
date, considerable effort has been expended on developing very detailed,
computationally intensive, and spatially explicit computer simulation
models to predict, for example, the abundance of mosquito vectors such
as *Aedes aegypti*, a common vector for dengue fever. However, these highly
complex models can be difficult to implement and parameterize requiring a great deal of data. While there is considerable value in continuing
to develop highly detailed computer simulation models, here we explain
and explore the use of simpler, spatially explicit rule-based models that
can be used to quickly develop relative risk maps of vector abundance and
disease risk. With additional parameterizations, these models may yield
outcomes that accurately track mosquito abundance data. The modeling
framework is implemented using ArcGIS software and is adaptable to the
level and quality of data available. The rule-based approach posits that
a generalized understanding of the ecological requirements for mosquitoes can be used to develop a spatially explicit model focused on suitable
mosquito habitat. Combined with human census data, the highest relative
risk of vector-borne diseases would lie where mosquito habitat suitability
and human density were highest. This approach is quasi-mechanistic in
that the ecological information incorporated into the model relates to the
reproductive biology of the vector, although detailed data are not required.
As more and better data become available, however, this information can
be added to improve model predictions and confidence. Although we
think detailed, computationally intensive vector models are relevant, in
some cases a streamlined, rule-based approach may be more appropriate
especially when data and time are limited. We provide an example of the
application of this spatially explicit modeling approach to the mosquito
vector *Culex tarsalis* in West Texas. Our approach can be broadly applied to
a range of vectors or other risk factors and may be of use to municipalities
or can have applications relevant to the military in foreign lands.

2.1.1   Background

Infectious diseases are responsible for approximately 25% of human
deaths worldwide (World Health Organization, 2004) and two-thirds of
childhood deaths (Black et al., 2010). There are about 1425 known human

pathogens of which 217 are viruses or prions and 518 are bacteria or rickettsia. Of the total, about 868 (or 61%) are zoonotic and can therefore be transmitted from nonhuman animals to humans (Cleaveland et al., 2001). Emerging infectious disease is an ongoing and significant concern (Daszak et al., 2000; Jones et al., 2008). The rise in concern over emerging and resurgent vector-borne diseases can, to some degree, be attributed to changes in public health policy, insecticide and drug resistance, shifts in emphasis from prevention to emergency response, demographic and societal changes, and genetic changes in pathogens (Gubler, 1998). Now more than ever, there is a strong need to develop and implement tools to help predict and then effectively prevent spread of infectious disease.

One specific concern lies in the impact of infectious diseases on military personnel deployed in foreign lands where exposure to multiple and different pathogens is likely (Zapor and Moran, 2005). History is replete with examples of the impacts of disease on military campaigns as in the case of diarrheal diseases during the Napoleonic wars where disease accounted for eight times more deaths than combat (Cook, 2001). To this day, infectious diseases continue to account for significant effects on force health. Recent concerns for U.S. military personnel stem from deployment in foreign lands where it is unlikely that soldiers have immunity to pathogens and where hygienic conditions may promote spread of disease. Because of the prevalence of infectious disease among military personnel, measures to predict, prevent, and treat infectious disease are of paramount importance.

Mathematical disease models are useful tools for understanding disease dynamics, predicting epidemics, and identifying treatment options and efficacies (Keeling and Rohani, 2008). Concern within the military and the general public over the spread of emerging infectious diseases is increasing largely driven by the observed spread of infectious diseases such as West Nile virus in recent decades. This is in spite of historical claims by the U.S. Surgeon General that: "the war against infectious diseases has been won" in the 1960s. Indeed, there are multiple current examples of emerging and reemerging infectious diseases (Daszak et al., 2000; Jones et al., 2008), some purposefully engineered and distributed for use as bioweapons. In this latter case, the intentional introduction of infectious disease into areas inhabited by U.S. military and/or U.S. lands used by livestock or human populations is a serious area of concern. As mentioned, zoonotic diseases infect both human and nonhuman animals and the majority of emerging, infectious human diseases are zoonoses.

The need for force health protection is mirrored by concern for homeland security as well. The National Center for Foreign Animal and Zoonotic Disease Defense (FAZD) is a Department of Homeland Security National Center of Excellence aimed at protecting the United States against zoonotic diseases. These activities are in support of Homeland

Security Presidential Directive 9: Defense of United States Agriculture and Food. As stated in the directive

> The United States agriculture and food systems are vulnerable to disease, pest, or poisonous agents that occur naturally, are unintentionally introduced, or are intentionally delivered by acts of terrorism. America's agriculture and food system is an extensive, open, interconnected, diverse, and complex structure providing potential target for terrorist attacks. We should provide the best protection possible against a successful attack on the United States agriculture and food system, which could have catastrophic health and economic effects.

Emerging zoonotic infectious diseases have the potential to be significant burdens on U.S. public health, the economy, military readiness and effectiveness, and the intended and unintended spread of important and competent disease vectors may represent a significant risk to a range of vulnerable subpopulations. Hence, there is a need for an effective, multipronged approach to reducing the spread and impact of emerging diseases. This is particularly true when we consider novel or potentially introduced pathogens.

One important area of research is in the generation of mathematical computer-based models that can be used to reduce risks to civilian populations, military personnel, and U.S. food sources by (1) improving our understanding of how diseases are and can be transmitted; (2) identifying environmental, ecological, or socioeconomic factors that are drivers of emerging infectious disease risk; and (3) generating scenarios or predictions that represent vulnerable conditions that favor disease spread. A generalized framework for assessing zoonotic disease risk is shown in Figure 2.1. This framework utilizes the three-tiered approach common to risk assessment, including a "problem formulation and information gathering" tier, "risk assessment and monitoring" tier, and a "characterization" tier. Within the first two tiers are identified aspects critical to the assessment of zoonotic disease risk and actual estimation of potential risk. The third tier describes how these aspects apply to the real world taking into consideration identified uncertainties and limitations. Underpinning this entire framework are mathematical models, which characterize how different elements act and interact to influence disease risk. Indeed, mathematical models have played a critical role in advancing our understanding of infectious diseases (SIR models, etc.) and in the prevention and treatment of diseases that had already spread to exposed populations. Models are powerful tools that can aid in disease control and prevention,

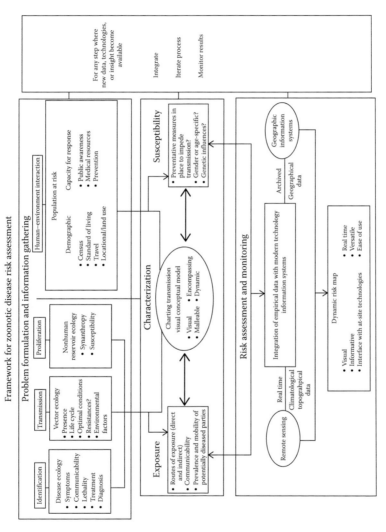

Figure 2.1 Schematic conceptual model for a framework for disease risk estimation. This is a comprehensive conceptual model encompassing several different approaches for risk assessments of vector-borne diseases. Within this framework, mechanistic, statistical, and rule-based models can all be developed and implemented.

allowing optimization of limited resources, or in identification of the most potent control measures (Keeling and Rohani, 2008). In the case of the latter, although multiple control measures exist, they all function by reducing the average amount of transmission to susceptible individuals. By comparing simulated results, models can prove useful for determining which strategy (or strategies) are most likely to yield favorable results given the constraints on time and resources.

2.1.2   *Modeling arthropod-borne vectors of disease*

While there are many potential agents or activities that can put humans at risk, arthropod-borne vectors specifically represent a particularly damaging and vexing problem (CDC, 2014a) that may only be getting worse due to factors such as insecticide resistance, public health policy changes (Gubler, 1998), and climate change (Githeko et al., 2000). On a global scale, arthropod-borne diseases are sources of significant human misery and economic loss, accounting for an estimated 17% of all infection disease (CDC, 2014b). Assessing and reducing disease risk prior to disease outbreak is a vital component to an arthropod vector-borne disease control program (hereafter known simply as "vector control"). Disease risk posed by arthropod-borne vectors can be viewed as the likelihood of humans (or other hosts of interest) being infected by a pathogenic agent via an arthropod vector and, generally, increases when vector abundance increases. Hence, predicting the occurrence, abundance, and population growth of arthropod vectors represents an important step in predicting and preventing the manifestation of disease. And, indeed, much effort has been spent developing mathematical models to describe vector population dynamics. However, while mathematical models, like all models, are simplifications of reality, factors such as spatial heterogeneity, environmental variability, and human intervention (vector control methods) all increase the complexity of interactions between organisms and their environments. Thus, accurately capturing population dynamics, that is, reproducing observed population patterns, of organisms outside of a controlled environment is a significant challenge of population biology and ecology.

As mentioned before, the predominant approach to predicting vector species dynamics is to develop mathematical models that incorporate varying degrees of complexity and stochasticity or variability. Mechanistic models of vector population growth and dispersal, for example (Magori et al., 2009; Legros et al., 2011), are generally based on laboratory experiments that provide estimates of survival, growth, and reproduction that are then used to parameterize stage or age-structured population models. Alternatively, statistical models based on field-collected data (Winters et al., 2008; Schurich et al., 2014) can be constructed based on counts of mosquitoes and a collection of factors known or thought to be important

drivers of arthropod population growth and abundance (e.g., temperature, habitat characteristics, etc.). These regression-based models are then
used as predictive tools that allow for an estimate of abundance (or density) to be generated when model factors are known. Both mechanistic
and statistical models require a great deal of information/data to perform
well, with explicit knowledge of life history parameters required for the
former and sufficient (and sometimes extensive) monitoring data required
for the latter. Also, in many cases, vector density data do not exist yet
or may be prohibitively impractical to obtain, or there is a need to make
decisions involving risk in a rapid manner. This could especially be true
in cases where a new vector is introduced or suspected, or conversely, in
cases where there would be exposure of people in novel areas suspected
to be populated with arthropod vectors. This latter case is particularly
relevant to military personnel deployed in foreign lands.

2.1.3   Mechanistic models: Pros and cons

Figure 2.2 shows an example of a mechanistic, cohort-based population model and highlights the data requirements to parameterize such a
model. This model was developed to better understand and potentially
predict population dynamics of *A. aegypti* in a heterogeneous landscape
subjected to human management activities in the form of pesticide application. The model is stage and age-based for each transition and operates
on a 1-day time step. Data are needed to describe the probability of mosquitoes surviving from one age class/developmental stage to the next on a
per day basis. In Figure 2.2, each arrow represents an important data need
often filled by conducting detailed laboratory studies. There are many

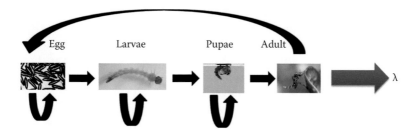

Figure 2.2 A life cycle graph of a mosquito vector. This diagram serves as the first
step in creating a mathematical model describing mosquito population dynamics.
Each arrow represents a transition between life cycle stages, and hence, estimates
for these rates are needed in order to build the model. The blue arrow indicates
an output from the model describing λ, a population level parameter describing
population growth ($\lambda > 1$) or decline ($\lambda < 1$). For mosquitoes, the estimates often
come from laboratory studies or may be assumed.

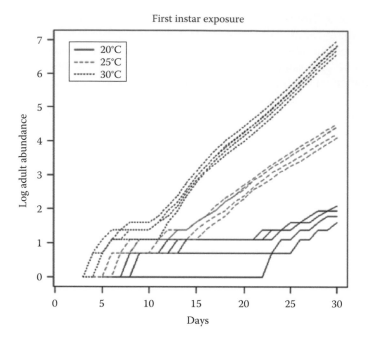

First instar exposure

Figure 2.3 Output from stage/age matrix model on a 1-day time step of *Aedes aegypti* assuming exponential growth. The model was created based on experimental data in which larvae were reared at three temperatures and first instars were exposed to five concentrations of malathion, including two controls, an LC_5, and LC_{25}, and LC_{50}. It can easily be seen that population growth is driven primarily by temperature and secondarily by concentration.

cases and examples of this type of model for a variety of mosquito species, many of which are important disease vectors.

A key advantage of more mechanistic models is that if the different life cycle traits are well characterized and if it is known how those traits respond to different environmental conditions, the model can be quite flexible. A simple example is shown in Figure 2.3, which corresponds to output from the life cycle matrix model shown in Figure 2.2. In this example, the larvae were reared to adulthood at three different temperatures and were exposed to three sublethal concentrations of malathion, an organophosphate pesticide, and two controls. It is easy to see from this Figure 2.3 that when only two factors are considered, including temperature and the concentration of a dose of pesticide to the first cohort only, and when exponential growth is assumed, temperature is the primary driver of population growth. Chemical concentration is a secondary driver, with the highest line in each temperature group corresponding to the control, and the lowest line corresponding to the highest exposure dose (LC_{50}).

An excellent example of a complex, highly parameterized model is Skeeter Buster (Magori et al., 2009). This freely downloadable model (Gould and Lloyd, 2011) is based on the life cycle and breeding habits of *A. aegypti* and is extremely detailed including movement of mosquitoes in and among houses as well as vector control efficacies (Magori et al., 2009; Legros et al., 2011). This modeling platform is based on detailed physiological models of mosquito development, including the incorporation of density effects, nutrient availability, and temperature, to govern aquatic stage (egg, larval, pupa) development, and individual-based models governing adult dispersal and oviposition behavior. The overall model then integrates the two into a spatially explicit environment in which the user can provide highly detailed, real-world information to simulate projected mosquito population dynamics, including the number and size of individual breeding containers at individual houses, local weather conditions, and whether mosquito control methods have been applied. This highly detailed model was found to produce field-accurate predictions (Legros et al., 2011), verifying its utility. However, the extensive effort required for data collection and model development for Skeeter Buster should be noted. Skeeter Buster was developed from a preexisting model platform of the population dynamics of container breeding mosquitoes (CIMSiM) that was developed based on work done by Focks et al. (1993a,b). Skeeter Buster improved on this model by adding in a number of additional considerations, including stochasticity, adult dispersal behavior, and the consideration of genetics (Magori et al., 2009). The performance of the model was also tested against field-collected data (Legros et al., 2011). Lastly, the completed model was outfitted with an easy to use interface and made available online. In total, these considerable efforts required the work of a team of researchers over a period of many years to complete.

Despite the difficulties of building such detailed mechanistic models, these types of model can provide a means of modeling important species interactions such as competition or predation, factors known to contribute strongly to population dynamics. These interspecies interactions can be especially important when (1) species have different biology and/or ecology, (2) there is a risk of nonnative species entering an area, (3) different species show differences in their competence to vector a pathogen, and (4) the modeling effort is geared to supporting an integrated pest management strategy. As an example of the application of a multispecies, mechanistic model, we parameterized a larval competition model in which *A. aegypti* and *A. albopictus* were present in the same location and were using the same breeding habitats. The species share similar traits with regard to development, survival, growth, and reproduction but differ in some key traits. Both species are container breeders, and when larvae from both species are developing in the same container, *A. albopictus* larvae are competitively superior (Braks et al., 2004; Yee et al., 2004; Murrell and Juliano, 2008). The presumption is that under baseline conditions with adequate availability of breeding habitat, *A. albopictus* would competitively dominate and would likely be the important potential vector. However, eggs from *A. aegypti* are more desiccation tolerant than eggs from *A. albopictus*. Under climatic conditions where precipitation patterns are characterized by high variability with long periods between rainfall events, *A. aegypti* can dominate because there is a greater pulse of viable eggs after dry periods. Even when precipitation events are modeled as stochastic, a generally dryer climate can favor *A. aegypti* (Figure 2.4).

While mechanistic models like those described earlier can yield important predictions and novel insights, they are also very data hungry and can be somewhat difficult to use or explain. Moreover, many such models may not have the flexibility to be applied to a wider range

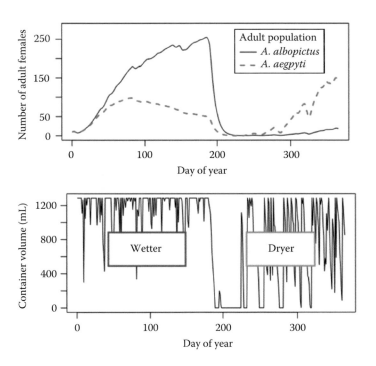

Figure 2.4 Abundance of *Aedes aegypti* and *Aedes albopictus* through time as a function of stochastic rainfall. Earlier time points are generally wetter (more overall precipitation), while later time points are dryer. Differences in larval competitive ability and desiccation tolerance of eggs of each species contribute to dominance under different conditions. This is a good example of how specific species traits (desiccation tolerance) can have a profound impact on which vector is dominant and, hence, which diseases may be more prevalent.

of species, habitats, or climates simply because data are not available. Alternative approaches that follow a more heuristic process of modeling that incorporates basic knowledge and readily available information could be beneficial. As an added benefit, this type of modeling is likely more user friendly, easily communicated and the modeling framework could be flexible enough to accommodate more detailed information as available.

2.1.4   "Fuzzy logic" and streamlined mosquito modeling

A potential way to estimate spatially explicit arthropod-borne disease risk without the need for the intensive data required for highly mechanistic models is to construct a measure of relative risk using a weighted overlay approach in the geographic information systems framework (Mitchell, 2012). In this approach, information (known or suspected) about the biology and habitat associations of the vector species is combined using fuzzy logic rules to construct a spatial dataset representing relative potential vector density within a landscape. The logic behind these rules can be considered "fuzzy" because it is not necessarily empirically derived, but instead may depend upon prior knowledge and expert opinion to describe how contributing spatial attributes relate to vector density, and how different spatial attributes interact with each other to produce the projected density surface. The resulting vector density layer is then overlaid with a spatial dataset of the relative density of humans (perhaps derived from a census) in the landscape. In the simplest case, information regarding habitat associations and the occurrence of humans are all that are needed to construct a preliminary model. Importantly, if better or new data are available, this information can be added to further improve the model. Hence, this modeling approach is tiered where each tier may represent the addition of more information or submodels that can help focus overall estimates of mosquito occurrence and abundance in a spatial context. This approach can be visualized as a series of stacked lenses, all bringing better focus on an image, with the lenses being spatial datasets or submodels, and the image being the projected population density. With each additional lens, the projection becomes more focused. As images can be distorted depending upon the lens, population projections can be altered depending upon the spatial datasets used and the fuzzy logic rules used to associate them to the population projection.

Once basic data layers are available and incorporated, estimates of relative (or absolute) risk for a location can be calculated by incorporating the values of the two density layers into a synthesized index. A similar index using projected mosquito numbers based on a linear regression model was suggested by Winters et al. (2008). For example, both human density and vector density may be previously converted to percentiles, and the relative risk may be calculated for a given location using the following simple formula: relative risk quotient (RRQ) = (VD + HD)/MIV, where VD is the vector density, HD is the human density, and MIV is the maximum index value. In this index, areas of highest vector density and highest human density would receive the highest RRQs, areas of high vector/low human density or low vector/high human density would receive moderate RRQs, and areas of low vector/low human density would receive low RRQs. More quantitative estimates of risk can again be obtained when more and stronger data are available. From a modeling perspective, estimates of relative risk may be adequate to inform either management or prevention activities. Further, exact estimates of mosquito population size are extremely difficult to obtain given the vast number of stochastic factors that act on living systems. In many cases, a relative risk perspective may be all that is attainable.

It should be noted that weighted overlay approaches to estimating mosquito-borne disease have been employed by other authors. For example, Hanafi-Bojd et al. (2012) constructed a complex weighted overlay model including the consideration of climatic, habitat, and anthropogenic (human density, epidemiological data, and mosquito control) data to create a detailed malaria disease risk maps over an Iranian district. In addition, Bindu and Janak (2009) constructed a similar model for an Indian city in which different types of wetlands contributed to risk differently depending upon perceived mosquito production capacity. Although similar in their end result and indeed may share many of the model refinement we later suggest, our methodology (as discussed in the following) differs from these prior efforts in that (1) we construct a potential density surface prior to estimating risk and (2) we explicitly consider mosquito dispersal behavior in the construction of this surface.

As an illustration, we applied this rule-based modeling approach here to develop a measure of relative disease risk posed by *C. tarsalis*, a mosquito species commonly found in the Western United States, to human populations in Lubbock County, Texas. *C. tarsalis* is a known vector of both West Nile Virus and Western Equine Encephalitis. The research described here was conducted using three, readily available spatial datasets, including the US Fish and Wildlife Service/National Wetland Inventory Service (USFWS/NWIS; USFWS, 2014) wetland dataset for Texas, the 2010 US Census dataset (by block) for Lubbock county, Texas (USCB, 2013), and an outline of the extent of Lubbock County (Lubbock, 2013). In the most basic sense, the wetland data layers represent available mosquito breeding habitat for this particular species, which is known to use larger bodies of water for breeding as opposed to species such as *A. albopictus*, which are almost entirely container breeders. All of these datasets are free and publically available online. All spatial analyses were carried out using ArcGIS 10.1.

2.2   Methods

2.2.1   Methodology for rule-based mosquito modeling

2.2.1.1   Creating a potential mosquito density surface: General overview

The first step in the rule-based modeling process is determining how to represent relative vector density within the landscape. This can be accomplished by making the simple assumption that more available suitable breeding habitat will generally translate to more individual organisms (e.g., Shaman et al., 2002, 2006; Shaman and Day, 2005), and therefore, larger habitat patches will have more individuals relative to smaller patches. Although this assumption is not universally the case for all mosquitoes, and such a relationship may not be linear, it is also not unreasonable for species that are common, abundant, and have specific habitat requirements. For all species of mosquitoes in particular, wetland habitat is required to reproduce, as they have several aquatic developmental stages. Because larger wetlands offer more habitat, there is an expected positive relationship between wetland size and the density of mosquitoes that can be supported. To gain an estimate of relative potential population density contributed by each wetland patch, patches within a landscape can be ranked by size, and then assigned those ranks. For example, wetland patches can be ranked by deciles (i.e., 1–10), and then assigned those values. We realize this is a simplified way of characterizing mosquito breeding habitat but additional information and characterization is easily implemented. As an example, a habitat quality index could be used in addition or instead of habitat size if information on habitat suitability of particular wetlands is known.

The disease risk mosquitoes pose is due in large part to their ability to disperse and to find suitable hosts. Actual dispersal behavior of individuals can be complex, but at a larger scale it can be simplified and captured by taking advantage of readily available species information. First, it is known that most individual mosquitoes do not travel far from their location of emergence as adults (often within a few hundred meters) over the course of their lives. However, some individuals are known to be more mobile, for example, *C. tarsalis* females can travel 2–4 km on average away from breeding areas over the course of several days. Therefore, given a single wetland, we would expect that the highest density of mosquitoes would be near the wetland, and as distance increases from breeding sources, the density of mosquitoes would quickly and proportionately (relative to the density at the wetland) decrease. Another basic, but important assumption is that as more patches of habitat are available, overall abundance tends to increase (Reiskind and Wilson, 2004), with more patches of suitable wetland habitat producing higher overall abundances than fewer wetland patches. When multiple wetlands are within close proximity of each other (i.e., within the maximum dispersal distance), the density of mosquitoes at any given point between the patches could be expected to be additive (assuming no density-dependence).

Such a relationship can be approximated with a kernel density estimation (KDE) function (O'Sullivan and Unwin, 2010), with each wetland (represented by a point, or a line) weighted with the relative potential density of mosquitoes (based on their size), and the bandwidth determined by a dispersal distance expected for the species. The kernel function itself, which models the decay of density away from the origin, can be selected based on available empirical information. For example, Estep et al. (2010) used an exponential decay function when constructing kernels to describe the dispersal behavior of *Culex erraticus*. If such information does not exist, different functions can be modeled to capture abundance projections under different dispersal scenarios. Lastly, by converting the resulting density surface into ranks or quantiles, relative potential density across the landscape can be represented.

This structure and computation for this modeling approach could be accomplished using both commercially available (e.g., ArcGIS) as well as open-source platforms (program R, GRASS). In this exercise, we conducted the modeling process using ArcGIS 10.1, which has a graphically based, menu-driven user interface. A feature of ArcMap (included within ArcGIS) that is particularly useful for this approach is the ModelBuilder tool. This tool allows for the construction of a graphical model diagram, which can then be used for model implementation. The overall structure of the model described in the following is shown in Figure 2.5. Model components are represented via polygons connected by arrows, with the left-most circles representing data input files, subsequent circles representing the results of processes, and rectangles representing processes and tools. The arrows indicate the linear nature of this model; that is, both a human density spatial layer and a habitat spatial layer are run progressively through a series of processes before being combined at the end to construct the risk index layer. Aside from being an effective way to visualize the model structure and process, the ModelBuilder tool also allows for multiple model scenarios to be run quickly and easily by simply changing which input files and processes are used and how processes are specified. At any time, additional and more detailed information can be added by modifying existing model structures or adding new ones.

2.2.2   Application to Lubbock, Texas

2.2.2.1   Mosquito density surface

Lubbock County, Texas, lies in the West Texas Pan Handle and is characterized by significant mosquito communities. In part, mosquito communities are supported by abundant potential breeding habitat.

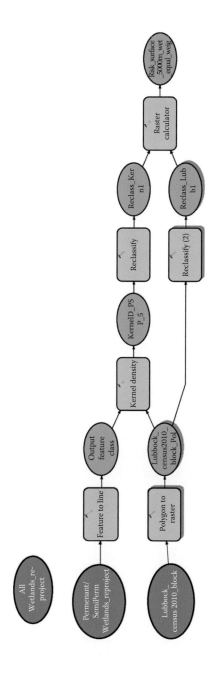

Figure 2.5 Diagram of model structure using the ArcGIS ModelBuilder tool. Blue circles are data input files, yellow rectangles are processes/tools, and green circles are the results of processes.

West Texas is dotted with several thousand mostly small wetlands (man-made and natural), most of which are at least partially ephemeral, which potentially serve as habitat for *C. tarsalis*, particularly if emergent vegetation is present (personal observation). The spatial location and attributes of these wetland patches have been mapped by the USFWS and are included in the Texas NWIS dataset (Figure 2.6). In addition, other attributes, including wetland classification, are included within a code associated with each wetland patch. To prepare this set for the previously described procedure, it was imported into ArcMap 10.1 and clipped to spatially match the Lubbock County layer. The attribute table for the clipped file was then exported, and programs R and MS Excel were used to convert wetland classification codes for each patch into descriptive categories, such as "permanent," "semipermanent," "seasonally flooded," "temporarily flooded," and "intermittently flooded," which correspond to water regime classifications by the USFWS. Lastly, the table was imported back into ArcGIS and joined with the clipped wetland file.

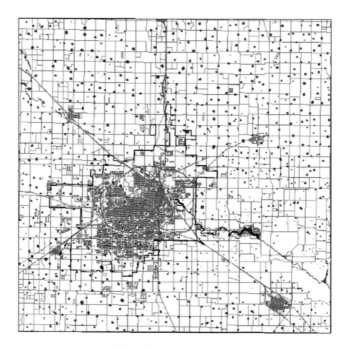

Figure 2.6 Lubbock County, Texas, census blocks with wetland locations in blue. Lubbock city limits are outlined in black. Census spatial data were obtained from the U.S. Census Bureau. Wetland spatial data were obtained from the USFWS. City boundary data were obtained from the city of Lubbock. All other layers incorporated or developed were scaled to the area represented here.

To begin the process of generating a mosquito density surface, the wetland patches were classified by size into deciles. In essence, assigning a decile value to wetland patches ranks the wetlands on a scale from 1 to 10. This classification was then used as the basis of a new layer in which the size decile of a patch is included as a field (i.e., an attribute) in the attribute table of the layer. In order to construct density kernels, we used the built-in KDE tool in ArcMap 10.1. This requires either a polyline or point feature as an input. A point feature, which can be created for each wetland at its center, could have been used. However, we use a polyline for two reasons. First, we are not interested in mosquito density in the space between the boundary of the wetland and the center of the wetland, and second, suitable habitat is generally found along the boundaries of wetlands, where water is shallow and there is more emergent vegetation. Therefore, we converted the polygon file into a polyline shapefile, which we used as the input to the KDE tool. To weight each wetland by their relative size, we specified that the decile classification should be the quantity considered for each point (i.e., used in the "population field" of the KDE tool). Lastly, we used dispersal distance as the bandwidth/search radius, which we derived from previous studies (see Section 2.2.2.4). The default kernel function in ArcMap is the quadratic function (Silverman, 1986; ESRI, 2012), and is the only one available when operating through the graphic user interface. Other functions can be implemented using extensions such as the Geospatial Modeling Environment (Beyer, 2012). Lastly, the classification tool was used to convert the resulting raster surface into deciles again, to estimate relative potential abundance across Lubbock County. Figure 2.7 shows an example of the output from this procedure. In this example, a subset of permanent and semipermanent wetlands in Lubbock county were selected, and the KDE tool was applied in ArcMap 10.1 using a shorter estimate of dispersal distance (500 m) as the bandwidth. After renormalizing, it can clearly be seen that projected densities decrease (move from red to green) as distance from wetlands increase, but that in places where the dispersal distances from different wetlands overlay, the densities increase. This is particularly evident where there are clusters of wetlands, such as within the city limits of Lubbock, the black outline in the center of the figure.

2.2.2.2   Human density surface

Human density was estimated with a dataset from the US Census Bureau that mapped the population of people per polygonal census block in Texas. This areal dataset was imported into ArcMap and clipped to match the areal extent of Lubbock County. The field calculator tool was used to convert the raw population numbers of each census block into a density by dividing the block's area, producing a density surface. In order to use this information along with the mosquito density surface, the human density polygon

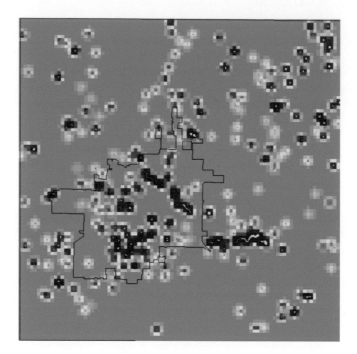

***Figure* 2.7** Result of the kernel density estimation function to project relative population density of *Culex tarsalis* mosquitoes as functions of wetland size and distance from the wetland. In this example, all permanent and semipermanent wetlands in Lubbock are included, and a lower-end dispersal distance of 500 m was used for the function bandwidth.

shapefile was converted to a raster, using the same cell size. To ensure that the extent of the mosquito and human density surfaces aligned, this raster was used as a snap raster when creating the mosquito density surface.

2.2.2.3   *Relative risk surface*

To estimate the relative risk, the mosquito density and the human density surfaces were overlaid with each other, and the raster calculator tool was used to calculate the RRQ using the following expression: 0.5*human density + 0.5*mosquito density. This resulted in a final "risk surface" with a value ranging from 0 to 10, with higher numbers representing higher relative risk. Although the current specification of the risk index is very simple, other specifications need not be. For instance, the index used by Winters et al. (2008) incorporated epidemiological information. Moreover, this relative risk quotient could just as easily be the absolute risk if more detailed information were available related to human and mosquito behaviors, infection rates, and habitat suitability. It should be noted that this point in the process amounts to a weighted overlay approach, and the calculations demonstrated here can be carried out in ArcGIS 10.1 using the weighted overlay tool. This tool proportionately weights each constituent layer, in this case 50% for both layers, in producing a final surface. However, we use the raster calculator tool because it allows greater flexibility in specifying how the final surface is produced. This is particularly useful if more complex mathematical relationships than simple proportional weighting are desired in producing the risk surface.

2.2.2.4 Scenarios

An advantage of this particular approach, other than its relative simplicity, is the ability to easily compare how risk is impacted by different scenarios, taking multiple factors into consideration such as habitat availability and association, behavior, and anthropogenic activity. Here, we compared six different, but plausible scenarios, including differences in habitat availability and differences in dispersal ability. In essence, this amounts to an analysis of uncertainty. In many real cases, there is high uncertainty with regard to the behavior of natural systems. By exploring the impacts on model outcomes of a range of values for given parameters, managers and scientists can better understand the system and better direct information gathering or management activities.

In the first case, we compared the difference in risk during a wet year, in which all wetlands were included as potential contributors of mosquito abundance, and a dry year, in which only permanent and semipermanent wetlands were included. This particular stratification ignores the fact that particular wetlands may be better at producing mosquitoes than others, particularly wetlands with emergent vegetation along their edges. This type of information, however, could be incorporated by the identification and quantification of such habitat via the classification of areal imagery. However, this is beyond the scope of this particular exercise, and a wet/dry year difference is sufficiently drastic to illustrate the overall approach. In the second example, several different dispersal ranges were compared and included (1) a short reported expected dispersal distance (0.5 km, Winters et al., 2008), (2) a medium reported average dispersal distance (2.5 km, Clements, 1999), and (3) a longer reported average dispersal distance (4 km, Clements, 1999). Using the methods described earlier, the three dispersal distances and two habitat availability factors were combined to model and compare the relative risk surfaces of six scenarios.

2.2.3 Model output and interpretation

A comparison of the six scenarios (Figure 2.8) revealed that changes in both number of included wetlands and dispersal radius have a large influence on the distribution of the relative risk across the landscape. Several important patterns emerged from the exercise. First, as the number

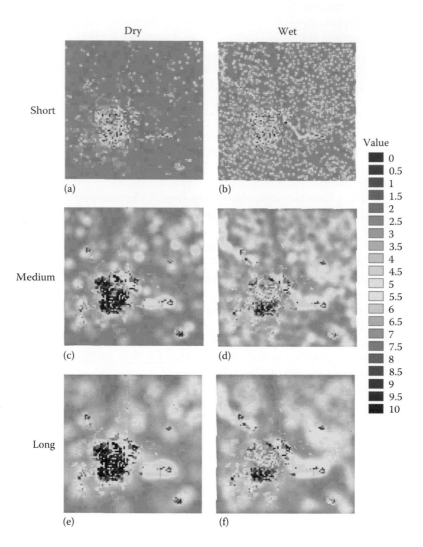

Figure 2.8 All six modeled scenarios, including (a) dry year, short dispersal; (b) wet year, short dispersal; (c) dry year, medium dispersal; (d) wet year, medium dispersal; (e) dry year, long dispersal; and (f) wet year, long dispersal. The figure shows clearly that species traits (dispersal) and environmental conditions (precipitation) both play critical roles in defining the risk landscape. In this case, identifying critical features of mosquito population dynamics is critical for developing informative risk maps.

of wetlands increases, the number of overlapping kernels increases, and the risk surface became more generalized, meaning that risk, in essence, becomes more homogeneous. This results in more areas of moderate risk, relative to high- and low-risk areas. Similarly, as the dispersal radius increased, the risk surface also became more generalized, with more areas of moderate risk surrounding areas of higher risk. When the dispersal radius is very small (500 m), higher risk is concentrated immediately around wetlands (Figure 2.8a and b). As dispersal distance increases, kernels become wider, spreading risk further away from wetlands. When dispersal distance reaches the point where kernels begin to overlap, the result is large clusters of high and moderate risk surrounded by a matrix of relatively lower risk (Figure 2.8c and e). When there are many wetlands and longer dispersal distances, the most generalized relative risk surfaces are produced due to the normalization process, with only the highest combinations of human and mosquito densities resulting in large high risk clusters (Figure 2.8d and f).

Other insights can also be obtained by directly comparing scenarios via raster calculator subtraction. Essentially, this calculation allows the user to clearly identify how changes in parameter values or assumptions relate to net differences in relative risk. In Figure 2.9, the

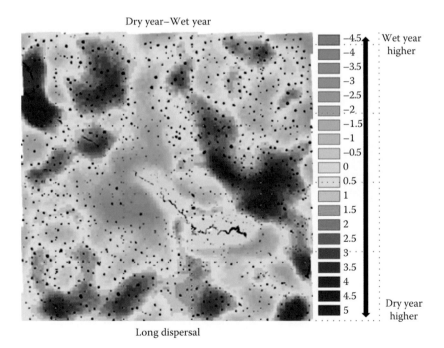

Figure 2.9 Comparison of wet versus dry year scenarios (long dispersal) using raster calculator. This simple analytical approach provides immediate insight into how (in this case) wet years increase the relative spatial risk of mosquito-borne disease.

risk surface of the wet year, long dispersal scenario is subtracted from the dry year, long dispersal surface. In this image, the purple polygons are permanent and semipermanent wetlands, while the black polygons are all other wetland classifications. This analysis clearly indicates that the level of relative risk is higher (in this example becomes greener) in the dry scenario around the permanent and semipermanent wetlands (especially in the center of the county where most people live), while relative risk is higher (in this example becomes redder) in the wet scenario around larger concentrations of other wetlands. This suggests that when there are fewer wetlands available, individual wetland productivity and proximity to humans is important in determining relative risk, and when there are more wetlands available, relative risk may be more influenced by the proximity of wetlands to each other. In Figure 2.10, the risk surface of the long dispersal, wet year scenario was subtracted from the short dispersal, wet year scenario. As shown in the image, relative risk is higher (i.e., more red regions on map) in the short dispersal scenario in the immediate areas around mostly larger, isolated wetlands. Conversely, relative risk is higher (i.e., greener) in

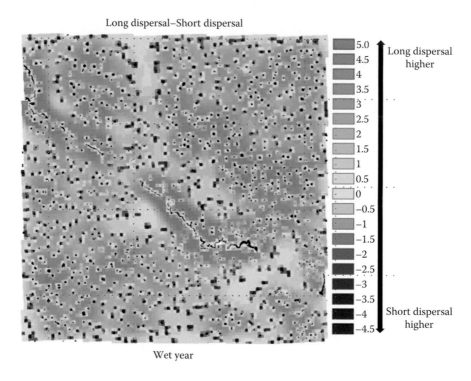

Long dispersal–Short dispersal

Wet year

Figure 2.10 Comparison of long versus short dispersal (dry year) using raster calculator.

the long dispersal scenario in areas where wetlands are clustered. This suggests that when dispersal distance is short or wetlands are isolated, relative risk in close proximity to a given wetland would be expected to be higher than with longer dispersal ability and clustered wetlands. This further indicates that spatial location of wetlands, in addition to size and dispersal ability, is an important factor in determining relative disease risk.

This exercise points to the utility of using a rule-based modeling approach in at least identifying areas that may be considered "high relative risk" to focus monitoring and/or control efforts. Given dwindling resources available for vector control, a spatially explicit, knowledge-based model that provides clear maps of relative risk could prove extremely valuable in guiding future disease risk efforts. As well, the uncertainty analysis we conducted further helps identify the impact on relative risk of changes in information or conditions. We emphasize that the spatially explicit insights into relative mosquito risk were obtained with a minimum of data collection and fundamentally based on preexisting spatial data layers.

2.2.4 Refining the model

As mentioned earlier, the advantage of the rule-based modeling framework is that valuable insights and outputs can be obtained from a minimum of available data. Refining the model can result in appreciable increases in realism in model projections. In the earlier case, for example, the model was based on two particularly important assumptions: that mosquito abundance increased only as a factor of wetland size and that density tends to decrease away from wetlands due to dispersal behavior. While there is ample evidence that breeding habitat quantity relates strongly to total mosquito population size, our fieldwork has indicated and others have found (i.e., Chase and Knight, 2003) that certain wetland features such as long hydroperiod favor the support of a strong predator community that can serve to effectively reduce mosquito production. In reality, then mosquito production will be a function of availability and suitability of breeding habitat. In addition, dispersal behaviors of some species, including *C. tarsalis*, may differ depending upon the surrounding habitat, with some habitats more likely than others to be used as dispersal corridors (Barker et al., 2009). Such a data refinement can drastically alter estimates of mosquito abundance and therefore disease risk, and if this information can be incorporated into the model, it would increase confidence in the model projections. Three important ways that model refinements can be made are (1) the addition of focusing rules, (2) through more informed specification of fuzzy logic relationships, and

(3) through refinement of the risk index. For example, habitat suitability can be incorporated into the model by perhaps assuming that at a certain size, water regime, or combination thereof, wetlands will support a more diverse predator community and hence mosquito production will decrease with larger wetlands. Adding such a rule will also require that the basic habitat-size relationship be altered, either by weighting nonsuitable wetlands differently or perhaps by creating an entirely new habitat–abundance relationship scheme. A predator community-size or water regime relationship could be developed with some field sampling of wetlands, or by literature review. Also, an actual data layer of mosquito abundance, perhaps developed via surveying over a subset of the area of interest, would be useful here. In addition to the mosquito density layer, the human density layer could also be refined to better reflect that some human populations may be more at higher risk than others. For example, relative income level may be found to relate to people spending more or less time outdoors, and children are often at greater risk from infectious diseases than adults. These patterns could be employed as model refinements by using demographic and economic data to impose additional refining rules, and by developing a modified scheme for ranking the human data. Lastly, the computation of the risk index in this case was also quite rudimentary, with both potential mosquito density and human density layers equally weighted in an additive index. However, a risk index may be improved with the addition of epidemiological data, similar to Winters et al. (2008), or by using the economic or demographic data suggested earlier. Table 2.1 provides a list of potential refinements and a qualitative assessment of the effort needed to acquire the information and implement the refinement.

It is important to note that although the actual creation and implementation of the rule-based model does not require actual data, the process of specifying and refining the model will require careful consideration and research, and the rules and fuzzy logic relationships implemented in the model should be biologically based and logically sound. As with any model, the model output is only as good as the information used to build it, and expert judgment should be utilized whenever possible. For example, in the weighted overlay model to predict malaria risk by Hanafi-Bojd et al. (2012), the authors report conducting a survey of malaria experts to determine factors important in the malarial cycle, and the relative importance of these factors when developing their weighting scheme. In general, as more and better information becomes available, better refining layers to the model can be made, more informed fuzzy logic relationships can be determined, and better population and/or risk projections can be made. Ultimately, with increasingly specific refining layers and relationships, this approach may develop into a combination mechanistic and

Table 2.1 Potential refinements to the model projecting relative density of *Culex tarsalis* in the southern high plains of Texas

Information layer	Category	Potential approach to refinement	Relative implementation difficulty
Vector density	Habitat suitability	1. Reweighting by patch size or length	Easy
		2. Stratifying and reweighting by predefined habitat	Easy
		3. Stratifying and reweighting by classes defined through image analysis	Moderately difficult
	Dispersal behavior	1. Using or altering other existing kernels	Moderately easy
		2. Developing custom kernel based on field data	Difficult
		3. Wind influence: directional, sequentially applied	Moderately difficult
		4. Differential habitat permeability to dispersal: cost surface and diffusion-based dispersion	Difficult
	Mosquito control	1. Larvicide: Removing or reducing contribution from	Easy
		2. Adulticide: Masking treated areas, renormalizing density surface	Moderately easy
Human density	Demographic factors Economic factors	If data are available (via census or municipal data), classifying and reweighting human density layer	Moderately easy
Risk index	Epidemiological data	If data are available (via health department), incorporating incidences of disease in the risk index	Moderately easy

Note: Relative difficulty refers to the difficulty for the average ArcGIS user of implementing the refinement in ArcMap 10.1 and does not take into consideration the fuzzy logic rules by which the refinement will operate on model projections.

fuzzy framework for predicting disease risk. This would give the benefit of rapid model development for decision making with the flexibility to improve as more data and incidences become available.

2.3   Discussion

2.3.1   Broader application of rule-based models for risk estimation

While the examples here focused on estimating mosquito abundance and, by extension, disease risk, the spatially explicit rule-based approach can likely be applied to a range of potential management or risk scenarios. Many of the issues identified in other chapters of this text, for example, may be well served by such a modeling approach. With any such exercise, the key lies in identifying the important drivers of potential risk or vulnerability and to then assemble as much knowledge (or a good guess) and the associated spatial data layers as possible with which to start formalizing the model. In many cases, there is a wealth of data and information available that can be used to inform model development and use. As such, this type of framework would work well inside a public health informatics program where a large quantity of data are obtained and managed.

In an extreme case, a spatially explicit modeling environment can be used to help identify a risk as posed from, for example, a biopathogen weapon attack (see Chapter 3). Here, the actual risk agent (vector) may not be known but available data may be useful in at least first identifying a pattern of infection that may provide insight into the nature of the attack and, better yet, the potential agent involved.

Public health agencies and the Department of Defense collect information regarding the potential for a biopathogen attack. Table 2.1 provides a list of potentially available data that could be used to start building a rule-based model that identifies patterns of risk. Data that may be commonly recorded that could potentially be useful for building rule-based models might include unusual etiology of disease, infections downwind or downstream, unusual numbers of dead livestock or wildlife, and/or a large number of nonnative arthropods.

2.3.2   Conclusions and further research

Understanding, predicting, and managing disease risk are critical to maintain public health and, for the military, to maintain readiness and limit casualties. Here, we provide examples of mechanistic models as well as a newly developing, streamlined modeling approach that can be implemented with varying degrees of data. We show that mechanistic models, while extremely valuable and useful for providing detailed and important insights into vector ecology and abundance, are frequently limited by data availability and, in many cases, expertise. Alternatively, the rule-based approach can be implemented in a heuristic manner with less hard data but is flexible enough to incorporate detailed information when available. The clear drawback to the rule-based approach is that in our example, we only assessed relative risk, not absolute risk. That is, we do not differentiate between high or low overall numbers of vector organisms, only relative numbers. A potential solution to this may be to adjust the overall scale used to represent potential mosquito density to represent higher (i.e., warmer, wetter) and lower (i.e., cooler, dryer weather) potential density conditions. Also, the model could be calibrated to actual data numbers instead of using a decile approach.

Despite the limitations of the approach, the results from this type of analysis have clear and practical management implications. For instance, it was shown here that during dryer years, areas of higher relative risk are distributed throughout populated areas near larger wetlands, while in wetter years, areas of highest risk are distributed where the largest human and mosquito densities overlap. In addition, if a species or population is known to have a more restricted dispersal ability, risk may be higher immediately adjacent to wetlands than with longer dispersers. For vector control authorities with limited resources, such risk maps may be helpful in guiding the use of their resources to better effect. And, because the approach is flexible, management implications can improve with additional model specification. For example, anthropogenic stressors, such as larvicides or wetland draining, could be included by removing particular wetlands. The impact of wind could be included by masking portions of the density kernels in particular directions. Likewise, habitat permeability to dispersal may be included by modeling dispersal in other ways, including through diffusion, and by incorporating barriers or cost surfaces. As mentioned in Section 2.2.4, the amount of available habitat could be refined by further specifying habitat types, and/or weighting how different wetlands contribute to relative potential abundance. The impact of human density on risk could be altered by utilizing demographic or economic data to differentially weight the density layer. Lastly, the function used to calculate the risk surface itself can be altered to better reflect risk conditions, including the consideration of epidemiological information. In conclusion, this approach is a flexible, streamlined method of estimating disease risk in situations where data are limited.

References

Barker, C.M., Bolling, B.G., Moore, C.G., and Eisen, L. 2009. Relationship between distance from major larval habitats and abundance of adult mosquitoes in semiarid plains landscapes in Colorado. *J. Med. Entomol.* 46(6):1290–1298.

Beyer, H.L. 2012. Geospatial modeling environment [WWW Document]. http://www.spatialecology.com/gme/index.htm (accessed November 27, 2015).

Bindu, B. and Janak, J. 2009. Identifying malaria risk zones using GIS—A study of Vadodara City. *J. Commun. Dis.* 41:239–248.

Black, R.E. et al. 2010. Global, regional, and national causes of child mortality in 2008: A systematic analysis. *Lancet* 375(9730):1969–1987.

Braks, M.A.H, Honório, Lounibos, L.P., Lourenço-de-Oliveira, and Juliano, S.A. 2004. Interspecific competition between two invasive species of container mosquitoes, *Aedes aegypti* and *Aedes albopictus* (Diptera:Culcidae), in Brazil. Annals of the Entomological Society of America. 97 (1):130–139.

CDC. 2014a. Division of vector-borne diseases [WWW Document]. Centers for Disease Control. Atlanta, GA. http://www.cdc.gov/ncezid/dvbd/ (accessed November 27, 2015).

CDC. 2014b. World Health Day: Vector-borne diseases. [WWW Document]. Centers for Disease Control. Atlanta, GA. http://www.cdc.gov/Features/worldhealthday2014/ (accessed November 27, 2015).

Chase, J.M. and Knight, T.M. 2003. Drought-induced mosquito outbreaks in wetlands. *Ecol. Lett.* 6:1017–1024. doi:10.1046/j.1461-0248.2003.00533.x.

Cleaveland, S., Laurenson, M.K., and Taylor, L.H. 2001. Diseases of humans and their domestic mammals: Pathogen characteristics, host range and the risk of emergence. *Philos. Trans. R. Soc. B* 356(1411):991–999.

Clements, A.N. 1999. *The Biology of Mosquitoes*, Vol. 2: *Sensory Reception and Behavior.* CABI, New York.

Cook, G.C. 2001. Influence of diarrhoeal diseas on miliatry and naval campaigns. *J. R. Soc. Med.* 94(2):95–97.

Daszak, P., Cunningham, A.A., and Hyatt, A.D. 2000. Emerging infectious diseases of wildlife—Threats to biodiversity and human health. *Science* 287(5452):443–449.

ESRI. 2012. ArcGIS Help 10.1 [WWW Document]. ArcGIS Resour. http://resources.arcgis.com/en/help/main/10.1/index.html#//009z00000011000000 (accessed November 27, 2015).

Estep, L.K., Burkett-Cadena, N.D., Hill, G.E., Unnasch, R.S., and Unnasch, T.R. 2010. Estimation of the dispersal distances of Culex erraticus in a Focus of Eastern Equine Encephalitis virus in the Southeastern United States. *J. Med. Entomol.* 47(6):977–986.

Focks, D.A., Haile, D.G., Daniels, E., and Mount, G.A. 1993a. Dynamic life table model for *Aedes aegypti* (Diptera: Culicidae): Analysis of the literature and model development. *J. Med. Entomol.* 30:1003–1017.

Focks, D.A., Haile, D.G., Daniels, E., and Mount, G.A. 1993b. Dynamic life table model for *Aedes aegypti* (Diptera: Culcidae): Siulation results and validation. *J. Med. Entomol.* 30:1018–1028.

Githeko, K., Lindsay, S., Confalonieri, U., and Patz, J. 2000. Climate change and vector-borne diseases: A regional analysis. *Bull. World Health Organ.* 78:1136–1147.

Gould, F. and Lloyd, A.L. 2011. SkeeterBuster [WWW Document]. http://www.skeeterbuster.net/ (accessed November 27, 2015).

Gubler, D.J. 1998. Resurgent vector-borne diseases as a global health problem. *Emerg. Infect. Dis.* 4:442–450. doi:10.3201/eid0403.980326.

Hanafi-Bojda, A.A. et al. 2012. Spatial analysis and mapping of malaria risk in an endemic area, south of Iran: A GIS based decision making for planning of control. *Acta Trop.* 122:132–137.

Jones, K.E. et al. 2008. Global trends in emerging infectious diseases. *Nature* 451:990–993.

Keeling, M.J. and Rohani, P. 2008. *Modeling Infectious Diseases in Humans and Animals.* Princeton University Press, Princeton, NJ.

Legros, M., Magori, K., Morrison, A.C., Xu, C., Scott, T.W., Lloyd, A.L., and Gould, F. 2011. Evaluation of location-specific predictions by a detailed simulation model of *Aedes aegypti* populations. *PLoS One* 6:1–11. doi:10.1371/journal.pone.0022701.

Lubbock, C. 2013. The City of Lubbock: GIS and data services [WWW Document]. http://www.mylubbock.us/departmental-websites/departments/gis-data-services/home (accessed November 27, 2015).

Magori, K., Legros, M., Puente, M.E., Focks, D.A., Scott, T.W., Lloyd, A.L., and Gould, F. 2009. Skeeter Buster: A stochastic, spatially explicit modeling tool for studying *Aedes aegypti* population replacement and population suppression strategies. *PLoS Negl. Trop. Dis.* 3:e508. doi:10.1371/journal.pntd.0000508.

Mitchell, A. 2012. *The ESRI Guide to GIS Analysis,* Vol 3: *Modeling Suitability, Movement, and Interaction.* ESRI Press, Redlands, CA.

Murrell, E.G. and Juliano, S.A. 2008. Detritus type alters and outcome of inter-specific competition between *Aedes aegypti* and *Aedes albopictus* (Diptera: Culicidae). *J. Med. Entomol.* 45(3):375–383.

O'Sullivan, D. and Unwin, D.J. 2010. *Geographic Information Analysis,* 2nd edn. Wiley & Sons, Inc., Hoboken, NJ.

Reiskind, M.H. and Wilson, M.L. 2004. *Culex restuans* (Diptera: Culicidae) oviposition behavior determined by larval habitat quality and quantity in Southeastern Michigan. *J. Med. Entomol.* 41:179–186.

Schurich, J., Kumar, S., Eisen, L., and Moore, C.G. 2014. Modeling *Culex tarsalis* abundance on the northern Colorado front range using a landscape-level approach. *J. Am. Mosq. Control Assoc.* 20:7–20.

Shaman, J. and Day, J.F. 2005. Achieving operational hydrologic monitoring of mosquitoborne disease. *Emerg. Infect. Dis.* 11:1343–1350.

Shaman, J., Spiegelman, M., Cane, M., and Stieglitz, M. 2006. A hydrologically driven model of swamp water mosquito population dynamics. *Ecol. Modell.* 194:395–404. doi:10.1016/j.ecolmodel.2005.10.037.

Shaman, J., Stieglitz, M., Stark, C., Le Blancq, S., and Cane, M. 2002. Using a dynamic hydrology model to predict mosquito abundances in flood and swamp water. *Emerg. Infect. Dis.* 8:6–13.

Silverman, B.W. 1986. *Density Estimation for Statistics and Data Analysis.* Chapman and Hall, London, U.K./New York.

USCB. 2013. United States Census Bureau: Geography [WWW Document]. TIGER Prod. https://www.census.gov/geo/maps-data/data/tiger.html.

USFWS. 2014. National wetlands inventory [WWW Document]. http://www.fws.gov/wetlands/.

Winters, A.M., Bolling, B.G., Beaty, B.J., Blair, C.D., Eisen, R.J., Meyer, A.M., Pape, W.J., Moore, C.G., and Eisen, L. 2008. Combining mosquito vector and human disease data for improved assessment of spatial West Nile virus disease risk. *Am.J. Trop. Med. Hyg.* 78:654–665.

World Health Organization. 2004. *International Statistical Classification of Diseases and Related Health Problems*, Vol. 1. World Health Organization, Geneva, Switzerland.

Yee, D.A., Kesavaraju, B., and Juniano, S.A. 2004. Larval feeding behavior of three co-occurring species of container mosquitoes. *J Vector Ecol.* 29(2):315–322.

Zapor, M.J. and Moran, K.A. 2005. Infectious diseases during wartime. *Curr. Opin. Infect. Dis.* 18(5):395–399.

chapter three

Threats and vulnerabilities associated with biological agents

Steven M. Presley, Kristyn N. Urban, and Anna G. Gibson

Contents

> The fear that new plagues are in the making is not unjustified. In most parts of the world we are unprepared for any new pestilence. We have not enough water, not enough food, not enough shelter, and no peace.
>
> **—I.J.P. Loefler (1996)**

3.1   Introduction

Human morbidity and mortality resulting from infectious diseases associated with famine, pestilence, and epidemics have shaped history, cultures, and societies far more than the direct effects of war and political struggles. Conversely, the indirect effects and unintended consequences of political struggles and wars have oftentimes perpetuated famine, pestilence, and infectious disease epidemics and pandemics. Ironically, or perhaps efficiently, many of the infectious disease-causing organisms historically associated with the famine, pestilence, and epidemics resulting from war and political unrest have been utilized in their natural or an altered state as weapons to wage war or coerce societies and governments to change through terroristic campaigns. History is replete with examples of individuals, militant groups, and nation-states employing biological threat agents, including both pathogens and toxins, to disrupt, coerce, and destroy their enemies. From the most simple and expedient tactical use of a natural-state pathogen (i.e., *Yersinia pestis* in the corpses of plague victims) delivered to the besieged Genoese defenders of Kaffa by the Tarters in 1346 to the highly organized and strategic development and use of *Y. pestis* and various other pathogens by the Imperial Japanese Army at Unit 731 in the mid- to late 1930s, the employment of disease and terror for the purposes of defeating one's enemies is not novel (Arnon et al., 2001; Rosenau, 2001; Wheelis, 2002; Wheelis et al. 2006; Witkowski and Parish, 2002; Barenblatt, 2004; Riedel, 2004; Shukla and Sharma 2005; Koblentz, 2009).

We define a biological threat agent as any living microorganism (pathogen), or the toxic product derived from a living organism (toxin), that may cause disease or adverse physiological response in animals, humans, and plants. Disease infers a state of "not at ease/normal" and is typically a progressive unhealthy condition; whereas an adverse physiological response may include allergic reactions, and temporary or permanent physiological damage (e.g., organ damage). Biological threat agents occurring in the environment include any pathogenic or toxic agent that naturally exists and are maintained in animals, plants, or elsewhere and may be acquired by or transmitted to humans. Such agents include anthroponoses, zoonoses, other infectious diseases, and toxins, and may be representatives of various taxa and genera, including bacterial, chlamydial, protozoan, rickettsial, viral, fungal, and prion species. When we consider biological weapon agents, they are biological threat agents that have been "weaponized" to facilitate their delivery, environmental stability, infectivity properties, and virulence. There are approximately 1400 species of infectious microorganisms and agents that are known to cause human disease (bacteria, fungi, helminths, prions, protozoa, rickettsia, viruses, etc.) (Taylor et al., 2001). Of those infectious microorganisms and agents, roughly 61% are zoonotic and 13% are considered to be emerging. Additionally, approximately 75% of those emerging agents are zoonotic, and 28% of those emerging zoonoses are vector-borne. Of those 1400 infectious agents, 25 are designated as Select Agents by the U.S. Centers for Disease Control and Prevention (2010).

From a global perspective, naturally occurring vector-borne and zoonotic infectious diseases cause approximately two million human deaths each year and immeasurable morbidity resulting in lost productivity and reduced quality of life for untold numbers of people. Additionally, vast numbers of people suffer from the long-term health effects and chronic disease conditions that are a result of their exposure to pathogens, toxins in the foods they eat, or from the environments in which they live. These biological toxins are typically classified with regard to the living organism source from which they are produced or derived. This classification includes mycotoxins (fungal toxins; e.g., aflatoxin), microbial toxins (bacterial toxins; e.g., botulinum toxin), phytotoxins (plant toxins; e.g., ricin), and animal toxins (e.g., arthropod and snake venoms). There are a wide array of mycotoxins that are produced by highly invasive fungal species, such as numerous *Aspergillus* species (approximately 40 species known to cause disease in humans), that naturally occur in most human environments.

Human activities that alter natural ecosystems likely also affect the transmission cycles and dynamics of naturally occurring biological agents in the environment. An example for consideration is the creation or enhancement of phytotelmata-rich environments as a result of agricultural practices or urbanization in an area, and the resultant increase in container-breeding mosquito species that may be vectors of disease pathogens (Yanoviak et al., 2006). Additionally and as a result of urbanization, there is often an increase in the potential exposure of humans and domestic animals to wildlife and enzootic vectors at the WUI (wildlife/urban interface). It is critical to understand the oftentimes complex relationships that exist between the pathogen, its various hosts, and the environment to effectively prevent or control threats to human public health. Additionally, recognizing the extensive diversity and vast numbers of biological agents is essential for one to understand the threat they pose to human, animal, and plant health globally, both naturally occurring and intentionally introduced.

3.2   Biological threats

The incidence and frequency of naturally occurring disease outbreaks are significantly influenced by infrastructure, cultural and social factors. Host factors influence the degree to which an individual is susceptible to becoming infected and vulnerable to the disease process. An individual's genotype, nutritional status, immune status, cultural and social behavior, etc. are all critical factors in their potential for infection. Biologic agent (pathogen) factors influence the capacity of the pathogenic microorganism to infect and cause pathology. Environmental factors influence or possibly facilitate the interaction between the potential host and biologic agent, and transmission. Surroundings, both natural and manmade, vegetation, weather, structures, roads, economy, political, vectors (arthropods, other invertebrates, vertebrate animals, people), etc., all influence to some degree the transmission dynamics of a biologic agent. Additionally, there are auxiliary factors that directly and indirectly influence the occurrence of disease, and include those that are physical, biological, and social/cultural.

Physical factors include climate (rainfall, humidity, temperature, sunlight intensity, wind, etc.), topography, soils, and hydrology. Biological factors include flora and fauna in an area, prevalent and endemic diseases in an area, "herd immunity," dominant blood groups of the population, and the degree of parasitism in the potential host population. Social factors include population distribution and density, standard of living (housing, diet, clothing, sanitation, economics, etc.), and religious and cultural norms.

Other than active and passive biological threat agent detection technologies, there are several key indicators that can be relied upon to recognize, or strongly suspect, that a biological weapon has been deployed in an area. These indicators include occurrence of a large outbreak or epidemic of a disease not normally occurring in the region, with higher than normal case fatality rates; an unusual etiology of the diagnosed disease (e.g., disease normally acquired through flea bite, but pulmonary presentations most common in outbreak); multiple epizootics and crossover human infections; no disease in persons in isolated environments, but within same area of outbreak; casualties only downwind or downstream (monitor trends); large numbers of dead livestock or wildlife in the area; and large numbers of nonindigenous arthropods observed in the area.

3.3   Historic perspective

Naturally occurring disease outbreaks, epidemics, and pandemics have significantly shaped human history, and the psychological terror associated with such historic events are most certainly associated with the contemporary perspective and effectiveness of biological threats. The massive mortality resulting from the last of a long series of plague (*Y. pestis*) epidemics that devastated the city of London, England, from 1499 through 1665 was truly terrifying. The weekly total number of reported human deaths caused by plague during the summer and fall of 1665 was approximately 8000. "The Great Plague of London" in 1665 killed between 16% and 22% of London's population of about 460,000 (Moote and Moote, 2004). The devastating morbidity and mortality resulting from the "Spanish flu" pandemic of 1918–1919 affected human populations throughout the world. In the United States, morbidity estimates in the autumn of 1918 included 500,000 ill in New York State, 350,000 ill in Pennsylvania, 220,000 ill in Virginia, 150,000 ill in Ohio, and 100,000 ill in New Jersey. Estimates of percentage mortality caused by the influenza virus in major U.S. cities included 14.8% in Baltimore, 15.8% in Philadelphia, and 10.9% in Washington, DC (Iezzoni, 1999). Worldwide, estimated mortality attributed to the pandemic influenza included 2.2% of the population of Guatemala, 1.0% of the population of Chile, and 0.6% of the population of France (Oldstone, 1998). During the 1918 Meuse-Argonne offensive of World War I, it is estimated that 69,000 U.S. soldiers were incapacitated by influenza. Additionally, it is estimated that approximately 43% of U.S. casualties in World War I were due to the pandemic influenza (Byerly, 2010).

The United States government did not officially establish a biological warfare research program until late 1941 or early 1942, when President

F.D. Roosevelt signed it into being. George Merck was selected by the president and appointed to lead the program. Initially Merck and the program were tasked to investigate the potential uses and efficacies of various agriculture-related pathogens as weapons to cripple the economies and agricultural resources of enemy nations. The specific pathogens identified for study included Newcastle disease virus, highly pathogenic avian influenza virus (fowl plague), foot and mouth disease virus, classical swine fever virus (hog cholera), rice blast fungus, cereals stem rust fungus, wheat scab fungus, and late blight fungus. It was not until the Korean War period (1950–1953) that human disease–causing pathogens were added to the list of specific biological weapon agents designated for study by the U.S. biological warfare research program, including *Bacillus anthracis, Francisella tularensis, Brucella* species, *Coxiella burnetii*, Venezuelan equine encephalitis virus, *Clostridium botulinum* toxin, and *Staphylococcal* enterotoxin-B (Croddy et al., 2002; Smart, 1997; Wheelis et al., 2006). Additionally, research toward the development of at least 15 other pathogens that cause disease in livestock and domestic animals was conducted for the development of biological weapons to devastate the agricultural animal industry—thus the economy. Among those 15 anti-animal pathogens were included African swine fever virus (7 strains), blue tongue virus (5 strains), bovine influenza virus (1 strain), foot and mouth disease virus (11 strains), fowl plague virus (34 strains), goat pneumonitis virus (4 strains), Newcastle disease virus (3 strains), Rift Valley fever virus (4 strains), Rinderpest virus (41 strains), and vesicular stomatitis virus (7 strains) (Wilson et al., 2000).

In recent years, there have been numerous reviews published regarding the historical uses and effects of biological threat agents, both as weapons of war and as weapons of terrorism. For the purposes of this chapter, we only briefly describe a few such historic events to remind the reader that the effective employment of biological agents (i.e., pathogens and toxins) does not necessarily require high-tech formulation and culturing equipment, nor complicated delivery and dissemination devices to achieve effective results, whether those results include significant morbidity, mortality, or widespread terror. From the very simple delivery approach used by sixth-century BC Assyrians to deliver a toxin derived from ergot-infected rye by poisoning the water wells of besieged enemies to the more complicated semicovert use of weaponized *Bacillus anthracis* spores disseminated through the "anthrax letters" of October and November 2001, the real threat to societies posed by such pathogens and toxins is their respective adaptability to be effectively weaponized for use as weapons of war and terrorism. In-depth reviews of the historical uses and development of biological weapons for warfare, terrorism, and biological crimes are provided in Smart (1997) and Dudley and Woodford (2002).

3.4   Current threats

The occurrence of an infectious disease agent in a specific geographic region or human population may be a significant indication for social, demographic, and economic factors. Whether through natural, accidental, or intentional introduction of an infectious disease agent into human or animal populations, recognizing and understanding the specific identity, biology, and transmission dynamics of the pathogen are extremely important in developing and implementing the appropriate therapeutic and preventative course of action.

Over the past decade, there has been significant global concern regarding emerging and resurgent pathogens. Emerging pathogens may be defined by three characteristics, and include (1) a previously recognized infectious disease agent occurring in a new host species, (2) a previously recognized infectious disease agent occurring in a new geographic area, and (3) the occurrence of a previously unknown disease agent. Resurgent pathogens may also be defined by three characteristics, including (1) the reappearance of an infectious disease agent that previously occurred in a particular host species, (2) the reappearance of an infectious disease agent that previously occurred in a particular geographic area, and (3) the reestablishment of previously endemic/enzootic foci of disease in a particular area. The natural reintroduction and establishment of a vector-transmitted infectious disease agent in an area, or population, is highly dependent on the occurrence of adequate numbers of the vector species to facilitate amplification of the pathogen. We also must consider "designer" vectors (i.e., genetically engineered mosquitoes, ticks, fleas, or biting flies that are more effective or efficient in vectoring weaponized zoonotic pathogens).

Recognition and concern regarding the significant threat from emerging and resurgent diseases of wildlife and domestic animals has continued increase over the past 25 years. In addition to the public health threat posed, the economic and ecological threats have been increasingly considered (Daszak et al., 2000). Table 3.1 provides a listing of the diseases and pathogenic agents that are considered to pose the greatest threat to the agricultural industry, and thus the economy of the United States.

As an example of the significant threat to both human health, animal health, as well as the agricultural economy, we summarize a multicounty, regional survey of feral swine (*Sus scrofa*) populations for specific zoonotic and agriculture-relevant pathogens. In the United States, feral swine have been documented to occur in at least 38 states. The feral swine population is estimated to be approximately four to five million in United States, with an estimated two to three million in Texas. They cause an estimated annual loss of more than $1 billion nationwide, and approximately $63 million in Texas. Additionally, feral swine populations have been reported to be

Table 3.1 Diseases posing the greatest threat to the agricultural industry and economy within the United States[a]

Specific disease/ pathogen	Species typically infected						
	Avian	Bovine	Caprine	Equine	Swine	Wildlife	Zoonotic
African horse sickness[b]				X			
African swine fever[b]					X		
Anthrax[c]		X	X		X	X	X
Avian influenza virus[b]	X					X	X
Bluetongue virus[b]		X	X			X	
Chlamydia psittaci	X						X
Classical swine fever[b]					X	X	
Foot and mouth disease[b]		X	X			X	
Heartwater, cowdriosis[b]		X	X			X	
Lumpy skin disease virus[b]		X				X	
Lyssaviruses and rabies viruses		X	X	X	X	X	X
Newcastle disease[b]	X					X	
Porcine enterovirus 1					X	X	
Porcine enterovirus 9					X	X	
Porcine reproductive and respiratory syndrome					X	X	
Primary screwworm		X	X	X	X	X	
Pseudorabies virus		X	X	X	X	X	X
Rift Valley fever virus[c]		X	X				
Rinderpest virus[b]		X				X	
Sheep and goat pox virus[b]			X			X	
Venezuelan equine encephalomyelitis[c]				X			X
Vesicular stomatitis[b]		X	X	X		X	

[a] Information compiled from multiple sources, including 9 CFR 121.3, 9 CFR 121.4, and OIE-listed diseases, World Organization for Animal Health.
[b] Animal diseases and agents listed as Select Agents exclusively by APHIS (9 CFR 121.3).
[c] Overlap diseases and agents listed as Select Agents by both APHIS and CDC (9 CFR 121.4).

infected with a range of zoonotic and agriculturally relevant pathogens, including *Brucella abortus* and *suis* (brucellosis), *Coxiella burnetii* (Q fever), and *Francisella tularensis* (tularemia) (Gresham et al., 2002; Wyckoff et al., 2009; Pedersen et al., 2014). Seroprevalence of *Brucella* spp. in feral swine has ranged from 3.1% (9/124) in Texas (Corn et al., 1986; Hoffarth, 2011) to 77.5% (62/80) in South Carolina (Stoffregen et al., 2007).

From 2009 through 2012, a serosurvey was conducted to gain a better understanding of the extent to which feral swine in northern and western Texas were exposed to/infected with six different zoonotic and agriculturally relevant pathogens. A total of 383 feral swine serum samples were collected and serologically screened for antibodies to *B. abortus*, *C. burnetii*, *F. tularensis*, porcine reproductive and respiratory syndrome (PRRS), pseudorabies virus (PRV), and *Y. pestis*. Overall, we found that 1.42% (5/352) feral swine serum samples were positive for antibodies to *B. abortus*, 1.57% (6/383) were seropositive for *C. burnetii*, 19.19% (57/297) were seropositive for *F. tularensis*, 0.35% (1/283) were seropositive for PRRS, 24.03% (68/283) were seropositive for PRV, and 1.35% (4/297) were seropositive for *Y. pestis*. Our findings suggest that feral swine populations may play a significant role in the maintenance and geospatial dissemination of these pathogens.

Recently, significant concern has developed related to emerging zootic and zoonotic disease outbreaks affecting wildlife, domestic livestock, and humans. Epizootic hemorrhagic disease virus (EHDV; closely related to blue tongue virus) has occurred and caused disease in cervid populations throughout the United States. This disease causes extremely high mortality in both white-tailed and mule deer populations, but EHDV has been asymptomatic in cattle. New serotypes of the EHDV have been newly detected and are causing disease in cattle in the United States.

3.5   *Vulnerabilities*

The increasing threats to human public health, as well as to animal health (both domestic animals and wildlife) from the intentional and natural exposure to disease-causing pathogens can be directly related to our vulnerabilities as a result of a wide range of environmental, societal, cultural, and economic factors. Examples of such factors that facilitate our collective vulnerabilities include changes in land use and agricultural practices alter the ecological diversity and natural limiting biological factors that previously suppressed or prevented the establishment and persistence of diseases in an area. Explosive population growth, unprecedented urbanization, and establishment of urban slums without adequate water and waste management in many regions of the globe clearly perpetuate an ideal environment for communicable diseases to flourish. The evolution of affordable and fast air travel has significantly increased the likelihood for the spread of infectious diseases. Additionally, the increasing number of persons declining vaccination(s) over the last 20 years poses a real vulnerability to populations, thus resulting in a decrease in population immunity consequential of the decrease in vaccination coverage. For example, recently the world has seen a reemergence of threatening infectious diseases. Case examples include the 2014 measles outbreak in the United States from January through May (Alabama, California, Connecticut, Hawaii, Illinois, Kansas, Massachusetts, Minnesota, Missouri, New Jersey, New York, Ohio, Oregon, Pennsylvania, Tennessee, Texas, Virginia, Wisconsin, and Washington state) with these outbreaks representing 77% of reported cases from January to June 2014 (U.S. Centers for Disease Control and Prevention, 2014), the 2014 measles outbreak in Somalia (WHO/UNICEF, 2014), and the October 2013 reemergence of polio in Syria after a 15-year absence from the disease (WHO, 2013). Many health officials and institutions have suggested the declining trend in vaccination is related to a lack of communication, public confidence, and public demand for immunization, with demand including occupational, travel, age, health history, and seasonality (e.g., *B. anthracis*, tuberculosis, smallpox, yellow fever, influenza, shingles, and typhoid) needs. It is important to note that *B. anthracis*, yellow fever virus, and *Variola* major (smallpox), Category A biological threat agents, do have available vaccines, such that a "Smallpox Response Plan" has been outlined post-2001 terrorist events by the CDC for fear of an intentional exposure. Nationally, the vulnerability does exist, if an agent is released, from the likelihood of public and mass hysteria.

Infectious disease outbreaks and epidemics are typically highly correlated with extreme climatic conditions such as flood and drought. In 2010, a magnitude 7.0 earthquake ravaged Haiti killing an estimated 150,000 people. The essential infrastructure required to respond to the natural disaster was severely damage or destroyed. Ten months after the devastating magnitude 7.0 earthquake in Haiti, cholera reemerged for the first time in over a century. Over the 2 years following the earthquake, a total of 534,647 cases, 287,656 hospitalizations, and 7,091 deaths were reported as a result of the outbreak (U.S. Centers for Disease Control and Prevention, 2012). Attempts to develop predictive models to better understand and prepare for the potential increased incidence and prevalence of diseases, particularly vector-borne diseases, have revealed valuable results on the regional scale (Erickson et al., 2010a,b, 2012).

Figures 3.1 through 3.4 illustrate the prevalence of several infectious and zoonotic diseases in the United States from 1996 through 2013, and demonstrate the number of annual cases reported. The selected and depicted disease prevalence trends, particularly those for zoonoses such as hantavirus, plague, Q fever, Rocky Mountain spotted fever, and tularemia, clearly suggest the influence of environmental and weather influences.

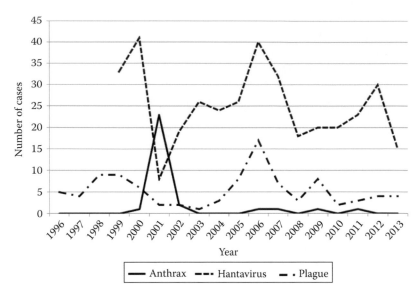

Figure 3.1 Reported human cases of anthrax, hantavirus pulmonary syndrome, and plague in the United States, 1996–2013 (Data derived from CDC-MMWR).

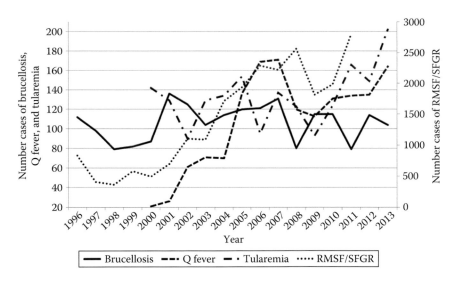

Figure 3.2 Reported human cases of brucellosis, Q fever, tularemia, and spotted fever group rickettsia (RMSF/SFGR) in the United States, 1996–2013 (Data derived from CDC-MMWR).

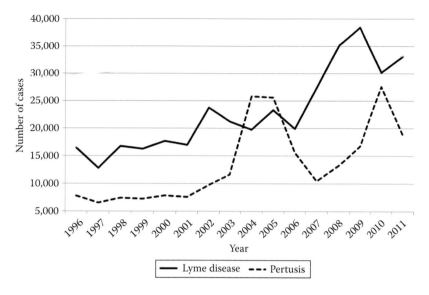

Figure 3.3 Reported human cases of Lyme disease and pertusis in the United States, 1996–2011 (Data derived from CDC-MMWR).

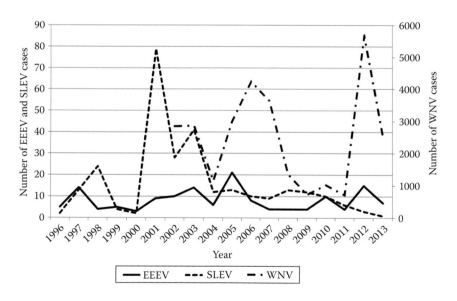

Figure 3.4 Reported cases of mosquito-vectored viruses (Eastern equine encephalitis virus [EEEV], St. Louis encephalitis virus [SLEV], and West Nile virus [WNV]) in the United States, 1996–2013 (Data derived from CDC-MMWR).

3.6   Preventing and protecting against biological threats

During testimony to the United States House Committee on Energy and Commerce, Subcommittee on Oversight and Investigations hearing in 2013, Mike Walter clearly stated the importance of and need for continued research and development in the field of biological threat detection and preparation: "Bioterrorism remains a continuing threat to the security of our nation. A biological attack could impact any sector of our society and place enormous burdens on our nation's public health, with a rippling effect on critical infrastructure. Biological attacks are particularly challenging because they can be difficult to detect. Detecting a biological attack as soon as it occurs and identifying the biological agent helps save lives." (Walter, 2013).

We can only prevent and be protected against biological threats through *intelligence* (our capacity for recognizing the threats, and leveraging advances in countermeasures science), *vigilance* (remaining alert and aware of the threat), *resilience* (ability to readily recover tactically, operationally, and strategically from attacks, incidents, and catastrophes), and *perseverance* (determination to continue the fight to achieve our goal despite difficulties, failure, or opposition). There are numerous resources, both governmental and nongovernmental agencies and entities, gathering and disseminating information related to both the natural occurrence of disease outbreaks and the potential intentional introduction of biological threat agents into human and livestock populations. The World Health Organization (WHO) established the International Health Regulations (IHR), which is an international legal instrument that is binding on 196 countries, including all the Member States of WHO (including the United States), and was entered into force on June 15, 2007. The goal of the IHR is to help the international community prevent and respond to acute public health risks that have the potential to cross borders and threaten people worldwide. The IHR requires participating countries to report certain disease outbreaks and public health events to WHO. International Health Regulations also establish a number of procedures that WHO must follow to ensure global public health security.

There was recently a national initiative launched in the United States called the "One Health Initiative," with a primary objective of establishing/fostering a coequal, all inclusive collaboration between physicians, osteopaths, veterinarians, dentists, nurses, and other scientific-health and environmentally related disciplines, including the American Medical Association, American Veterinary Medical Association, American Academy of Pediatrics, American Nurses Association, American Association of Public Health Physicians, the American Society of Tropical Medicine and Hygiene, the Centers for Disease Control and Prevention (CDC), the United States Department of Agriculture (USDA), and the U.S. National Environmental Health Association (NEHA). This initiative will, if successful, significantly enhance and improve the capabilities and resources available to more effectively and rapidly respond to naturally occurring epidemics, emerging and resurging diseases, as well as intentional use of biological threat and weapon agents.

It is both imperative and essential for the greater public health that local, state, and federal government public health agencies and entities, as well as veterinarians, academic, and private allied health scientists, continue to inform the civil public of the emerging threats and challenges related to naturally occurring and intentionally introduced biological agents. We as a nation will be more prepared for any infectious pathogen-related incidents, or event through the free-flow of such information, the open discussion of scientific advances in preventative treatments, pathogen detection technology, and personal protective capabilities.

References

Arnon, S.S., Schechter, R., Inglesby, T.V., Henderson, D.A., Bartlett, J.G., Ascher, M.S., and Layton, M. 2001. Botulinum toxin as biological weapon. *J. Am. Med. Assoc.* 285:1059–1070.

Barenblatt, D. 2004. *A Plague upon Humanity: The Secret Genocide of Axis Japan's Germ Warfare Operation.* Harper, New York.

Byerly, C.R. 2010. The U.S. military and the influenza pandemic of 1918–1919. *Public Health Rep.* 125(Suppl. 3):82–91.

Corn, J.L., Swiderek, P.K., Blackburn, B.O., Erickson, G.E., Thiermann, A.B., and Nettles, V.F. 1986. Survey of selected diseases in wild swine in Texas. *J. Am. Vet. Med. Assoc.* 189:1029–1032.

Croddy, E., Hart, J., and Perez-Armendariz, C. 2002. *Chemical and Biological Warfare.* Springer, New York, pp. 30–31.

Daszak, P., Cunningham, A.A., and Hyatt, A.D. 2000. Emerging infectious diseases of wildlife—Threats to biodiversity and human health. *Science* 287:443–449.

Dudley, J.P. and Woodford, M.H. 2002. Bioweapons, bioterrorism, and biodiversity: Potential impacts of biological weapons attacks on agricultural and biological diversity. *Rev. Sci. Tech. Off. Int. Epiz.* 21(1):125–137.

Erickson, R.A., Hayhoe, K., Presley, S.M., Allen, L.J.S., Long, K.R., and Cox, S.B. 2012. Potential impacts of climate change on the ecology of dengue and its mosquito vector the Asian tiger mosquito (*Aedes albopictus*). *Environ. Res. Lett.* 7(3):1–6.

Erickson, R.A., Presley, S.M., Allen, L.J.S., Long, K.R., and Cox, S.B. 2010a. A stage-structured, *Aedes albopictus* population model. *Ecol. Model.* 221(9):1273–1282.

Erickson, R.A., Presley, S.M., Allen, L.J.S., Long, K.R., and Cox, S.B. 2010b. A dengue model with a dynamic *Aedes albopictus* vector population. *Ecol. Model.* 221:2899–2908.

Gaston, W.D., and DeLiberto, T.J. 2014. Identification of *Brucella suis* from feral swine in the U.S.A. *J. Wildl. Dis.* 50(2):171–179.

Gresham, C.S., Gresham, C.A., Duffy, M.J., Faulkner, C.T., and Patton, S. 2002. Increased prevalence of *Brucella suis* and Pseudorabies Virus antibodies in adults of an isolated feral swine population in coastal South Carolina. *J. Wildl. Dis.* 38:653–656.

Hoffarth, A.K. 2011. Selected Diseases and Antimicrobial Resistance in Feral Swine in West Texas. M.S. Thesis, Texas Tech University, Lubbock, TX, 58 pp.

Iezzoni, L. 1999. *Influenza 1918: The Worst Epidemic in American History*. TV Books, L.L.C., NY, 256 pp.

Koblentz, G.D. 2009. *Living Weapons: Biological Warfare and International Security*. Cornell University Press, Ithaca, NY.

Moote, A.L. and Moote, D.C. 2004. *The Great Plague: The Story of London's Most Deadly Year*. Johns Hopkins University Press, Baltimore, MD.

Oldstone, M.B.A. 1998. *Viruses, Plagues, & History*. Oxford University Press, New York.

Pedersen, K., Quance, C.R., Robbe-Austerman, S., Piaggio, A.J., Bevins, S.N., Goldstein, S.M., Gaston, W.D., and DeLiberto, T.J. 2014. Identification of *Brucella suis* from feral swine in the U.S.A. *J. Wildl. Dis.* 50(2):171–179.

Riedel, S. 2004. Biological warfare and bioterrorism: A historical review. *Proc. Baylor Univ. Med. Cent.* 17(4):400–406.

Rosenau, W. 2001. Aum Shinrikyo's biological weapons program: Why did it fail? *Stud. Confl. Terror.* 24:289–301.

Shukla, H.D. and Sharma, S.K. 2005. Clostridium botulinum: A bug with beauty and weapon. *Crit. Rev. Microbiol.* 31:11–18.

Smart, J.K. 1997. History of chemical and biological warfare: An American perspective. In *Textbook of Military Medicine: Medical Aspects of Chemical and Biological Warfare*, eds. F.R. Sidell, E.T. Takafugi, and D.R. Franz, pp. 9–86. Office of the Surgeon General, Washington, DC. http://www.usuhs.mil/cbw/history.htm (accessed January 2007).

Stoffregen, W.C., Olsen, S.C., Wheeler, J., Bricker, B.J., Palmer, M.V., Jensen, A.E., Halling, S.M., and Alt, D.P. 2007. Diagnostic characterization of a feral swine herd enzootically infected with *Brucella. J. Vet. Diagn. Invest.* 19:227–237.

Taylor, L.H., Latham, S.M., and Woolhouse, M.E.J. 2001. Risk factors for human disease emergence. *Philos. Trans. R. Soc. Lond. B, Biol. Sci.* 356:983–989.

U.S. Centers for Disease Control and Prevention (CDC). 2010. Bioterrorism agents/diseases. Retrieved from http://emergency.cdc.gov/agent/agentlist-category.asp#a (accessed June 2014).

U.S. Centers for Disease Control and Prevention (CDC). 2012. Identification of *Vibrio cholerae* Serogroup O1, Serotype *Inaba*, Biotype *El Tor Strain—Haiti*, March 2012. *MMWR* 61(17):309–309.

U.S. Centers for Disease Control and Prevention (CDC). 2014. Measles—United States, January 1–May 23, 2014. *MMWR* 63(22):496–499.

Walter, M. 2013. Continuing concerns over BioWatch and the surveillance of bioterrorism (testimony). U.S. House Committee on Energy and Commerce, Subcommittee on Oversight, Release Date: June 18, 2013. Available at http://docs.house.gov/meetings/IF/IF02/20130618/101001/HHRG-113-IF02-Wstate-WalterM-20130618.pdf (accessed October 30, 2015).

Wheelis, M. 2002. Biological warfare at the 1346 siege of Caffa. *Emerg. Infect. Dis.* 8(9):971–975.

Wheelis, M., Rózsa, L., and Dando, M. 2006. *Deadly Cultures: Biological Weapons since 1945*. Harvard University Press, Cambridge, MA, pp. 284–293, 301–303.

Wilson, T.M., Logan-Henfrey, L., Weller, R., Kellman, B. 2000. Agroterrorism, biological crimes and biological warfare targeting animal agriculture. In *Emerging Diseases of Animals*, eds. C. Brown and C. Bolin, pp. 23–57. American Socicty for Microbiology Press, Washington, DC.

Witkowski, J.A. and Parish, L.C. 2002. The story of anthrax from antiquity to the present: A biological weapon of nature and humans. *Clin. Dermatol.* 20:336–342.

World Health Organization (WHO). 2013. Polio in Syria report. WHO, Geneva, Switzerland.

World Health Organization/United Nations (WHO/UNICEF). 2014. Measles in Somolia report. WHO, Geneva, Switzerland.

Wyckoff, A.C., Henke, S.E., Campbell, T.A., Hewitt, D.G., and VerCauteren, K.C. 2009. Feral swine contact with domestic swine: A serologic survey and assessment of potential for disease transmission. *J. Wildl. Dis.* 45:422–429.

Yanoviak, S.P., Paredes, J.E., Lounibos, L.P., and Weaver, S.C. 2006. Deforestation alters phytotelm habitat availability and mosquito production in the Peruvian Amazon. *Ecol. Appl.* 16:1854–1864.

chapter four

Pathogenic and toxic effects of biological threat agents

Jia-Sheng Wang, Lili Tang, Angella Gentles, and Ernest E. Smith

Contents

4.1   Introduction

Pathogenesis describes the mechanisms involved in the production of a disease. This includes the spread of microorganisms and anthropogenic and natural toxins through the body and the physiological responses of the host organism. Biological threat agents, by definition, are biologically originated or bioengineered bacteria, rickettsiae, viruses, toxins, or prions that may be intentionally employed to cause morbidity or mortality in humans or other living organisms (Burrows and Renner, 1999; Lindler et al., 2005). Biological threat agents are a wide range of toxic materials produced from pathogenic organisms, usually microbes, or artificially manufactured toxic substances that are used intentionally to interfere with the biological processes of a host. These substances work to kill or incapacitate the host and may be used to target humans, animals, or vegetation. They may also be used to contaminate nonliving substances such as air, water, soil, or food (Leitenburg and Smith, 2005; IOM, 2006; Wang, 2007). Biological weapons are a special group of biological threat agents that have been enhanced or modified to more effectively deliver and efficiently cause incapacitation, morbidity, or mortality in humans (army soldiers or civilians) or other living organisms at usually a confined region (Langford, 2004). On the other hand, biological terrorism, or bioterrorism, can be defined as the calculated use of biological threat agents that may cause diseases in civilian populations and debilitate or kill people or other living organisms in an attempt to intimidate or coerce a government, the civilians, or any segment in furtherance of political, religious, or social objectives (Christopher et al., 1997; Ashford, 2003; Lindler et al., 2005; Wang, 2007).

Because many biological threat agents are characterized by their low visibility, high potency, accessibility, inexpensive to produce, and easy delivery, the use of these bioagents as possible terrorist attacks has drawn great attention since the World Trade Center attack in September 11, 2000 (Langford, 2004). Many pathogenic agents that cause infectious diseases are considered as ideal selective agents by terrorist groups, which include anthrax, ebola, pneumonic plaque, cholera, tularemia, brucellosis, Q fever, Venezuelan equine encephalitis, smallpox, and more recently, swine and avian influenza. Biotoxins might also be used as biological threat agents that include staphylococcal enterotoxin B, botulism toxin, ricin, and various mycotoxins (Kortepeter and Parker, 1999). While it is possible to develop biological threat agents, finding a means of distributing these substances is usually difficult (Leitenburg and Smith, 2005; IOM, 2006). The most likely method of spreading the pathogenic agents would be by use of an aerosol generator like a pesticide spray apparatus or a crop dusting airplane (Langford, 2004). Another possible area of concern for the terrorist's using pathogens is contaminating water or food supply (Falkenrath et al., 2001) or infected animals or animal tissues/biofluids (Belay, 1999). Likewise, biological contamination of food would have to be done after processing for most foods. The extent of the disease would be limited to a local region in most scenarios; however, the fear factor would offer the terrorists justification for such action (Langford, 2004; Wang, 2007).

While biological threat agents, biological weapons, and bioterrorism have been well described and reviewed by many books or government publications and were also briefly introduced in Chapters 3 and 5, focus of this chapter will be on reviewing the general pathogenic effects of common biological threat agents with great public concerns in the United States and the biotoxins we have researched on. In addition, emerging swine and avian influenza viruses and prion diseases are also included.

4.2   Bacterial agents

From a microbiological view, bacteria are single-celled microorganisms that possess cell walls (membrane). They have chromosomes composed of DNA and reproduce very fast via cell division. They are described by their appearance, for example, *cocci* (spherical), *bacilli* (rod-shaped), *strepto-* (chains), or *staphylo-* (clumps) (Murray et al., 2005). Bacterial agents are the most common category of biological threat agents because of their natural occurrence and easy growth (Christopher et al., 1997). Bacteria species listed in Table 1.3 are pathogenic agents known to cause human disease and *Bacillus anthracis* and *Salmonella* have been used by terrorists. *Francisella tularensis* has been developed as a biological weapon (Ashford, 2003).

4.2.1   Anthrax

Anthrax is considered an effective bioterrorism agent because the bacterial spore is highly stable and storable, and because the disease has a relatively high lethality. Anthrax is caused by the bacteria *B. anthracis* (Murray et al., 2005). In nature, anthrax occurs in cows and other herd animals and can be transmitted to humans if they come in contact with infected animals or animal products. Various strains of anthrax exhibit different levels of lethality. Humans can become infected with anthrax in three ways: ingestion, inhalation, and cutaneous (skin) exposure. Finely milled powder and aerosolized spray anthrax are easily inhaled. A deliberate anthrax attack, however, would likely rely on inhalation since it is the most deadly, as demonstrated by the anthrax attack delivered via the postal system in the fall of 2001 in the United States (Jernigan et al., 2002).

Once the organism enters the body, anthrax becomes active, multiplies, and releases a three-part protein toxin of which one part is deadly to humans: the lethal factor (LF). The LF interferes with the normal functioning of the body's immune system cells. The virulence factor of anthrax is related to the product of three genes—LF, protective antigen (PA), and edema factor (EF)—by the gram-positive spore-forming bacteria *B. anthracis*. In the cytoplasm, LF acts as a protease that cleaves essential enzymes resulting in the inhibition of pathways that result in cell death. Furthermore, the EF inhibits the immune response, including phagocytosis by macrophages. Characterization of these factors provides the opportunity to develop countermeasures with the potential to block anthrax toxic effects (Leppla, 1982; Duesbery et al., 1998; Beauregard et al., 2000; Bradley et al., 2001; Mourez et al., 2001; Croston, 2014). Cutaneous (skin) anthrax infection is rarely fatal if treated. Symptoms appear within days of exposure, beginning with an itchy bump that develops into a black sore, sometimes accompanied by flu-like symptoms. Ingestion of anthrax (e.g., via contaminated food) causes food poisoning–like symptoms and can be fatal. Inhalation of anthrax is the most serious form—mild respiratory symptoms develop into severe symptoms, breathing difficulties, shock, and eventually death if not treated. Symptoms normally appear within a week of exposure, but may not appear for 2 months (Inglesby et al., 2002).

Prevention can be achieved via vaccination, which is only available to those who are at risk for anthrax exposure, such as the military. Generally, anthrax is treated with a course of antibiotics as soon as symptoms appear or before symptoms appear if exposure is suspected. If treated promptly, anthrax infection usually responds well to antibiotics; however, it may depend on dose exposed and individual susceptibility factors. As a result, the 2001 anthrax attacks resulted in a 45% fatality rate (5 deaths of 11 infected) (Jernigan et al., 2002).

4.2.2   Salmonellosis

Salmonella is a large group of bacteria that infects humans and many animals. The bacteria cause an illness commonly associated with food poisoning, salmonellosis. The flu-like typhoid fever, which only affects humans, is caused by the *Salmonella typhi* serotype. Transmission of the *Salmonella* bacteria occurs through ingestion of contaminated food and drinks. A bioterrorist could simply drop samples of the bacteria onto food or drinks ready to be consumed. Historically, in New York City from 1900 to 1915, Mary Mallon, also known as Typhoid Mary, spread typhoid fever to 47 people, killing three, through food that she handled. In 1984, the Rajneeshee religious cult contaminated the salad bars of 10 restaurants in Wasco County, Oregon, with *Salmonella typhimurium* in a plot to lower voter turnout for a local election. The attack resulted in 751 cases of salmonellosis with no deaths (Christopher et al., 1997; Falkenrath et al., 2001).

Outbreaks of Salmonellosis in the United States commonly occur because of improperly cooked food such as meat, poultry, seafood, eggs, and improperly prepared fruits, vegetables, milk, and other foods and drinks. Foods and drinks can become contaminated when handled by an infected person who does not wash their hands, through contact with bacteria-infested surfaces, or through the feces of infected individuals or animals. Many different sub-species or serotypes of *Salmonella* can sicken humans (Chin and Ascher, 2000). Different *Salmonella* serotypes are found in a variety of different environments. These locations include water, soil, insects, factory and kitchen surfaces, animal feces, and raw meats, poultry, and seafood. The bacteria can be isolated from these sources and grown. Approximately 40,000 salmonellosis cases with 600 deaths are reported yearly in the United States. The number of actual cases may be 30 times higher, or more, since milder cases may not be reported or diagnosed. There are 400 cases of typhoid fever recorded in the United States yearly, but 75% of them are associated with international travel. Deaths are rare when medical attention is received, but occur in 12%–30% of untreated cases (Murray et al., 2005).

Most *Salmonella* species infect the small intestines upon ingestion. Illness can be caused by as few as 15–20 bacteria cells. The bacteria pass through the interior lining of the small intestines and into its middle layer, causing inflammation. Prolonged infection of *Salmonella* can spread to the bloodstream and other organs, increasing disease length and severity. The typhi serotype spreads from the small intestines to the bloodstream and infects the lymph nodes, liver, and spleen. Symptoms of salmonellosis begin 12–72 hours after infection and include nausea, diarrhea, fever, headaches, abdominal cramps, and vomiting. Salmonellosis usually lasts 4–7 days without treatment. A longer duration can lead to severe dehydration or the infection spreading into the bloodstream and other organs, which can cause death. When the infection is over, some people with salmonellosis develop Reiter's syndrome, characterized by joint pains, eye irritation, and painful urination that can last for months or years and lead to chronic arthritis. Different from salmonellosis, typhoid fever is characterized by fever, headache, constipation, weakness, chills, muscle ache, and a rash of flat, rose-colored spots in some cases. Untreated typhoid fever can last for 3–4 weeks and can cause death due to complications (Christopher et al., 1997; Falkenrath et al., 2001).

There are no vaccines for salmonellosis, but vaccines for typhoid fever are given to travelers going to countries where outbreaks are frequent. Antibiotics, specifically ampicillin, gentamicin, ciprofloxacin, and a combination of trimethoprim and sulfamethoxazole, are given to patients with typhoid fever or severe salmonellosis. Some serotypes have developed some antibiotics resistance due to its use in feed animals. Administering intravenous fluids and electrolytes can remedy severe dehydration due to diarrhea (Langford, 2004).

4.2.3   Tularemia

Tularemia is also known as "rabbit fever" and "deerfly fever" and is caused by infection with the bacteria *F. tularensis*, found throughout North America, Europe, and Asia. *F. tularensis* was initially identified in 1912 after ground squirrels in Tulare County, California, were observed to have a plague-like illness. Waterborne outbreaks occurred in Europe and the Soviet Union in the 1930s and 1940s. In 1939, tularemia cases in the United States peaked at 2291. Although the bacteria does not form spores, *F. tularensis* can survive for weeks at low temperatures in moist soil, water, hay, straw, and decaying plants and animals (Murray et al., 2005). The bacteria can be isolated from these sources and grown. *F. tularensis* is considered a potential bioterrorism agent because it can be aerosolized to enhance inhalation exposure and as few as 10–50 cells can cause disease. In the past, Japan, the Soviet Union, and the United States have worked to weaponize *F. tularensis*, with the Soviet Union continuing its work into the 1990s (Dennis, 2004).

There are two subspecies of the bacteria, Type A found in North America and Type B found in Europe. Type A is highly virulent, whereas Type B causes milder forms of the disease. In the United States, approximately 200 human cases are reported each year, with less than 2% being fatal. Most cases occur in rural areas of the south central and midwestern states during the summer months. From 1990 to 2000, 56% of all reported tularemia cases in the United States were in four states, Arkansas, Missouri, South Dakota, and Oklahoma. Tularemia is not transmissible from person to person, so infected humans do not need to be quarantined. The disease is acquired either by being bitten by infected ticks, deerflies, mosquitoes, or other insects that feed on infected animals, by handling infected animal carcasses, consuming contaminated food or water, inhaling the bacteria, or through the eyes. Animals that can be infected include rodents and rabbits. Upon entering the body, *F. tularensis* infects the lymph nodes, lungs, spleen, liver, and kidneys. The bacteria multiply at these locations and within macrophages, cells that play a role in the body's immune response to infections. Continued bacterial growth leads to lesions on and inside infected organs and inflammation and necrosis of surrounding tissue (Dennis, 2004).

Tularemia symptoms usually appear within 3–5 days of infection but can appear up to 2–3 weeks after infection. Initial symptoms include fever, chills, headaches, diarrhea, muscle aches, joint pain, dry cough, sore throat, and progressive weakness. Prolonged infection can result in pneumonia, chest pain, bloody sputum, difficult breathing, and death. Depending on the route of infection, skin or mouth ulcers, swollen and painful lymph glands, and swollen and painful eyes can occur as well. If aerosolized tularemia is used in a bioterrorist attack, the majority of symptoms would involve severe respiratory illness, including pneumonia and systemic infection. A tularemia vaccine produced by United States Army Medical Research Institute for Infectious Diseases has been given to laboratory workers and others at high risk for infection. That vaccine is classified as an investigational new drug and is not licensed by the Food and Drug Administration. No vaccines are currently available for public use. Before antibiotic treatments were available, pulmonary and blood poisoning cases of tularemia had a mortality rate of 30%–60%. Tularemia is rarely lethal when treated with antibiotics. Preliminary testing for tularemia infection can be done in 2 hours; however, confirmation can take another 24–48 hours. Antibiotic treatment is generally started before confirmation. Several different antibiotics can be used, including streptomycin, gentamicin, doxycycline, and ciprofloxacin (Langford, 2004). In an effort to focus countermeasures toward protection against biothreats, current and future effort should place resources on simple, rapid, and reliable techniques to identify infected source and patients. In addition, efforts should be placed on the development of rapid analytical techniques to identify *F. tularensis* in environmental and vulnerable samples. It would be advantageous to further improve our knowledge base of the genetic variants of this agent. The characterization of *F. tularensis* functional genes and mechanisms of action would be useful in the development of reagents or tools to reduce or eliminate exposure to these organisms. The identification and characterization of these proteins would provide significant benefits in the development of approved vaccines to protect exposed individuals (Dennis et al., 2001).

4.3   Viral agents

Viruses are a heterogeneous class of agents. They vary in size and morphology, complexity, host range, and how they affect their hosts. Viruses consist of a genome, either RNA or DNA, which is surrounded by a protective protein shell. Viral genomes are very small and only encode from fewer than 10 to about 200 genes, compared with the roughly 100,000 genes in the human genome. Viruses multiply only in living cells. They are absolutely dependent on the host cells' energy-yielding and protein-synthesizing apparatus; therefore, they are parasites at the genetic level (Murray et al., 2005). Many important infectious diseases that afflict humankind are caused by viruses. Some are important because they frequently are fatal, such as small pox, rabies, and acquired immune deficiency syndrome (AIDS). Others are important because they cause acute discomfort or death, such as influenza. There are some viruses that can cause congenital abnormalities, tumors, and cancers. It is established that the immune system will use the most effective mechanisms to reduce the effects of viral agents depending on the characteristics of the viral agent.

The sequence of mechanisms of action varies during viral infections, as the system responds to free viral particles as well as toward infected cells. At present, there is little that can be done to interfere with the growth of viruses; therefore, viral pathogens are believed to be the ideal selective agents for terrorist attacks. Therefore, these areas of countermeasures require continued support for basic and applied research support to develop strategies to reduce the threat from these bioagents.

4.3.1   Smallpox

Smallpox is caused by the double-stranded DNA orthopoxviruses *Variola major* and *Variola minor*. Some health experts believe that smallpox is responsible for more deaths than all other infectious diseases combined. Beginning in the 1600s, the Native American population of North and South America was exposed to *Variola*, carried by Europeans. Infections carried a 50% mortality rate. Due to an aggressive immunization program by the World Health Organization and its inability to survive for more than a week outside of its only host, humans, *Variola* was declared eradicated in 1980 (Murray et al., 2005). The two known stock of the virus are at the U.S. Center for Disease Control and Prevention in Atlanta and the State Research Center of Virology and Biotechnology in Koltsovo, Russia. Rumors are that other countries may have retained their stock of smallpox and the Russian stock may have been compromised. Researchers in the Soviet Union from 1980 until the mid 1990s reportedly developed a strain of *Variola* as a potent bioweapon, capable of causing illness within 2 days instead of the average 12 days. Two noted production methods include incubation inside the embryos of chicken eggs and culturing the virus with cells susceptible to infection. Ideally, *Variola* exists only in secure Biosafety Level 4 labs of the two facilities mentioned earlier (Henderson and Fenner, 2001).

The smallpox virus can infect humans through inhalation, ingestion, or injection. A smallpox attack would likely rely on victims inhaling *Variola* via an aerosol or through an infectious individual deliberately infected with the virus. Clothing, blankets, and other such material can harbor the virus for up to a week. Infection with *Variola* could be accomplished with as little as 10–100 viral particles. After inhalation and being trapped in mucus lining of the lungs, the virus is unsuccessfully "eaten" by macrophages. Taken to the lymph nodes, the virus manufactures more viruses while inside the macrophage. Entering the bloodstream 3–4 days after initial infection, *Variola* spreads throughout the body and incubates in the bone marrow, spleen, and other organs. The virus enters the bloodstream 5–6 days later triggering the first symptoms and targeting blood vessels near the skin. The tongue, inside the mouth, and skin develop flat, red lesions that rise into blisters before becoming pus-filled pimples. Flu-like symptoms, including headache, fever, and fatigue, usually first occur 12 days after exposure. The infected person is also contagious at this stage. Within the next 4 days, the initial lesions containing *Variola* appear and spread to the arms, torso, and legs. Over the next 2 weeks, the virus continues to damage the body, particularly the immune and circulatory systems. When the last rash has scabbed over and fallen off, the person is no longer contagious. Permanent scars, blindness, and arthritis can result from the infection. Smallpox is fatal in 30% of infections. In 2%–6% of smallpox infections, lesions are classified as hemorrhagic, characterized by bleeding sores, or flat, where the lesions are soft and flat. The mortality rates for those types of infections are over 95% (Henderson, 1999).

The vaccine used to eradicate *Variola*, routinely used in the United States until 1972, prevents infections for an undetermined amount of time. It can also prevent or lessen smallpox if administered within 4 days of exposure. Mild to life-threatening risks are associated with the vaccine. No antivirals are available for unvaccinated individuals who contract the virus. After the symptoms develop, medications and intravenous fluid can be administered to make the patient more comfortable. Antibiotics can reduce potential secondary bacterial infections (Henderson et al., 1999).

4.3.2   Ebola

Ebola is one of 18 viruses that cause viral hemorrhagic fever (VHF) in humans and other primates. Ebola exists naturally in primate populations (mainly in Africa) and occasionally spreads to human populations that are exposed to these animals (Murray et al., 2005). Ebola virus disease outbreaks in various populations in central and west African nations have been recently reported with the largest outbreak ever documented in Guinea, Conakry, and Liberia (Dixon and Schafer, 2014; WHO, 2014c), which included a combined total of 528 cases and 337 deaths (case-fatality rate = 64%). Ebola could serve as an effective biological threat agent since it is stable, lethal, and transmittable from person to person, and has no treatment. As a matter of fact, bioweapon programs such as the former Soviet Union's may have investigated weaponizing Ebola. However, Ebola has not been used as a bioweapon, although three incidents of research scientists becoming infected after being stuck with Ebola-contaminated syringes have been reported: England, 1976 (recovered); United States, February 2004 (recovered); Russia, May 2004 (died). It might be possible for a terrorist to obtain the virus from natural sources and carry the virus to a target population to initiate person-to-person transmission, which requires close contact with an infected individual or items used by an infected individual. Ebola could be intentionally transmitted by an infected individual. Currently, it is not possible to aerosolize Ebola in dry form. The possibility of transmission via aerosolized liquid droplets (such as produced by sneezing) is speculated but unconfirmed (Ashford, 2003; Langford, 2004).

Ebola virus multiplies within the body and, in fatal cases, prevents the body from mounting an effective immune response. The virus produces proteins that increase the permeability of blood vessel membranes, which leads to hemorrhaging (internal bleeding) throughout the body. Death results from pulmonary (lung) hemorrhage, gastrointestinal hemorrhage, hepatitis, or encephalitis (brain swelling). Ebola proves fatal in 50%–90% of symptomatic cases. Symptoms appear 2–21 days after exposure. Onset is rapid, beginning with flu-like symptoms and progressing to chest pain, red eyes, skin rash, jaundice, hiccups, and bleeding. In fatal cases, symptoms progress over 1–2 weeks until the patient dies in shock or in a coma. Patients who recover may remain infectious even after symptoms abate. There is no effective treatment for Ebola. Health-care workers wear protective gear, when available, and every attempt is made to quarantine patients so others do not become infected. Research into an Ebola vaccine is progressing. In 2003, the National Institutes of Health (NIH) demonstrated efficacy of a vaccine in monkeys. The results of Ebola vaccine trials in humans are anticipated (Langford, 2004). Based on the Ebola virus's significant public health threat as a potentially devastating biological weapon, it is critical to further the understanding of animal to animal transmission, the ability of the virus to evade the host immune system for the development of an effective vaccine to neutralize or reduce mortality. A recent report highlighted some of the challenges that are associated with the characterization of the mechanism of pathogenesis of these biological agents and the efforts to develop antibodies against selected viral surface protein to inactivate the virus (Mohan et al., 2012).

4.3.3   Influenza

Influenza has not been used as a biological weapon, but it is a potential biological threat agent to human populations. Naturally occurring influenza pandemics include the 1918 flu, which caused 20–50 million deaths worldwide and 675,000 in the United States; the 1957 flu, which resulted in 70,000 U.S. deaths; and the 1968 flu, which caused 34,000 U.S. deaths. Even with widely accessible vaccines, seasonal flu results in an average of 36,000 deaths/year in the United States, and there is concern that laboratory samples of previous pandemic strains could be acquired by bioterrorists (Murray et al., 2005). In the past decade, frequent outbreaks of swine influenza and avian influenza have drawn significant scientific and public attentions (Kapoor and Dhama, 2014). The importance of these highly pathogenic influenza viruses has also increased due to their potential to be used in bioterrorism. Besides causing heavy mortality, trade embargoes and barriers can be imposed on poultry/swine products from a region/ country in which highly pathogenic influenza viruses have been detected (Kapoor and Dhama, 2014). Ever since the first incidence of "bird flu" in humans in Hong Kong in the year 1997, researchers have raised concern about the possibility of a human pandemic in the near future (WHO, 2009, 2011). The functions and responsibilities of the WHO and the recommendations for national measures to be taken before and during pandemics have been outlined in "WHO Global Influenza Preparedness Plan" (WHO/CDS/CSR/GIP/2005.5).

Avian influenza virus H5N1 is the latest flu virus with the potential to trigger a pandemic outbreak of flu due to its high lethality in birds and humans (WHO, 2014). The human population has no known natural immunity to H5N1 because it is genetically distinct from the three flu strains currently circulating in humans (H1N1, H1N2, and H3N2). Bird disease and death from H5N1 have occurred throughout Asia and a few European countries. In endemic areas where close interaction between people and poultry is common, 114 human cases and 59 deaths occurred from late December 2003 to September 19, 2005 according to WHO (2007). Hundreds of millions of farm birds have been killed throughout Asia in an attempt to control the spread of the virus. New influenza strains like H5N1 arise when two different viruses infect the same animal such as a bird or pig. Since influenza has a segmented RNA genome, individual segments can be exchanged between viruses in a single infected cell creating a new virus. Further changes to the virus in the form of mutations result because influenza virus has no ability to proofread its genome as it replicates. These subtle changes to the characteristics of a strain are collectively called genetic drift and are seen in flu viruses every season. This is precisely why the flu vaccine must be updated every year. H5N1 is now common in the bird population of many Asian countries. The close proximity of birds, humans, and other animals susceptible to H5N1 and human flu strains are ideal for the genetic exchange needed to increase transmission (USCDC, 2007).

Currently, humans are thought to contract H5N1 through close contact with infected poultry or surfaces contaminated by feces and body fluids from infected birds. Although consistent and effective person-to-person transmission has not occurred, a probable transmission involved a mother caring for her sick child. Should genetic drift result in an increased ability to transmit the virus from person to person, infection is expected to occur through inhalation of expelled viruses or contact with contaminated surfaces, similar to current seasonal flu outbreaks (Richt and Webby, 2013).

Pathogenic mechanism involves the H and N proteins (Flu strains are named for), hemagglutinin and neuraminidase, which stick out from the surface of the virus-like spikes. These protein spikes allow influenza to infect and damage cells and are what the immune system recognizes. The hemagglutinin spike allows the virus to bind to and enter cells. After co-opting the cells molecular machinery to produce more viruses, the neuraminidase spike is used to escape the cell, destroying it in the process.

Symptoms in people infected by H5N1 are similar, but more severe than typical, seasonal flu. Viral pneumonia and acute respiratory distress has been the primary cause of death. Current treatment procedures include the use of antiviral drugs like Tamiflu and Relenza that inhibit the production of neuraminidase in infected cells, preventing viral escape, and reducing illness severity. Many countries are stockpiling Tamiflu from its sole producer, Roche Laboratories, to prepare for a pandemic flu. The U.S. stockpile contains enough Tamiflu to treat only 2.3 million adults and 100,000 children. Two other companies are currently developing vaccines, which are currently being tested in clinical trials. The efficacy of the vaccine against H5N1 in humans is unknown (USCDC, 2007; WHO, 2007, 2009, 2011, 2014).

A novel and unique virus of influenza A H1N1 subtype of swine origin was identified in April 2009. This virus infected humans and spread from person to person, causing a large number of outbreaks with an increasing number of diseased cases in the United States and other countries. Before April 2009, sporadic infections of humans with swine influenza have occurred. Most of these cases were observed in people who were directly exposed to pigs, and only in a few instances the disease was reported due to human-to-human transmission of the swine influenza virus (Richt and Webby, 2013). However, in the current swine influenza outbreak, WHO has reported that the virus is spread from human to human, and not from contact with infected pigs. Outbreaks of H1N1 and H3N2 swine influenza were reported worldwide from countries far apart from each other. Also, the observation of human-to-human transmission of these viruses and the ability of the virus to cause community-level outbreaks raises an important question on the chances of its prolonged transmission from human to human. The phylogenetic ancestry of the classical swine viruses and avian-like H1N1 swine viruses is quite discrete. The potential of this strain to cause pandemic was reported (Fraser et al., 2009). In response to escalating outbreaks in the United States and other countries of the world, caused by a new influenza virus of swine origin (S-OIV), the WHO on June 11, 2009, declared the present swine flu "H1N1" a pandemic in humans by raising the pandemic phase to level #6.

A novel avian influenza virus (H7N9) was recently identified in China in March 2013. There have been 179 confirmed human cases of H7N9 including about 60 confirmed deaths by April 2014 (WHO, 2014). Most cases of human infections are due to contact with infected poultry or surfaces that are contaminated with infected bird excretions: saliva, nasal secretions, and feces. People have killed hundreds of millions of birds around the world in an attempt to control the spread of the avian flu that has now reached three continents: Asia, Europe, and Africa. The eight genes of the H7N9 virus are closely related to avian influenza viruses found in domestic ducks, wild birds, and domestic poultry in Asia. The virus likely emerged from "reassortment," a process in which two or more influenza viruses coinfect a single host and exchange genes. These events may have occurred in habitats shared by wild and domestic birds and/or in live bird/poultry markets, where different species of birds are bought and sold for food. The H7N9 virus likely obtained its hemagglutinin gene from domestic ducks, its neuraminidase gene from wild birds, and its six remaining genes from multiple related H9N2 influenza viruses in domestic poultry. The potential of the emerging H7N9 virus to cause severe disease or of even becoming a future pandemic strain is speculated, as genetic mutants generated in the laboratory were observed to attach to both upper and lower respiratory tracts (Kapoor and Dhama, 2014; WHO, 2014).

4.3.4   Antimicrobial resistance

Antimicrobial resistance (AMR) is resistance of a microorganism to an antimicrobial drug that was originally effective for treatment of infections caused by it and increases the risk of spread to others. The development of resistant strains is a natural process but can be encouraged by various practices. Antimicrobial resistance is a global concern as new resistance mechanisms emerge and spread globally threatening and increasing death and disability of individuals. Without effective anti-infective treatment, many standard medical treatments will fail or turn into very high risk procedures. AMR has the potential to threaten health security and damage trade and economies (WHO, 2014).

4.4   Biotoxins

Biotoxins are naturally occurring toxic agents produced by bioorganisms such as bacteria, cyanobacteria, fungi, and some species of plants and marine fish, which are etiological agents of a variety of animal and human toxicoses (Keeler and Tu, 1983; Wang, 2007). Many biotoxins are listed as biological threat agents, such as aflatoxins, amatoxins, botulinum toxin, ergot alkaloids, microcystins, ricin, saxitoxin, staphylococcal enterotoxin, T-2 toxin, and tetrodotoxins (Franz, 1997; Burrows and Renner, 1999). Because of their potent toxicities in animal and humans, these biotoxins are major candidates for use as chemical and biological warfare (CBW) agents. Several biotoxins, such as aflatoxin, botulinum toxin, ricin, and T-2 toxin, have been known to be weaponized (Franz, 1997; Burrows and Renner, 1999).

4.4.1   Aflatoxins

Aflatoxins, produced by *Aspergillus flavus* and *A. parasiticus*, were discovered as the causative agent in turkey X disease in Britain (Ciegler et al., 1981; Cole and Cox, 1981). This syndrome resulted in death of thousands of turkey poults, ducklings, and chicks (Wang et al., 1998). AFB_1, the most potent and commonly occurring biotoxin, is acutely toxic to all species of animals, birds, and fish tested with LD_{50} range of 0.3–9.0 mg/kg (Busby and Wogan, 1984). Sheep and mice are the most resistant, whereas cats, dogs, rats, and rabbits are the most sensitive species. Acute toxic effects include death with or without signs of anorexia, depression, ataxia, dyspnea, anemia, and hemorrhage from body orifices. In humans, vomiting, convulsions, coma, and death with cerebral edema and fatty involvement of the liver, kidney, and heart characterized the acute toxicosis. In subchronic cases, icterus, hypoprothrombinemia, hematomas, and gastroenteritis are common. Chronic aflatoxicosis is characterized histologically by bile duct proliferation, periportal fibrosis, icterus, and cirrhosis of the liver. Prolonged exposure to low levels of AFB_1 leads to hepatoma, cholangiocarcinoma, hepatocellular carcinoma, and other tumors (Wang et al., 1998). The mechanism of acute aflatoxicosis includes DNA damage and protein synthesis and inhibition of enzyme activities in gastrointestinal system, mainly in liver. Avoidance of food contamination with aflatoxins is the primary measure for prevention. Specific binding agent, such as NovaSil, is available for reducing bioavailability of aflatoxins (Phillips et al., 2006). For the treatment of acute aflatoxicosis, amphotericin B (fungizone) and itraconazole may be helpful, but supportive procedures to protect liver function are critical for reducing the mortality.

4.4.2   Anatoxin

Anatoxin is an alkaloid neurotoxin produced by freshwater cyanobacteria *Anabaena flos-aquae* (Carmichael, 1988). The effect of anatoxin in freshwater environments has increased in severity in recent years, and poisoning episodes are becoming more common and more widespread. For example, in midwestern United States, the consumption of contaminated water has resulted in the deaths of ducks and geese by thousands. Anatoxin mainly affects the functioning of the nervous system, often causing death due to paralysis of the respiratory muscles. Anatoxin acts as a mimic of the neurotransmitter acetylcholine and irreversibly binds the nicotinic acetylcholine receptor to produce an action potential, but cannot be cleaved by the enzyme, acetylcholinesterase. The sodium channel is essentially locked open, and the muscles become over-stimulated and become fatigued and then paralyzed. Acute toxicosis symptoms include staggering, gasping, and convulsions. When respiratory muscles become affected, convulsions occur due to a lack of oxygen supply to the brain. Suffocation is the final result a few minutes after ingestion of the toxin. For this reason, anatoxin is also known as the death factor in animals. It is toxic to wild and domestic animals and 50% lethal dose (LD_{50})

range from 0.1 to 1.0 mg/kg body weight. Because anatoxin causes rapid death, treatment usually is not an option (Burrows and Renner, 1999).

4.4.3   Botulinum toxin

Botulism is a rare paralytic disease caused by botulinum neurotoxin (BT), a protein produced by the soil bacteria *Clostridium botulinum*. Different strains of the bacteria make different types of toxin. However, only four of the seven known BT types (A, B, E, and F) cause human botulism. As one of the most deadly known toxins, approximately 0.4 μg can kill an average adult (Murray et al., 2005). In theory, BT can be used as a biological weapon by contaminating food or drink with the toxin or the bacteria. It is also possible to weaponize BT as an aerosol. When *C. botulinum* is growing in ideal conditions, it produces toxin, which can be purified. However, processing the toxin into an aerosol is extremely difficult even for those with microbiology and bioweapons experience. Nevertheless, the Japanese terrorist cult Aum Shinrikyo attempted to spread it as an aerosol three times from 1990 to 1995 without success. In the years leading up to the 1991 Gulf War, Iraq had a biological weapons program that produced a significant amount of BT (Christopher et al., 1997; Shapiro et al., 1998).

Poisoning from BT can occur in several ways, the frequency of which varies from year to year. Approximately two-thirds of all infections are caused by consumption of bacterial spores, which can turn into bacteria. This type of infection is commonly referred to as infant botulism because it primarily affects babies fed contaminated honey. Consumption of food contaminated with the toxin or bacteria are responsible for less than a quarter of all cases. Finally, bacterial infection of a wound causes a handful of cases each year. There are a few isolated examples of aerosolized BT causing illness in researchers who accidentally inhaled it. This, however, does not occur naturally. Mechanistically, the BT toxin affects the connections between nerves and the muscles they control. It does this by interfering with the release of the chemical messenger, acetylcholine, which the nerve uses to signal the muscle to contract. After entering the cell, the toxin physically destroys proteins required for the release of acetylcholine, effectively silencing the nerve. Clinically, the first symptoms appear within 18–36 hours after ingestion of contaminated food or 12–80 hours after inhalation of the toxin, but they can occur as early as 6 hours or as late as 10 days from the time of initial exposure depending upon the amount of toxin or bacteria present. This initially causes slurred speech, dry mouth, double and blurred vision, as well as breathing and swallowing difficulty. The effects slowly progress down the body symmetrically, weakening it, reducing muscle reflexes, and paralyzing the limbs. Botulism-related deaths are caused by paralysis of muscles required for breathing including the diaphragm.

Of the approximate 140 cases/year in the United States, there are usually only 1–3 deaths (Shapiro et al., 1998; Simpson, 2004).

The main treatment for botulism is antitoxins, which are antibodies that bind to BT and prevent it from affecting nerve cells. Once the toxin is bound to the cell, antitoxin is ineffective against it, making rapid diagnosis critical to preventing further paralysis. Antibiotics are also administered to kill the bacteria. The currently available antitoxins are isolated from horses and can cause adverse reactions in people. Clinicians must request antitoxin from the USCDC to treat patients. The antitoxin effective against BT types A and B is licensed by the FDA. The U.S. Army also has an effective antitoxin, but it is not USFDA approved. Finally, a vaccine against BT is given to U.S. military troops and lab personnel at high risk of exposure. Extensive paralysis caused by the toxin may require assisted breathing, feeding, and physical therapy for months while new nerves connect to paralyze muscles (Franz, 1997; Langford, 2004).

4.4.4   Microcystins

Microcystins, produced mainly by *Microcystic aeruginosa*, are hepatotoxic products of freshwater cyanobacteria blooms and have been implicated in the death of human dialysis patients (Carmichael, 1988). Microcystin-LR (MCLR), also known as the fast death factor, is the most common form of microcystins and presumably the biotoxin of choice to be weaponized. Mice treated with MCLR aerosol died within hours with LD_{50} 67 µg/kg (Anonym, 1999). Although the aerosolized form is the most likely threat, ingestion through water, even from natural source, may constitute a significant threat (Burrows and Renner, 1999). Mechanistically, MCLR is a strong inhibitor of protein phosphatases, which disturb cellular functions and regulations. In addition, MCLR is a potent tumor promoter in animal models. MCLR contamination in drinking water sources has recently been an increasing concern for ecological hazards and public health threats.

4.4.5   Ricin

Ricin is a potent toxin that could be used as a biological threat agent or bioterrorism. Ricin can be produced relatively easily and inexpensively in large quantities in a fairly low-technology setting. Worldwide, one million tons of castor beans are processed annually in the production of castor oil; the waste mash from this process is 5%–10% ricin by weight. Ricin's significance as a potential bioweapon relates in part to its availability. Although ricin is not an ideal bioweapon agent, it has reportedly been used as a tool for assassinations (Langford, 2004; Leitenburg and Smith, 2005). During the 1980s Iran–Iraq war, ricin may have been used. In February 2004, ricin was detected in mail received at the U.S. Senate office complex. Ricin can be delivered via inhalation, injection, or ingestion. Liquid or crystalline ricin could be utilized as a food or water contaminant. For ricin to be delivered as an aerosol, it must be lyophilized—a process by which a liquid substance is dried by freezing in a high vacuum. While it is not overly difficult to aerosolize ricin, this step does present a technical challenge (Olsnes, 2004).

Ricin is a phytotoxalbumin protein derived from the beans of the castor plant (*Ricinus communis*). Mechanistically, Ricin prevents cells in the body from synthesizing proteins, which can lead to widespread organ damage as well as pulmonary, liver, renal, and immunological failure. Fever, coughing, and gastrointestinal problems are likely to be the first symptoms. If eaten, the toxin causes stomach irritation, gastroenteritis, bloody diarrhea, and vomiting. Inhalation causes severe lung damage, including pulmonary edema. It can also cause seizures and central nervous system depression. When inhaled, this toxin may produce pathologic changes within 8 hours and severe respiratory symptoms followed by acute respiratory failure in 36–72 hours. When ingested, the toxin causes severe gastrointestinal symptoms followed by vascular collapse and death. Since ricin is a relatively large protein, it is not easily absorbed across the skin and dermal exposure to ricin is of little concern. There is no treatment or prophylaxis currently available for ricin exposure. If exposure does not prove fatal within 3–5 days, the victim will usually recover (Doan, 2004).

4.4.6   Saxitoxin

Saxitoxin is produced by marine dinoflagellate *Gonyaulax catenella* and *G. tamarensis*, which are consumed by the Alaskan butter clam and the California sea mussel. Saxitoxin is also produced by *Anabaena circinalis* and other cyanobacteria (Schantz, 1986). It is the causative agent for paralytic shellfish poisoning. Saxitoxin is highly toxic through the oral route and LD_{50} calculated from shellfish poisoning cases ranged from 0.3 to 1.0 mg/person. It is even more toxic by aerosol inhalation with an LD_{50} of 2 μg/kg body weight; therefore, saxitoxin is possibly weaponized. Acute symptoms include abdominal distress, diarrhea, nausea, vomiting, vertigo, headache, and paralysis. Death usually appeared with 24 hours. Mechanistically, saxitoxin blocks sodium flow through the sodium channel. There is no specific treatment for poisoning by saxitoxin. Supportive care, including respiratory support, is the treatment of choice (Burrows and Renner, 1999; Langford, 2004).

4.4.7   Staphylococcal enterotoxin B

Staphylococcal enterotoxin B (SEB) is a protein toxin produced by bacterium *Staphylococcus aureus* with a molecular weight of 28 kDa. SEB is highly stable once produced and has caused many cases of food poisoning in humans (Jett et al., 2001). Many outbreaks have been produced by consumption of inadequately refrigerated raw milk or cheeses. In the United States, the unrefrigerated cream puffs or potato salad at summer picnics are common sources. It is weaponized by several countries in aerosol form, including the United States. Therefore, the intoxication can result from either ingestion or inhalation. It can also be used through food and water sources. The human LD_{50} is about 1.7 mg by inhalation, while the incapacitating dose is only 30 ng by inhalation. Symptoms develop in a few hours (1–6 hours) after exposure, including severe GI pain, projectile vomiting, and diarrhea if ingested; fever, chills, muscle aches, and shortness of breath if inhaled. In most conditions, symptoms will diminish after several hours; however, high exposure can lead to septic shock and death if left untreated. Treatment includes supportive care with close attention to oxygenation and hydration, and in severe cases, ventilation with positive end expiratory pressure and diuretics. Acetaminophen and antibiotics methicillin or vancomycin may be effective to a certain degree (Franz, 1997; Langford, 2004).

4.4.8   T-2 toxin

T-2 toxin, produced primarily by *Fusarium sporotrichioides*, has been reported in many parts of the world (Beasley, 1989; Wang et al., 1998). It is formed in large quantities under unusual circumstance of prolonged wet weather at harvest. T-2 toxin, as a representative trichothecene, has been well studied for its toxic effects in many animal models (Ueno, 1983). General signs of toxicity in animals include weight loss, feed refusal, vomiting, bloody diarrhea, severe dermatitis, hemorrhage, abortion, and death. Histological lesions consist of necrosis and hemorrhage in proliferating tissues of the intestinal mucosa, bone marrow, spleen, testis, and ovary. T-2 toxin can alter hemostasis and affect cellular immune response, as well as a strong inhibitor of protein and DNA synthesis. As the major trichothecene mycotoxin, T-2 has been implicated in a variety of animal and human toxicoses, such as alimentary toxic aleukia, Mseleni joint disease, scabby grain toxicosis, and Kashin–Beck disease (Ueno, 1983). T-2 toxin and its mixture have been known to be weaponized and were used as CBW agents in Laos, Cambodia, and Afghanistan (Christopher et al., 1997; Franz, 1997). Because of its low water solubility and high stability to heat and ultraviolet light, T-2 toxin can contaminate an area for a longer period. The toxin can enter the body through the skin, by inhalation or by ingestion. Treatment procedure includes supportive care, especially maintenance of electrolyte balance. There are no antidotes, so avoidance of contact is the only preventive measure. Topical dermal antibiotic creams may be helpful to prevent dermal pain and secondary infection.

4.4.9 Tetrodotoxin

Tetrodotoxin is naturally responsible for fugu (puffer fish) food poisoning and is found in the liver, gonads, intestines, and skin of many species of the fish order *Tetraodontidae*. It was reported that tetrodotoxin is produced by Dinoflagellate *Alexandrium tamarense* (Yasumoto et al., 1986). Tetrodotoxin is a potent neurotoxin that blocks sodium flow through sodium channel. The oral lethal dose to humans is 1–2 mg and LD_{50} is 30 µg/kg. The toxin can be possibly weaponized and may be used as a drinking water threat by bioterrorists. After ingestion, symptoms appeared within 10 minutes to 4 hours, including numbness of the lips, tongue, and fingers, anxiety, nausea, vomiting, and progressive paralysis. Death appears within 30 minutes to 6 hours. There is no specific treatment for tetrodotoxin poisoning. Supportive care, including respiratory support, is the treatment of choice (Burrows and Renner, 1999; Langford, 2004).

4.5 Prions

A prion is an infectious agent composed of protein in a misfolded form. Prion is not considered a living organism and is in contrast to all other known infectious agents (virus/bacteria/fungus/parasite) (Belay, 1999; Belay and Schonberger, 2005). The word *prion* is derived from the words *protein* and *infection*. Prion diseases, also known as transmissible spongiform encephalopathies (TSEs), are a group of animal and human brain diseases that are uniformly fatal and often characterized by a long incubation period and a multifocal neuropathologic picture of neuronal loss, spongiform changes, and astrogliosis (Belay, 1999). Prion diseases are usually rapidly progressive and always fatal. Animal prion diseases include bovine spongiform encephalopathy (BSE, also known as "mad cow disease"), chronic wasting disease (CWD) of deer and elk, scrapie, transmissible mink encephalopathy, feline spongiform encephalopathy, and ungulate spongiform encephalopathy. In humans, prions cause Creutzfeldt–Jakob disease (CJD), variant Creutzfeldt–Jakob disease (vCJD), Gerstmann–Sträussler–Scheinker syndrome, fatal familial insomnia, and kuru (Belay and Schonberger, 2005). Prion diseases attracted much attention and public concern after an outbreak of BSE occurred among >180,000 cattle in the United Kingdom in 1986, and scientific evidence indicated the food-borne transmission of BSE to humans (Smith and Bradley, 2003). Outbreaks of BSE have potentially affected over two million U.K. cattle. Approximately 750,000 BSE-infected cattle were estimated to have been slaughtered between 1980 and 1996 (Ghani et al., 2000) and potentially consumed by millions of U.K. residents. As the U.K. BSE outbreak progressed, several important public health preventive measures were implemented before and after evidence of BSE transmission to humans surfaced in 1996. These measures included a 1989 specified risk material ban for human food, a 1996 prohibition of the processing of cattle ≥30 months old for human food, and total ban on the feeding of mammalian protein to any farmed animals (Belay and Schonberger, 2005). The measures introduced in 1996 were intended to contain the BSE outbreak aggressively by keeping potentially BSE-contaminated feed off the farms and to remove as many BSE-infected materials as possible from the human food supply system. Unfortunately, BSE continued to be detected, albeit at a very low rate, in cattle born after the 1996 ban, and was found in cattle over 15 different countries, including the United States (Collee and Bradley, 1997; Smith and Bradley, 2003). In addition to BSE, CWD in free-ranging cervids has been endemic in a tricorner area of Colorado, Nebraska, and Wyoming, and new foci of infection have been detected in others parts of the United States and the Canadian province of Saskatchewan (Belay et al., 2004).

All known prion diseases affect the structure of the brain or other neural tissue and all are currently untreatable and universally fatal. TSEs are distinguished by long incubation periods, characteristic spongiform changes associated with neuronal loss, and a failure to induce inflammatory response (Belay, 1999). If a prion enters a healthy organism, it induces existing, properly folded proteins to convert into the disease-associated, prion form; the prion acts as a template to guide the misfolding of more proteins into prion form. These newly formed prions can then go on to convert more proteins themselves; this triggers a chain reaction that produces large amounts of the prion form (Belay and Schonberger, 2005). All known prions induce the formation of an amyloid fold, in which the protein polymerizes into an aggregate consisting of tightly packed beta sheets. Amyloid aggregates are fibrils, growing at their ends, and replicating when breakage causes two growing ends to become four growing ends. The incubation period of prion diseases is determined by the exponential growth rate associated with prion replication, which is a balance between the linear growth and the breakage of aggregates. This altered structure is extremely stable and accumulates in infected tissue, causing tissue damage and cell death (Belay and Schonberger, 2005). This structural stability means that prions are resistant to denaturation by chemical and physical agents, making disposal and containment of these particles difficult. Prions come in different strains, each with a slightly different structure, and, most of the time, strains breed true. Prion replication is nevertheless subject to occasional epimutation and then natural selection just like other forms of replication (Belay and Schonberger, 2005).

In humans, the prion protein is encoded by genes located on the short arm of chromosome 20. Although the exact function of this protein is unknown, a protein found in such abundance in mammals, particularly in neurons, could have multiple functional roles. Several putative functions of the prion protein have been proposed, including supporting neuronal synaptic activity, binding copper, and interacting with other cell surface proteins to provide neuroprotective functions (Lasmezas, 2003). Prions are primarily distinguished from the cellular prion protein by their 3D structure. The cellular prion protein is predominantly composed of the α-helix structure and is almost devoid of β-sheet, whereas about 43% of scrapie prions are composed of β-sheet. Other distinguishing characteristics of prions include their resistance to inactivation by proteolytic enzymes, conventional disinfectants, and standard sterilization methods. Prions are abnormal conformers of the cellular prion protein, the presence of which appears to be a prerequisite for the replication and propagation of prions. Although the exact mechanism of prion replication remains unclear, the agent is believed to promote the conversion of the cellular prion protein into the abnormal conformer by an autocatalytic or other unidentified process (Belay and Schonberger, 2005).

4.6   Understanding mixtures and mechanisms of action for countermeasures

It is clear that there is a need for countermeasures to combat pathogenic and toxic threats of agents. While this chapter has focused on individual pathogenic or toxic agents, it is important to bring into focus the need to understand the effects and mechanisms of action from exposure to mixture of these agents. Data on the synergistic and/or antagonistic effects of these agents are significantly lacking. There is the potential for acute and chronic exposure to several of the agents summarized earlier. It is also imperative to understand how exposure to any pathogenic or toxic agent may neutralize the protective mechanism of counteragents administered during pre- or postexposure scenarios. For example, we should develop a mechanistic understanding of the immune system activation of the natural or adaptive response and how these immune cell populations as well as the purpose of the secreted molecules in the elimination of foreign agents. We should consider the potential of exposure to mixtures of these agents to reduce the capacity of the immune system or physiological response, thus increasing susceptibility of the exposed individuals or groups. What we know about pathogenic and toxic agents is constantly updated together with improvements in technology. Although important progress has been achieved in the last years, there are still many areas of weaknesses that are not yet well known about the effects of pathogenic and toxic agents, as well as protective mechanisms and techniques for countermeasures. Additional effort is required to study both the innate and adaptive immune response mechanisms to fight against microbial agents. Furthermore, continued effort and resource should be put in place to study sensor to prevent exposure to toxic agents. The biological effects of some of these agents are induced following their activation and binding to serum protein. As such this may increase their toxicity, therefore, from a mechanistic point of view, some toxic agents cannot be classified as a group. The mechanism of action of a number of these agents could result in the inhibition of protective biomolecules as well as the disruption of cell cycle and normal physiology. As potent inhibitors of protein and DNA and RNA synthesis, these bio-agents will be especially toxic to tissues with a high cell division rate.

4.6.1   Individual and community training needs

Various levels of training on potential pathologic and toxic agents are needed to ensure that individuals and communities get involved in countermeasure activities and have a good understanding of the potential threats and their role, as well as its consequences. It will be important that everyone involved in providing information to the community gives the correct information. Therefore, training workshops should be organized with clear aims and objectives.

4.7   Research recommendations and focus for future efforts

Research efforts conducted through the Admiral Elmo R. Zumwalt, Jr. National Program for Countermeasures to Biological and Chemical Threats at Texas Tech University have focused on studying combinative toxicity of biotoxins with emphasis on the newly identified food-borne and waterborne toxins. There is a historical precedence for the use of toxins as biological weapons against unprotected enemy or innocent people (Falkenrath et al., 2001; Langford, 2004). During the sixth and fourth centuries BCE, Assyrians and Persians poisoned drinking water wells with ergot alkaloids, a mycotoxin. More recently, trichothecene mycotoxins (T-2 toxin and diacetoxyscirpenol, produced by various *Fusarium* strains) were found to be the cause of the "yellow rain" episodes, which occurred in people in Afghanistan, Kampuchea, and Laos in the late 1970s. And plans were being developed for missile delivery of aflatoxin by Iraq (Zilinskas, 1997; Langford, 2004).

Even though for many years research efforts have been focused on the study of single toxins, or single categories of toxins, and a great deal of data regarding individual toxins has been documented, little attention has been paid in the study of combinative toxic effects of biotoxin mixtures, which may be more potent and cause more damage to human and animal health. The nature of coexistence of many types of chemicals and toxins in complex environmental samples has drawn the attention of federal governmental agencies and the scientific community in recent years. The great challenge currently facing the preventive medicine community is how to prevent chronic human diseases caused by complex toxin mixtures. Therefore, there is an urgent need for improved understanding of the mechanism of combinative toxicity of biotoxin mixtures, as well as the development of rapid and sensitive methods to detect multiple toxins in both the field and body fluids of animal and humans.

Additionally, developing prevention strategies against the possible use of these toxin mixtures is critical.

The new challenge currently faced is the potential use of highly pathogenic influenza viruses or prions by bioterrorist groups, which are urgent issues because these new viruses or prions can cause heavy mortality in humans, as well as trade embargoes and barriers on poultry/swine/beef and their products from a region/country in which highly pathogenic viruses or prions are detected. In addition to public health impact, food security and economic impact are extremely prominent.

Acknowledgment

The author is grateful to RDECOM for their financial support of this project, especially for the great help from Drs. William Lagna, John White, Ronald Kendall, Steve Presley, and Galen Austin.

References

Anonym. 1999. New understanding of algae. *Environ. Health Perspect.* 107:A13.

Ashford, D. 2003. Planning against biological terrorism: Lessons from outbreak investigations. *Emerg. Infect. Dis.* 9(5):515–519.

Beasley, V.R. 1989. *Trichothecene Mycotoxicosis: Pathophysiologic Effects*, Vols. I and II. CRC Press, Boca Raton, FL.

Beauregard, K.E., Collier, R.J., and Swanson, J.A. 2000. Proteolytic activation of receptor-bound anthrax protective antigen on macrophages promotes its internalization. *Cell. Microbiol.* 2(3):251–258.

Belay, E.D. 1999. Transmissible spongiform encephalopathies in humans. *Annu. Rev. Microbiol.* 53:283–314.

Belay, E.D., Maddox, R.A., Williams, E.S., Miller, M.W., Gambetti, P., and Schonberger, L. 2004. Chronic wasting disease and potential transmission to humans. *Emerg. Infect. Dis.* 10:977–984.

Belay, E.D. and Schonberger, L.B. 2005. The public health impact of prion diseases. *Annu. Rev. Public Health* 26:191–212.

Bradley, K.A. et al. 2001. Identification of the cellular receptor for anthrax toxin. *Nature* 414(6860):225–229.

Burrows, W.D. and Renner, S.E. 1999. Biological warfare agents as threats to potable water. *Environ. Health Perspect.* 107:975–984.

Busby, W.F. and Wogan, G.N. 1984. Aflatoxins. In *Chemical Carcinogenesis*, ed. C. Searle, pp. 945–1136. American Chemical Society, Washington, DC.

Carmichael, W.W. 1988. Toxins of freshwater algae. In *Handbook of Natural Toxins: Marine Toxins and Venoms*, Vol. 3, ed. A. Tu, pp. 121–147. Marcel Dekker, New York.

Chin, J. and Ascher, M. 2000. Salmonellosis. In *Control of Communicable Diseases*, eds. J. Chin and M. Ascher. American Public Health Association, Washington, DC.

Christopher, G.W., Cieslak, T.J., Pavlin, J.A., and Eitzen, E.M. Jr. 1997. Biological warfare. A historical perspective. *JAMA* 278:412–417.

Ciegler, A., Burmaister, H.R., Vesonder, R.F., and Hesseltine, C.W. 1981. Mycotoxins and N-nitro-compounds: Environmental risks. In *Mycotoxins: Occurrence in the Environment*, ed. R. Shank, pp. 1–50. CRC Press, Boca Raton, FL.

Cole, R.J. and Cox, R.H. 1981. *Handbook of Toxic Fungal Metabolites*. Academic Press, Inc, New York.

Collee, J.G. and Bradley, R. 1997. BSE: A decade on—Part 1. *Lancet* 349:636–641.

Croston, G. 2014. Pathways: Anthrax toxin mechanism of action. http://www.biocarta.com/pathfiles/h_anthraxPathway.asp# (accessed July 3, 2014).

Dennis, D.T. 2004. Tularemia. In *Infectious Diseases*, Vol. II, 2nd edn., eds. J. Cohen and W.G. Powderly, pp. 1649–1653. Mosby, Edinburgh, U.K.

Dennis, D.T. et al. 2001. Working Group on Civilian Biodefense. Tularemia as a biological weapon medical and public health management. *JAMA* 285(21):2763–2773. doi:10.1001/jama.285.21.2763.

Dixon, M.G. and Schafer, I.J. 2014. Ebola viral disease outbreak-West Africa, 2014. *Morb. Mortal. Wkly. Rep.* 63(25):545–551.

Doan, L.G. 2004. Ricin: Mechanism of toxicity, clinical manifestation, and vaccine development: A review. *J. Toxicol. Clin. Toxicol.* 42:201–208.

Duesbery, N.S. et al. 1998. Proteolytic inactivation of MAP-kinase-kinase by anthrax lethal factor. *Science* 280(5364):734–737.

Falkenrath, R.A., Newman, R.D., and Thayer, B.A. 2001. *America's Achilles' Heel: Nuclear, Biological, and Chemical Terrorism and Covert Attack*. MIT Press, Cambridge, MA.

Franz, D.R. 1997. Defense against toxin weapons. In *Medical Aspects of Chemical and Biological* Warfare, eds. F. Sidell, E. Takafugi, and D. Franz, pp. 603–619. TMM Publications, Washington, DC.

Fraser, C. et al. June 19, 2009. Pandemic potential of a strain of influenza A (H1N1): Early findings. *Science* 324(5934):1557–1561. doi:10.1126/science.1176062.

Ghani, A.C., Ferguson, N.M., Donnelly, C.A., and Anderson, R.M. 2000. Predicted vCJD mortality in Great Britain. *Nature* 406:583–584.

Henderson, D.A. 1999. Smallpox: Clinical and epidemiologic features. *Emerg. Infect. Dis.* 5:537–539.

Henderson, D.A. et al. 1999. Smallpox as a biological weapon: Medical and public health management. Working Group on Civilian Biodefense. *JAMA* 281:2127–2137.

Henderson, D.A. and Fenner, F. 2001. Recent events and observations pertaining to smallpox virus destruction in 2002. *Clin. Infect. Dis.* 33:1057–1059.

Inglesby, T.V. et al. 2002. Anthrax as a biological weapon, 2002: Updated recommendations for management. *JAMA* 287:2236–2252.

Institute of Medicine (IOM). 2006. *Addressing Foodborne Threats to Health: Policies, Practices, and Global Coordination, Workshop Summary*. The National Academies Press, Washington, DC.

Jernigan, D.B., Raghunathan, P.S., and Bell, B.P. 2002. Investigation of bioterrorism-related anthrax, United States, 2001: Epidemiologic findings. *Emerg. Infect. Dis.* 8:1019–1028.

Jett, M., Ionin, B., and Da, R. 2001. The Staphylococcal enterotoxins. In *Molecular Medical Microbiology*, Vol. 2, ed. M. Sussman, pp. 1089–1116. Academic Press, San Diego, CA.

Kapoor, S. and Dhama, K. 2014. *Insight into Influenza Viruses of Animals and Humans.* Springer, Cham, Switzerland. doi:10.1007/978-3-319-05512-1.

Keeler, R.F. and Tu, A.T. 1983. *Handbook of Natural Toxins.* Marcel Dekker, New York.

Kortepeter, M.G. and Parker, G.W. 1999. Potential biological weapons threats. Special Issue. *Emerg. Infect. Dis.* 5:523–527.

Langford, R.E. 2004. *Introduction to Weapons of Mass Destruction: Radiological, Chemical, and Biological.* Wiley-Interscience, Hoboken, NJ.

Lasmezas, C.I. 2003. Putative functions of PrPC. *Br. Med. Bull.* 60:61–70.

Leitenberg, M. and Smith, G. June 17, 2005. "Got toxic milk?": A rejoinder, Federation of American Scientists. http://www.fas.org/sgp/eprint/milk.html (accessed July 3, 2014).

Leppla, S.H. 1982. Anthrax toxin edema factor: A bacterial adenylate cyclase that increases cyclic AMP concentrations of eukaryotic cells. *Proc. Natl. Acad. Sci. USA* 79(10):3162–3166.

Lindler, L.E., Lebeda, F.J., and Korch, G.W. 2005. *Biological Weapon Defense: Infectious Diseases and Counter Bioterrorism.* Humana Press, Inc., Totowa, NJ.

Mohan, G.S., Li, W., Ye, L., Compans, R.W., and Yang, C. 2012. Antigenic subversion: A novel mechanism of host immune evasion by Ebola virus. *PLoS Pathog.* 8(12):e1003065. doi:10.1371/journal.ppat.1003065.

Mourez, M., Kane, R.S., Mogridge, J., Metallo, S., Deschatelets, P., Sellman, B.R., Whitesides, G.M., and Collier, R.J. 2001. Designing a polyvalent inhibitor of anthrax toxin. *Nat. Biotechnol.* 19(10):958–961.

Murray, P.R., Rosenthal, K.S., and Pfaller, M.A. 2005. *Medical Microbiology*, 5th edn. Elsevier Mosby, Philadelphia, PA, pp. 191–706.

Olsnes, S. 2004. The history of ricin, abrin and related toxins. *Toxicon* 44:361–370.

Phillips, T.D., Afriyie-Gyawu, E., Wang, J.-S., Williams, J., and Huebner, H. 2006. The potential of aflatoxin sequestering clay. In *The Mycotoxin Factbook*, eds. B. Barug, D. Bhatnagar, H.P. van Egmond, J.W. van der Kamp, W.A. van Osenbruggen, and A. Visconti, pp. 329–346. Wageningen Academic Publishers, Wageningen, the Netherlands.

Richt, J.A. and Webby, R.J. 2013. *Swine Influenza.* Springer, Basel, Switzerland. doi:10.1007/978-3-642-36871-4.

Schantz, E.J. 1986. Chemistry and biology of saxitoxin and related toxins. *Ann. N.Y. Acad. Sci.* 479:15–23.

Shapiro, R.L., Hatheway, C., and Swerdlow, D.L. 1998. Botulism in the United States: A clinical and epidemiologic review. *Ann. Intern. Med.* 129:221–228.

Simpson, L.L. 2004. Identification of the major steps in botulinum toxin action. *Annu. Rev. Pharmacol. Toxicol.* 44:167–193.

Smith, P.G. and Bradley, R. 2003. Bovine spongiform encephalopathy (BSE) and its epidemiology. *Br. Med. Bull.* 66:185–198.

Ueno, Y. 1983. General toxicology. In *Trichothecenes: Chemical, Biological and Toxicological Aspects*, ed. Y. Ueno, pp. 135–146. Elsevier, New York.

United States Center for Disease Control and Prevention. 2007. Key facts about influenza and the influenza vaccine: Fact sheet. http://www.cdc.gov/flu/keyfacts.htm (accessed September 25, 2007).

Wang, J.-S. 2007. Pathogenic and toxic effects of biological threat agents. In *Advances in Biological and Chemical Terrorism Countermeasures*, eds. R.J. Kendall, S.R. Presley, G.P. Austin, and P.N. Smith, pp. 229–241. CRC Press, Boca Raton, FL.

Wang, J.-S., Kensler, T.W., and Groopman, J.D. 1998. Toxicants in food: Fungal contaminants In *Current Toxicology Series. Nutrition and Chemical Toxicity*, ed. C. Ioannides, pp. 29–57. John Wiley & Sons, New York.

World Health Organization. 2007. Avian influenza. www.who.int/csr/disease/avian_influenza/en/ (accessed September 25, 2007).

World Health Organization. April 2009. Influenza (seasonal). World Health Organization, Geneva, Switzerland. http://www.who.int/topics/influenza/en/ (accessed April 28, 2014).

World Health Organization. 2011. Cumulative number of confirmed human cases of avian influenza A/(H5N1) reported to WHO. http://www.who.int/csr/disease/avian_influenza/country/cases_table_2011_04_11/en/index.html (accessed April 29, 2014).

World Health Organization. March 2014a. Avian influenza, fact sheet. http://www.who.int/mediacentre/factsheets/avian_influenza/en/ (accessed May 3, 2014).

World Health Organization. 2014b. Antimicrobial resistance. http://www.who.int/mediacentre/factsheets/fs194/en/ (accessed May 22, 2014).

World Health Organization. 2014c. Global alert and response: Ebola virus disease (EVD). World Health Organization, Geneva, Switzerland. http://www.who.int/csr/don/archive/disease/ebola/en (accessed May 22,2014).

Yasumoto, T., Nagai, H., and Yasumura, D. 1986. Interspecies distribution and possible origin of tetrodotoxin. *Ann. N.Y. Acad. Sci.* 479:44–51.

Zilinskas, R.A. 1997. Iraq's biological weapons. The past as future? *JAMA* 278:418–424.

chapter five

Ricin history, toxicity, adsorption, mobility, and palliative actions

Richard E. Zartman and William F. Jaynes

Contents

5.1   Introduction

Probably a few words in the United States are more associated with bioterrorism than the word "ricin." Ricin is a naturally occurring, highly toxic protein produced in the seeds of the castor plant (*Ricinus communis*). The use of castor oil and castor toxin (ricin) goes back many thousands of years (Ogunniyi, 2006). The castor plant is thought to have originated in Africa, but there are wild forms of castor that grow in India. While there are reports of castor grown in the United States dating back to 1803 (Martin et al., 1976), Ogunniyi (2006) stated that "generally the toxicity of the castor seed is a reason why US farmers no longer grow the crop extensively." India, China, and Brazil are the leaders in exported castor oil. The castor seed is not a bean as commonly reported because the castor plant is not a legume. It is thought that ricin is a plant-specific toxin that protects the castor plant and the seed of the castor plant from insect destruction. Ricin, however, is produced in the seed and nowhere else in the plant. Ricin notoriety (or infamy) is associated with the Markov case and from the numerous envelopes that contained a "white powder," such as at the Dirksen Building in Washington, DC, and numerous post offices and business offices (CDC, 2003; Hale, 2014).

5.1.1 Ricin properties

Castor seeds contain 1%–5% ricin by weight (Franz and Jaax, 1997). Ricin is a dimeric cytotoxin that is produced and stored in castor seed. The toxin is comprised of two chains that are joined by a disulfide bond (Figure 5.1). The ricin A chain is the ribosome inactivator while the B chain is the galactose binder. The B chain attaches to the cell surface and the A chain enters and begins the enzymatic deactivation. A single molecule of ricin A chain can inactivate 1500 ribosomes/minute, causing rapid inhibition of protein synthesis leading to cell death (Audi et al., 2005). Wannemacher et al. (1990) reported that the median lethal dose to kill 50% of the population (LD_{50}) for intravenous ricin injection into mice was 3.7 µg/kg of body weight and that it was 50–100 times more toxic when administered as an aerosol than when administered intravenously. Orally ingested ricin is much less toxic. The median lethal dose for orally ingested ricin in mice is 30 mg/kg or about 1000 times greater than for injected or inhaled ricin (Audi et al., 2005). The lethal oral ricin dose for humans was estimated to be 1–20 mg/kg of body weight (Audi et al., 2005). Vitetta et al. (2006) identified a site on ricin

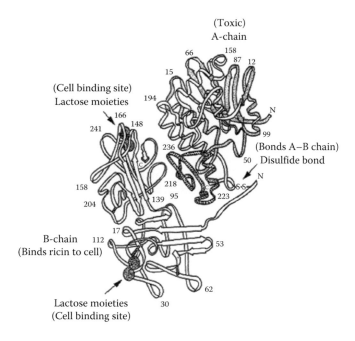

Figure 5.1 Ricin protein structure depicted as ribbons showing A-chain and B-chain subunits after Montfort et al. (1987). Lactose moieties on the B-chain allow ricin attachment to cell surfaces.

A-chain that induces vascular leak syndrome (VLS) in humans. There is no antidote to ricin poisoning, but Vitetta et al. (2006) developed a recombinant A-chain vaccine in which two amino acids in the ricin A-chain have been genetically engineered to inactivate the ribotoxic site and the VLS site. Buonocore et al. (2011) used liposome-encapsulated N-acetylcysteine to reverse ricin A-chain–induced hepatoxicity in test animals. They concluded that liposome-encapsulated N-acetylcysteine might potentially serve as an effective treatment for ricin-induced liver injuries.

Ricin is a probable weapon of choice by terrorists because a large quantity of castor seed could easily be obtained by cultivation or other means. Separation of the toxin from castor seed can be accomplished using low-tech equipment and materials available in a kitchen or garage (see Hale, 2014 for a detailed list of events in which ricin was identified). Ricin is classified as a lectin, which is a protein that specifically binds to particular sugars (Zentz et al., 1978). Lectins are highly specific for particular sugar moieties. Ricin (RCA60) toxin and *Ricinus communis* Agglutinin (RCA120) are galactose-binding lectins. Other lectins specifically bind to mannose, fructose, or other sugars. The larger and much less toxic RCA120 lectin occurs with ricin in castor seed. Much of the research conducted on lectins concerns the specific binding to cell surfaces (d'Avila-Levy et al., 2004; Wigglesworth-Cooksey and Cooksey, 2005). Ricin has been attached to antibodies in research to kill cancer cells (de Virgilio and Degryse, 2014).

5.1.2   Ricin used as a weapon

As mentioned earlier, ricin is perceived to be a weapon of mass destruction. In actuality, ricin has limited mass destruction capabilities (Schep et al., 2009). Ricin is much more a weapon for individuals rather than for large masses of people. Targeted individuals and people in offices are much likelier to be potential victims of ricin intoxication than are the masses of people in an open stadium. This is based on the method of ricin uptake (inhaled, injected, or orally ingested) and amounts needed to cause harm. Ricin is a toxin and is not a disease-causing organism, such as anthrax. Anthrax or a neurotoxic gas such as sarin could more easily be deployed against crowds of people to produce a large number of fatalities.

5.1.2.1   Antiquity

The origin of the castor plant is thought to be Africa and castor seeds have been found in 6000-year-old Egyptian tombs (Hale, 2014). Castor oil has been used as a skin lotion, laxative, and to induce hair growth. In addition to the medicinal properties, castor oil was used as a lamp oil and a machine lubricant. Ricin has been found mixed with 35,000-year-old beeswax making it the earliest known use of a poison (d'Errico et al., 2012).

It has been speculated that the beeswax/ricin mixture was used to poison the tips of stones or spearheads to improve the lethality of those weapons (d'Errico et al., 2012).

5.1.2.2   Pre-9/11

The Markov case in which ricin was injected into the leg of a Bulgarian dissident is probably the most famous ricin poisoning event (Crompton and Gall, 1980). Georgi Markov was assassinated in London, England, when a ricin-filled platinum pellet was injected into his leg at Waterloo Bridge (Owen, 2000). Within the United States, one of the first incidents of ricin use as a terrorist weapon was the Minnesota Patriots Council in 1994 (Tucker and Pate, 2000). Castor is widely cultivated in Iraq and other semiarid countries. In 1989, approximately 10 L of concentrated ricin solution was manufactured at the Salman Pak biological weapons facility just south of Bagdad (Zilinskas, 1997). Even before the events of September 11, 2001 (9/11), the U.S. Centers for Disease Control and Prevention (CDC) identified ricin as a high-priority threat agent for biological and chemical terrorism. Ricin was placed on the CDC's "Category B" list because of its ease of dissemination and moderate morbidity.

5.1.2.3   Post-9/11

After the events of 9/11, biosecurity issues have been an increasing concern. These security issues led to the passage of the Public Health Security and Bioterrorism Preparedness and Response Act of 2002 (Bioterrorism Act). The Bioterrorism Act (2002) takes steps to protect the U.S. public from a threatened or actual terrorist attack. Biological and chemical threat agents are used in terrorism to create instability and paranoia within the population. A brief historic summary of biological and chemical weapon use is provided in Presley et al. (2008) with further details available in the U.S. Department of Defense "Bluebook" (USAMRID, 2011) and the *Medical Aspects of Chemical and Biological Warfare* (Sidell et al., 1997). Even before the events of September 11, 2001, the U.S. CDC had identified ricin as a high-priority threat material for biological terrorism. Ricin is considered a "Category B" biological threat agent because of its ease of dissemination, moderate morbidity rates, and low (2%–6% from ingestion) mortality rates (Arizona Department of Health Services, 2004). There were arrests in Great Britain in 2003 for the potential contamination of the military food supply with ricin (Risen and van Natta, 2003).

The primary concern about contamination of our food supply is that it is a very "low-technology" threat. This threat, however, continues to be largely ignored by the agricultural and environmental community. Brandenberger and McGlynn (2003) in the December 2003 Council for Agricultural Science and Technology Commentary stated, "Therefore, *any* disease-causing microbes present on fruits or vegetables are there because of *inadvertent contamination....*" [Emphasis added]. The agricultural and environmental communities need to be aware of intentional contamination and available remediation methods. While there is abundant public geospatial information that could aid terrorists, it is not the greatest environmental vulnerability. "Human expertise" is a much more critical problem in the "more demanding attack planning part of the targeting problem" (Baker et al., 2004).

Toxins need not be "weaponized" to contaminate food. It was determined that the ricin in the October 15, 2003, letter was not in a weaponized form (CDC, 2003). The sophistication of these bioterrorists is in their subtle use of low-technology methods. Contamination of fresh fruits and vegetables with toxins would be an example of a sophisticated, low-technology terrorist attack. The food and feedstuffs supply chain is highly vulnerable to this type of attack from on-farm production through consumer sales. It is a standard practice to keep vegetables fresh in the supermarket with water rinses. If the water sources used to rinse fresh produce were contaminated by ricin, the consumer would be harmed without immediate knowledge. Our vulnerability to this form of covert biological attack against our food supply may be enhanced by the fact that the persons washing the fresh fruits and vegetables are generally low-paid employees, who might more easily be duped or persuaded to participate. The most common ricin toxicity events were mailed letters containing a "white powder." About the same time as the September 11, 2001, attacks on the World Trade center in New York and the Pentagon in Washington, DC, there were ricin "attacks" in letters.

5.1.3   Modes of ricin dissemination

Biological and chemical threat agents associated with terrorism are directed not only toward vulnerable humans but also toward the environment that supports life. This chapter, however, focuses only on the threat to humans through our environment including food. More general and direct biological and chemical threats to humans are more thoroughly discussed in Kendall et al. (2008). The environment consists of three fundamental components—air, land, and water. As humans, we live in and interact with and depend on each of these environments for our health and well-being. Related to this chapter, biological and chemical threat agents in the environment were modeled and individual personal protection from threat agents is discussed in Kendall et al. (2008).

5.1.3.1   Soil

Ricin, as a natural protein, is a high-molecular-weight polymer like the synthetic polymers nylon 6–6 (poly adipic acid/hexamethylenediamine), polyacrylamide, and polyethylene glycol. Dissolved natural and synthetic polymers are thought to nonspecifically sorb to surfaces via weak van der Waals bonds. The terms "sorb" or "sorption" are used here to indicate removal from solution without specifying a particular mechanism. Although each individual polymer bond is weak, the collective effect of multiple bond attachments can result in strong sorption. This is true especially for high-molecular-weight polymers. Polymer sorption is considered essentially irreversible in that most of the adsorbed polymer cannot be desorbed. Ricin has amino, carboxylic acid, and other functional side chain groups that cause the solubility to vary with pH. At a particular pH, a protein can be anionic, cationic, or have both anionic and cationic groups. Stryer (1975) noted that 20 different side chains commonly occur in proteins from the 20 essential amino acids. The isoelectric point of a protein is the pH where the molecule has a net charge of zero (i.e., equal number of anionic and cationic groups). The isoelectric point of ricin is 7.1 (Merck, 2001). At pH below the isoelectric point, ricin has a net positive charge while at pH above the isoelectric point, it has a net negative charge. A pH that maximizes the number of cationic groups is expected to maximize sorption to materials with a high cation exchange capacity (CEC). Similarly, a pH that maximizes the number of anionic groups would maximize sorption to a high anion exchange capacity (AEC) material.

5.1.3.2   Air

Some speculations were made that ricin could be released into the atmosphere causing injury to the general population. In that scenario, the key controlling factors are boundary layer depth and processes in the air. That scenario is improbable because vast quantities of ricin would be needed to likely produce a significant number of casualties. Of more concern is ricin-filled letters, in which the kinetic energy applied in opening mail can suspend microscopic ricin particles in the air. This can contaminate a small room or a person's face and inhaled air. There certainly have been many incidents in which ricin-laden letters have been sent through the mail.

Toxins, such as ricin, can move as very small particles in the air. Airborne ricin is a concern since inhaled ricin is ~1000 times more toxic than when orally ingested (Audi et al., 2005). Particle-tracking models provide the primary tools for predicting dispersion (Leggoe et al., 2008). To begin any useful effort in mitigating a terrorist incident, the modeling center must be promptly notified that an event has occurred and provided with an initial description of the source (Leggoe et al., 2008). Since ricin is often released in buildings, the volumes of contamination would be small. For ricin release, toxic exposure would mostly occur immediately after the initial release. Immediately after 9/11, aerial spray planes were grounded because there were concerns of aerial applications of biological terror agents.

5.1.3.3   Water

The introduction of ricin into surface waters and municipal water supplies poses several different problems. The nature of the problems posed will depend on the biological and physical properties of ricin and the nature of the water body. Water treatment processes would remove ricin, but small, treated water supplies and consumer products would remain vulnerable to ricin contamination. The large amount of ricin needed to effectively contaminate a large municipal water supply after treatment (e.g., water towers) would make that threat unlikely. The terrorism value of contaminating a municipal water supply might, however, remain attractive to terrorists even though the potential number of fatalities is minimal. The solubility of purified ricin in water is >3 mg/mL. The lethal oral ricin dose for a 70 kg person is 70–1400 mg (1–20 mg/kg body weight), which is 23–467 mL of a 3 mg ricin/mL solution. A 16 oz (473 mL) bottle of water could easily contain the maximum lethal oral dose of ricin for a 70 kg (154 lb) person. Only three 500 mg ricin pills made to look like vitamin tablets would be enough to exceed the maximum lethal oral dose. Because the ricin content is only 1%–5%, a greater weight of castor seeds is needed to get a lethal dose. Four castor seeds weigh about 1 g. Hence, 8 castor seeds with 5% ricin contain 100 mg of ricin, which is more than the minimum lethal dose for a 70 kg person. Only 112 castor seeds (28 g or 1 oz) with 5% ricin would be required for the 1400 mg maximum lethal dose for a 70 kg person. While the earth's surface is mostly water (78%), it is too saline to be potable. We depend on a small, vulnerable fraction of the earth's water (~3%) (Manahan, 2004) to sustain our lives. The environmental destruction caused by biological and chemical weapons would first endanger the surface water and might subsequently be transmitted to groundwater. The environmental effects of biological and chemical weapons would be catastrophic because we all depend on water. Not only would human life be compromised, but our plant and animal communities would also suffer.

5.1.3.4   Clothing

Ricin can contaminate clothing when it is applied as a liquid or when it is embedded within the fabric as fine particles of a solid powder. Greater amounts of ricin could be retained by clothing surfaces from ricin dissolved in water than from ricin powder. Ricin contact to the skin (except eyes and mucous membranes) is not toxic because ricin is too large to pass through the skin and oral ingestion of ricin from clothing is unlikely. Ricin toxicity from dried ricin on clothing, however, is a concern. Powdered ricin can be easily transferred to the eyes or airways after initial ricin contamination of clothing. Natural fibers, such as wool and cotton, are porous and are more amenable to ricin transfer than are synthetic fibers, such as nylon and polyester.

5.1.3.5   Food

There already have been limited biological attacks on fresh fruit and vegetables. The Rajneeshee cult contaminated salad bars in Oregon with *Salmonella typhimurium* to influence the outcome of an election (Torok et al., 1997). In 2003, there were arrests in England for the attempted contamination of military food supplies with ricin (BBC, 2003). These two examples demonstrate that intentional contamination of fresh fruit and vegetables can occur. The simplicity of contaminating food supplies is that it is a very "low-technology" threat.

Ricin need not be "weaponized" to contaminate food (Friedlander, 1997; U.S. Food and Drug Administration 2003). The letter containing ricin (dated approximately October 23, 2003) had not been weaponized (CDC, 2003). Terrorists can be clever by the subtle use of low-technology methods. Contamination of fresh fruits and vegetables by ricin (Franz and Jaax, 1997) would be an example of a sophisticated, low-technology terrorist attack. The food supply chain is vulnerable to this type of attack from farm production, transportation, and delivery all the way to consumer sales (BBC, 2003). It is a standard practice to keep vegetables fresh in the supermarket with water rinses. If the rinse water were contaminated with ricin, the consumer could be harmed without immediate knowledge. This type of biological attack on food security could easily occur because supermarket employees might contaminate the food or customers might surreptitiously contaminate the food as was done by the Rajneeshee cult.

5.1.4   Ricin sorption, movement, and degradation

Ricin is a water-soluble toxin that must be absorbed into the body to be toxic. Ricin is a large (>60 kDa), globular protein and is much too large for absorption through the skin. Dissolved ricin solutions can move through soils and ricin can adsorb to soil particles. Small ricin particles can move in air and be inhaled into human and animal airways and lungs. Heat, chemicals, ultraviolet radiation, and microbes can degrade ricin.

5.1.4.1   Ricin adsorption/retention by soil

Soil is a dynamic, natural three-phase system comprised of solids, liquids, and gas. The transport and fate of biological and chemical threat agents depend upon the state of the agent and how the agent reacts with the soil. Threat agents such as ricin can be applied as solids, can be mixed with the soil solids, or be suspended or dissolved in the aqueous phase surrounding the solids. Once ricin comes in contact with the soil, it may sorb to the soil, move with the water, or be degraded within the soil.

Several articles have reported that the clay component of soils and sediments effectively sorbs proteins. Sorption to natural soils and other materials affects the migration and fate of toxins in the environment (Zartman et al., 2002). Soils contain inorganic minerals, organic matter, and microorganisms. These materials can sorb or degrade aqueous toxins. Soils contain a wide variety of materials with different sorptive properties and a wide range in particle size. Soil organic matter consists of a wide variety of materials that range from recalcitrant, highly altered materials, such as humus, to fresh plant material and animal remains. Humic acid, a component of humus, has been shown to sorb a variety of organic compounds, such as pesticides. Humic acid is the name (or misnomer) given to polydisperse biopolymers that occur in soil organic matter, sewage sludge, weathered lignite coal, and other organic materials.

The cation- and anion-exchange capacities of soils can strongly affect the sorption of many compounds. Temperate-region soils mostly contain minerals and materials with significant CECs. Most soils, however, contain minerals and materials with both a CEC and anion exchange capacity (AEC). Cationic compounds strongly adsorb to materials with a high CEC. Anionic compounds strongly adsorb to materials with a high AEC. Because like charges repel, small anionic compounds are not effectively sorbed by the negatively charged surfaces of high CEC materials and small cationic compounds are not effectively sorbed by high AEC materials. Large organic compounds, such as natural and synthetic polymers, sorb to a variety of materials. Proteins are natural polymers that can exist as cations, anions, or zwitterions depending on solution pH. The sorption of proteins and other charged polymers is affected both by charge and the polymeric character.

5.1.4.2   Soil texture

Soil texture is determined by the sand, silt, and clay content. Water movement into (infiltration) or through (permeability) a soil depends on textural class. Soil textural classes dominated by clay, such as sandy clay, clay, or silty clay, have low water infiltration rates and low permeabilities. Soil textural classes dominated by sand, such as sandy loam, loamy sand, or sand, have high water infiltration rates and high permeabilities. Silt textured soils have intermediate water infiltration rates and permeability. Sand, silt, and clay particles have different effects on the fate of biological and chemical threat agents in the environment. The sand (2–0.05 mm)— and silt (0.05–0.002 mm)—size fractions usually consist largely of quartz and feldspars. The clay (<0.002 mm) fraction usually consists mostly of silicate clay minerals and iron oxides. The clay-size minerals have a large specific surface area, which in part, explains the greater capacity of clays to adsorb a large variety of substances. The sand and silt fractions have low specific surface areas and are generally rather poor sorbents. Hence, soil texture has both physical and chemical effects on water and dissolved contaminants. A clayey soil both adsorbs contaminants and restricts surface water movement into groundwater. Sandy soils neither readily adsorb contaminants nor restrict surface water movement into groundwater. Cationic chemicals readily sorb to negatively charged clay particles and inhibit cation movement within the soil. Sandy or silty soils, however, would allow biological and chemical threat agents to pass rapidly through the soil and contaminate shallow ground water (Zartman and Jaynes, 2014). Therefore, the soil texture may determine the environmental fate of biological and chemical threat agents. To sequester, sorb, and remove cationic materials, a clay-textured soil is advantageous. Sand- and silt-textured soils would facilitate the mobility of biological and chemical materials within the environment.

5.1.4.3   Mineralogy

The silicate clays are classified into 1:1 and 2:1 types based on crystal structure and chemistry. Silicate clays are phyllosilicate minerals with a sheet-like structure typical of the micas—muscovite and biotite. The silicate clays are classified according to the number of tetrahedral (SiO_4) silica units and octahedral (AlO_6, MgO_6) alumina–magnesia units in the mineral structure. The tetrahedral and octahedral units are bonded together through shared oxygen or hydroxyl groups into a structural unit but are often described as if consisting of separate tetrahedral and octahedral layers. A 1:1 clay is a silicate clay with one silica tetrahedral layer and one alumina octahedral layer (Schulze, 1989). Kaolinite, also called "china clay," is a 1:1 clay and an important industrial mineral used to produce porcelain and fine chinaware ceramics. Montmorillonite, vermiculite, and illite are examples of 2:1 silicate clays. Montmorillonite and vermiculite have high CECs and can expand the clay lattice by adding water or other substances between the individual clay layers. Montmorillonite is the principal mineral in most bentonites, which are mined worldwide and are extensively used commercial products. Montmorillonite is used as an excipient in pharmaceuticals, food products, animal feed, well-drilling fluids, metal casting, paints, pet litter, as well as many other uses. Illite (or clay mica) is a nonexpandable clay with an intermediate CEC. Kaolinite and illite are nonexpanding minerals. The "total" surface areas of smectites can be as high as 800 m^2/g. Minerals, such as quartz (SiO_2), have a fixed composition. In contrast, vermiculite and montmorillonite chemical compositions and CECs vary within limits for different samples. Most clays in temperate-region soils have significant CECs. Amorphous or noncrystalline clays, which are more common in tropical climates or in areas blanketed by volcanic deposits, have large surface areas and a pH-dependent charge (AEC at low pH, CEC at high pH). Iron oxide minerals, such as hematite, goethite, and ferrihydrite, also have a pH-dependent charge. Iron oxides occur in most soils but are more abundant in the soils of tropical regions.

The clay mineral, sepiolite, and sorbed collagen protein, and the extent of sorption were affected by solution pH and ionic strength (Perez-Castells et al., 1985). They reported that collagen is positively charged in acid solution, which increases electrostatic interactions between the negatively charged sepiolite clay surface and the positively charged protein. Ding and Henrichs (2002) concluded that electrostatic interactions dominated in protein adsorption to clay minerals such as goethite, illite, and montmorillonite. Jaynes et al. (2005) reported that several types of clay minerals common in soils were effective in binding ricin. They reported that ricin sorption was greatest at pH ≤7 (i.e., below the ricin 7.1 isoelectric point), but much less ricin was sorbed at pH 10. At alkaline pH, ricin might sorb to positively charged minerals, such as hydrotalcites.

5.1.4.4   Organic matter

Organic matter in the soil also sorbs many ionic and nonionic chemicals. This is because the macromolecules that comprise organic matter contain both polar and nonpolar regions. These polar regions contain nitrogen, oxygen, and sulfur functional groups. On a weight-per-weight basis, organic matter has a greater CEC than inorganic clays. Organic matter, however, is less than 5% in most soils, and the more abundant inorganic clays can have a greater net sorptive capacity. The presence of organic matter within soils is specific to the soil depth and geographic region. Because organic matter is derived from plant material, it is generally greater near the soil surface than at greater depths. Soils in the hotter, drier areas (e.g., southwest United States) generally have very low soil organic matter contents. It is normal for soils in the southwestern United States to have less than 1% organic matter in the soil surface horizons. The soil organic matter percentages decrease significantly with depth. In contrast with these low organic matter levels, soils in the northeastern United States have higher soil organic matter levels. Soils in the northeast region have higher organic matter production since they have greater annual precipitation. Additionally, soils in the northeastern United States have lower mean annual temperatures, which results in less organic matter decomposition. The high organic matter production and the lower organic matter decay result in a greater net soil organic matter content.

5.1.4.5   Ion exchange capacity

As mentioned previously, there are many different kinds of clays; however, only phyllosilicate clays (1:1 and 2:1) and nonphyllosilicate materials will be discussed. Kaolinite is a low-CEC 1:1 clay that generally occurs in "old" highly weathered soils and is typical of the soil clay mineralogy that occurs in the southeastern United States. These soils typically also contain iron oxide minerals, a low CEC (2–10 centimoles per kilogram [cmol/kg] of material), and are not capable of sorbing large quantities of ricin. While 1:1 silicate clays have low CECs at low soil pH (>5), these clays have an AEC. The AEC allows these clay minerals to sorb anions within the soil. The nonphyllosilicate iron oxide minerals, however, also have an AEC at acidic pH and are generally more effective anionic sorbents than 1:1 clays. The properties of 2:1 silicate clays vary depending on the CEC magnitude and location (tetrahedral or octahedral layer) of the charge. The total charge imparts a CEC (net negative charge) or AEC (net positive charge) to clays. Vermiculites are 2:1 silicate clays with a very large CEC and are not as expandable as smectites, such as montmorillonite and beidellite. The 2:1 clay minerals with most of the charge from tetrahedral layers (e.g., beidellite) are not as expandable as clays with most of the charge from the octahedral layer, such as montmorillonite. Soils that contain smectite clays have high CECs and have high shrink/swell capabilities. These soils expand when wet and shrink when dry. The high CECs and large surface areas of smectites contribute to the sorption of ricin as a cation and a polymer.

5.1.5   Adsorption/retention by building materials

Ricin sorption to some building materials can be similar to some soil minerals. Building materials, such as concrete, contain calcite ($CaCO_3$) that is typically present in soils in the southwestern United States. The sand and gravel aggregate used in concrete are like the sand and gravel fractions in soils. Fired brick is made using soil minerals, such as quartz, feldspars, and kaolinite, but the intense heat used in the firing process changes the mineralogy. Fired brick has lost most of the cation exchange and sorptive properties of the constituent soil materials used in manufacture. Bricks can be porous and might absorb dissolved ricin solutions. Wood is a common building material with sorptive properties that are controlled by the porosity and by the cellulose, hemicellulose, and lignin chemical constituents. Ricin sorption would be minimal to metal, glass, vinyl, ceramic tile, linoleum, and other nonporous materials used as building structural or exterior facing materials. Curtains and other fabric materials used in building interiors would have the greatest potential to sorb or retain ricin. In general, ricin sorption to building exterior surfaces should be minimal, but ricin sorption to interior surfaces and materials would be the greatest concern.

5.1.6   Adsorption/retention by clothing

For clothing, the type of fabric would control ricin sorption. The fibers of synthetic fabrics, such as nylon, consist of solid rods formed by extrusion of a polymer melt through a small orifice. Ricin sorption to synthetic fabrics is minimal (Zartman and Jaynes, 2014). In contrast, natural fibers are hollow tubes with internal structures. Cotton fibers are cellulose seed hairs with primary and secondary cell walls and an interior lumen. Wool fibers are animal hairs with a complex interior structure formed of two helical proteins. Like other proteins, wool should have pH-dependent ion exchange properties.

5.1.7   *Ricin adsorption/retention and food contamination*

Food security issues have been an increasing homeland security and environmental concern. This concern is due to the simplicity of food supply contamination and that it is a very "low-technology" threat. Castor is easy to cultivate and is often used as an ornamental plant thereby making it accessible (Atlas, 1999). The grocery industry recognizes the food contamination problem can originate in the soil (Hennessy, 2000). In 2003, the U.S. Food and Drug Administration stated "the agency concludes that there is a high likelihood, over the course of a year, which a significant number of people will be affected by an act of food terrorism…" (U.S. Food and Drug Administration, 2003). The FDA Food Safety Modernization Act (FSMA) was signed into law on January 4, 2011, to further limit potential food contamination (U.S. Food and Drug Administration, 2011). Food safety was further emphasized by the Council for Agricultural Science and Technology, which stated that "recent outbreaks of food-related illnesses have increased many people's concern about the safety of fresh fruits and vegetables…." (Brandenberger and McGlynn, 2003).

5.1.7.1   *Surfaces*

From studies on ricin sorption to fruits and vegetables, it is clear that fruit/vegetable surfaces influence ricin sorption. Vegetables with porous, non-waxy surfaces retain significantly more ricin than vegetables that have smooth, waxy surfaces (Zartman et al., 2003). Once sorbed, most of the ricin sorbed to the fruits and vegetables might persist through multiple aqueous rinses. After fruits and vegetables have been contaminated with ricin, it is not certain that aqueous washing will render it safe or acceptable for human consumption (Zartman et al., 2003). Although the residual ricin might not pose a significant health risk to the general population, babies and people with compromised heath may be at a risk for ricin intoxication.

5.1.7.2   *Temperature*

Ricin is a protein that can be denatured with heat. Therefore, foods contaminated with ricin heated above 80°C should not be a problem. Fresh fruits or vegetables that are consumed cold or at room temperature would be problematic. While certainly not a food product, the meal remaining after castor oil is extracted from castor seeds can be used as an insecticide. From an industrial perspective, this meal is heated and or chemically treated to render it nontoxic (Barnes et al., 2009). Typically castor meal is heated to 100°C to insure the ricin protein is denatured.

5.1.8 Ricin movement through soils

As mentioned in Section 5.1.4.1, soil texture, mineralogy, and organic matter all influence ricin movement within soils. Ricin attacks most likely will be small in extent due to the relatively large amounts of ricin needed to cause illness or death. Ricin introduced in sandy soils, such as that which occur in Florida, would move rapidly with the soil water due to lack of ricin sorption sites. As the soil clay and organic matter increase, ricin is less readily transported. Even for soils with similar clay contents, the mineralogy would influence ricin movement. The kaolinitic clays of the southeast United States would allow greater movement and transmission of ricin than would the illitic clays of the Midwest or the montmorillonitic clays of the west (Zartman et al., 2008).

5.1.9 Ricin movement in dust

Ricin is more readily sorbed to the clay fraction of the soil than either the sand or silt fractions. Ricin powder can easily be transported long distances with the prevailing wind (Zartman et al., 2005). This was a concern with the US troop movement into Iraq. If the Iraqis had sufficient ricin to spread along the incursion path to Bagdad, the disabilities and death of coalition warfighters might have been horrific.

5.1.10 Degradation of ricin

Ricin is a dimeric cytotoxin that can be chemically or microbiologically degraded into nontoxic substances. For typical laboratory cleanup, sodium hypochlorite (Bleach) can be used to decompose or denature ricin (Mackinnon and Alderton, 2000). Alternatively, other oxidation agents, such as hydrogen peroxide, will decompose or denature ricin. Strong acids, such as nitric or sulfuric, are also capable of destroying ricin. de Oliviera et al. (2010) reported that microbiota in ruminates are able to degrade ricin, but ricin inhibits ruminate microbial growth. Ricin is deactivated irreversibly by heating. Heating above the critical temperature can denature ricin and eliminate the capacity of ricin to inhibit protein synthesis.

5.1.11 Modeling ricin transport

Ricin can exist as solid particles, sorbed to a solid, or dissolved in a liquid media. Ricin often occurs in a powdered form that could be disseminated into the air as an aerosol. While ricin is soluble in water and does not exert a significant vapor pressure, in nonaqueous media, ricin would exist as a solid. Relative amounts of dissolved versus adsorbed ricin can vary dynamically with quantity added and sorbent material. Solid ricin particles can move independently of soil particles. Ricin adsorbed to soil particles can only move with the soil particle. Dissolved ricin can move by diffusion, convection, or by both modes.

The partitioning of ricin between the solid and liquid phases in soil can be written as

$$C = \rho_b C_a + \theta_v C_l \tag{5.1}$$

where
C is the total ricin content (M/L^3)
ρ_b is the soil bulk density (M/L^3)
C_a is the adsorbed ricin concentration expressed as mass of ricin per mass of dry soil (M/M)
θ_v is the volumetric water content (L^3/L^3)
C_l is the dissolved ricin concentration expressed as mass of ricin per volume of soil solution (M/L^3)

Note that fundamental units M (mass), L (length), and T (time) are used.

5.1.11.1 Diffusion

Diffusion is defined as movement by a gradient from an area of high concentration to an area of low concentration. The gradient is the difference in ricin concentration divided by the distance between the two concentration areas. Molecular diffusion for steady-state transport is generally written as

$$J = -D \frac{\partial C}{\partial z} \tag{5.2}$$

where
J is the solute flux density $(M/L^2/T)$
D is the molecular diffusion coefficient (L^2/T)
z is the distance (L)

For transient-state conditions, the conservation of mass equation in one-dimension without generation or consumption is

$$\frac{\partial C}{\partial t} = -\frac{\partial J}{\partial z} \tag{5.3}$$

where *t* is the time. Combining Equation 5.2 with Equation 5.3 gives the following:

$$\frac{\partial C}{\partial t} = \frac{\partial}{\partial z}\left(D\frac{\partial C}{\partial z}\right) \tag{5.4}$$

This equation presents change of ricin concentration with time and the molecular diffusion coefficient in the *z* direction. Ricin would not be expected to diffuse to any great extent, due to the small diffusion coefficient.

5.1.11.2   Convection

Convection is movement of a substance with a carrier, such as air or water. Ricin moves as a particle in the air or as a solute dissolved in soil water. The kinetic energy produced by opening a ricin-laden envelop would cause ricin particles to be ejected into the air. One-dimensional flow rate, J_z, in the *z* direction can be represented by

$$J_z = -q_z C_a \tag{5.5}$$

where
   q_z is the air flow rate (L/T)
   C_a is the ricin concentration expressed as the mass per volume of
      air (M/L^3)

For ricin moved as a convective liquid, Equation 5.5 can be rewritten as

$$J_z = -v\theta_v C_l \tag{5.6}$$

where
   v is the average water velocity (L/T)
   θ_v is the volumetric water content (L^3/L^3)
   C_l is the dissolved ricin concentration expressed as the mass of ricin
      per volume of soil solution (M/L^3) in the *z* direction

If applied to the soil surface, the mathematical solution for the ricin solution would be as follows:

$$C(z,t) = \left[\frac{C_0 Z}{2\sqrt{\pi D t^3}}\right]\left[\exp\left\{-\frac{(z-vt)^2}{4Dt}\right\}\right] \tag{5.7}$$

given the appropriate boundary conditions of Jury et al. (1991).

Application of the Equation 5.7 to real-world problems is very limited. This type of flow assumes sharp wetting fronts of solution passing through the soil as "piston flow," which seldom, if ever, occurs in the environment. The diffusion portion of the diffusion–convection advances or retards the flow and precludes the sharp line of demarcation. Due to dispersion, preferential flow and fingering, solute flow is unstable and has diffuse flow boundaries (Hillel, 1998). Examples of ricin breakthrough curve data will be shown in the results Section 5.2.2 later in this document.

5.2   Results and discussion

5.2.1   Ricin adsorption to soil clays and other natural materials

Montmorillonite, illite, and kaolinite are common clay minerals in temperate-region soils and ricin adsorption to montmorillonite was much greater than to illite or kaolinite (Figure 5.2). Montmorillonite is an expandable clay mineral with a much larger specific surface area ($630 \ m^2/g$) and CEC than illite ($20 \ m^2/g$) or kaolinite ($11 \ m^2/g$) and these properties probably account for the greater ricin adsorption. Soils typically contain other minerals and materials, such as iron oxides, carbonates, and organic matter. The other soil materials adsorbed ricin (Figure 5.3), but not nearly as effectively as montmorillonite (Figure 5.2). Of the iron oxide minerals, the high surface area ferrihydrite ($227 \ m^2/g$) more effectively adsorbed

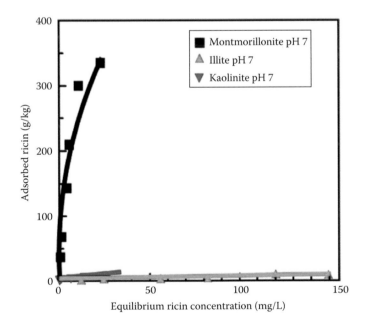

Figure 5.2 Ricin adsorption to common soil clay minerals at pH 7.

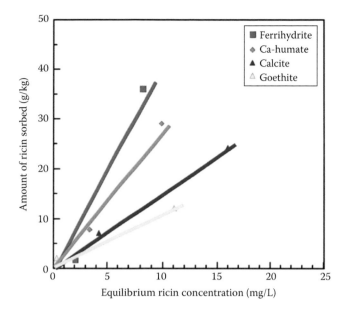

Figure 5.3 Ricin adsorption at neutral pH to nonsilicate soil materials: calcite (CaCO₃), ferrihydrite and goethite are iron oxides, and Ca-humate is soil organic matter or humus.

ricin than goethite (31 m²/g). Calcite, a carbonate mineral common in arid and semiarid region soils, also effectively adsorbed ricin. Calcium humate, a common type of soil organic matter, also effectively adsorbed ricin.

5.2.2 Ricin and peanut lectin adsorption and movement through soil

Ricin (mw = 65 kDa) and peanut lectin (PNA, mw = 110 kDa) are both glob-ular plant proteins and galactose-binding lectins. Peanut lectin is similar to ricin and was used as a nontoxic simulant in experiments before ricin use. Ricin adsorption to montmorillonite, however, was much greater than peanut lectin (Figure 5.4). Peanut lectin is a larger molecule than ricin and greater adsorption might be expected. Differences in the amino acid com-position between ricin and peanut lectin might explain the difference in adsorption. The ratio of basic amino acids (histidine, lysine, and arginine) to acidic amino acids (glutamate, aspartate) in ricin (1.02) is much greater than in peanut lectin (0.39). Basic amino acids are positively charged at neutral to acidic pH, which would favor ricin adsorption to a negatively charged high-CEC mineral like montmorillonite. Ricin and peanut lectin solutions at neutral pH were eluted through loamy fine sand and sandy

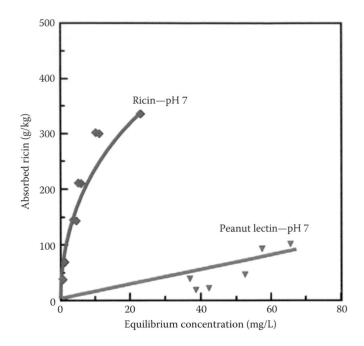

Figure 5.4 Relative adsorption of castor seed lectin (ricin) and peanut lectin (PNA) to montmorillonite at pH 7. Ricin (mw = 60 kDa) and peanut lectin (mw = 100 kDa) are both galactose-binding globular proteins.

clay loam soil columns (Figure 5.5). Soil column pore volume is the volume of all of the water-filled voids in a water-saturated soil column (Skaggs and Leij, 2002). Breakthrough is achieved when the initial (C_0) and eluted concentrations (C_e) of ricin and peanut lectin are equal (e.g., $C_e/C_0 = 1$). For the loamy fine sand columns, peanut lectin reached breakthrough in only 10 pore volumes, but 50 pore volumes were not quite enough ($C_e/C_0 = 0.9$) to achieve ricin breakthrough (Figure 5.5). The loamy fine sand (13% clay) soil column adsorbed more ricin than peanut lectin, which is consistent with the montmorillonite adsorption isotherms (Figure 5.4). For the sandy clay loam (28% clay) soil columns, peanut lectin achieved breakthrough in 55 pore volumes, but ricin breakthrough was not achieved ($C_e/C_0 = 0.1$) after 130 pore volumes. Even a relatively sandy soil, like loamy fine sand, can adsorb and limit the mobility of ricin.

5.2.3   *Ricin adsorption to activated carbon and building materials*

Ricin adsorption to decolorizing activated carbon (Norit-A) was 50 times less than to montmorillonite (Figure 5.2) and comparable to kaolinite (Figure 5.6). Ricin adsorption to powdered quartz, glass, and concrete

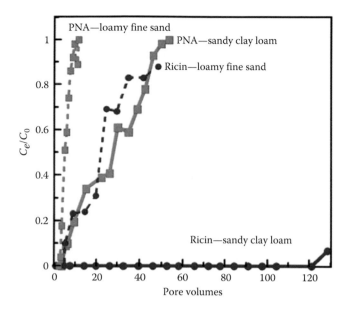

Figure 5.5 Breakthrough curves for elution of ricin and peanut lectin (PNA) through loamy fine sand (13% clay) and sandy clay loam (28% clay) soil columns. Ricin was strongly retained in the sandy clay loam soil column and breakthrough ($C_e/C_0 = 1$) was not achieved after 130 pore volumes.

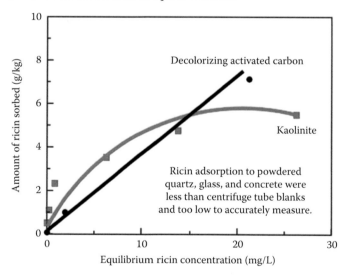

Figure 5.6 Adsorption of ricin to decolorizing activated carbon and kaolinite from neutral (pH ~7) solution. Ricin adsorption to decolorizing activated carbon and kaolinite were low and about 100 times less than montmorillonite. Ricin adsorption to quartz, glass, and concrete were even less than kaolinite.

was also measured, but the values were too low for accurate measurement. A blank correction was used because small amounts of ricin adsorbed to the centrifuge tubes used in the adsorption experiments. Equilibrium ricin concentrations in centrifuge tubes with added quartz, glass, and concrete powders were equal to or greater than that in centrifuge tube blanks. Building materials used in exterior surfaces should not retain ricin, but fabrics and other materials in building interiors might act differently.

5.2.4   *Ricin adsorption kinetics to montmorillonite and effect of ionic strength*

Timed ricin concentration measurements for ricin/montmorillonite suspensions were made (pH 7) in an attempt to measure the rate of ricin adsorption. After only 1 minute (Figure 5.7a), ricin adsorption was complete. Ricin adsorption was clearly too rapid for the experimental method and equipment used. The amount of adsorbed ricin slightly decreased between 1 and 240 minutes. This suggests that ricin is very rapidly adsorbed to montmorillonite and is later reorganized during equilibration with some ricin desorption. Cation exchange is a rapid process that might explain the rapid adsorption of ricin. Increasing the ionic strength from 0.02 to 0.5 (seawater ionic strength = 0.7) greatly reduced ricin adsorption to montmorillonite (Figure 5.7b). The decreased ricin adsorption with increased ionic strength also suggests that ion exchange is an important process in ricin adsorption. The greater Na^+ concentrations with increased ionic strength compete against ricin for cation exchange sites. It also suggests that high ionic strength solutions might be used to desorb adsorbed ricin.

5.2.5   *Ricin adsorption to clays, pH, CEC, and Langmuir model fit*

Ricin adsorption to montmorillonite was measured at different pH using buffer solutions to control pH. Ricin adsorption at pH 5 was greater than at pH 7, which in turn was greater than at pH 10 (Figure 5.8). The acidic pH 5 buffer solution should impart a net positive charge to ricin (isoelectric point pH 7.1), which could enhance adsorption to negatively charged montmorillonite particles. The ricin adsorption data were fitted to the Langmuir adsorption model, and monolayer ricin adsorption capacities (X_m) were calculated from the Langmuir fit parameters. The good fit of the adsorption data to the Langmuir adsorption model suggests that ricin adsorbs to a surface. Ricin adsorption to montmorillonite was five times greater at pH 5 than at pH 10 and three times greater at pH 7 than at pH 10. The pH 10 buffer solution should impart a net negative charge

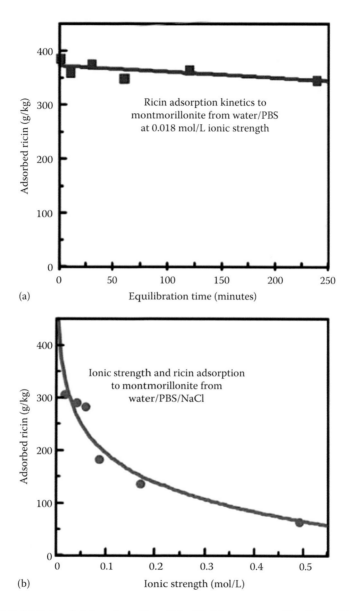

(a)

(b)

Figure 5.7 (a) Rate of ricin adsorption (kinetics) to montmorillonite and (b) effect of solution ionic strength on ricin adsorption.

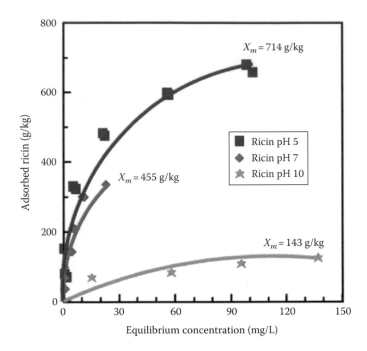

Figure 5.8 Ricin adsorption to montmorillonite at pH 5, 7, and 10. The adsorption data were fitted to the Langmuir adsorption model and monolayer (X_m) adsorption capacities were calculated.

to ricin, which could prevent or limit adsorption to negatively charged montmorillonite particles. Most (>80%) of the charge site on montmorillonite particles is on permanent negatively charged sites on interlayer surfaces, but montmorillonite particles also have pH-dependent exchange sites at the edges of particles. The relative amounts of ricin adsorbed at pH 5 and pH 10 suggest that ricin might adsorb to montmorillonite edge sites only at pH 10. Montmorillonite samples vary in CEC and the number of negatively charged sites. Clay Minerals Society sample SWy-2 (CEC = 87 cmol/kg) is a low-charge montmorillonite from Wyoming and sample SAz-1 (CEC = 130 cmol/kg) is a high-charge montmorillonite from Arizona. Ricin adsorption isotherms with pH 5 buffer were prepared for SWy-2 and SAz-1 (Figure 5.9). Despite the greater SAz-1 CEC, comparable amounts of ricin adsorbed to SWy-2 and SAz-1 and calculated Langmuir monolayer adsorption capacities were approximately the same. Based on montmorillonite, illite, and kaolinite CECs and the relative amounts of ricin adsorbed (Figure 5.2), CEC is an important factor in ricin adsorption. The 50% greater CEC of SAz-1 relative to SWy-2, however, did not increase ricin adsorption. Ricin molecules are large polymers and numerous relatively weak van der Waals bonds might contribute to ricin adsorption.

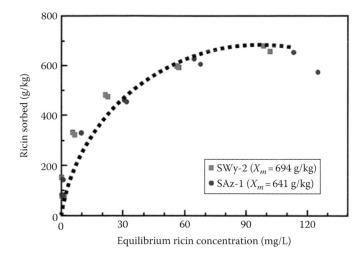

Figure 5.9 Ricin adsorption to low- (SWy-2) and high-charge (SAz-1) reference montmorillonite samples at pH 5. Monolayer ricin adsorption capacities (X_m) were calculated from a fit of adsorption data to the Langmuir adsorption model.

5.2.6   X-ray diffraction, ricin adsorption, and interlayer montmorillonite expansion

Montmorillonite samples were suspended in pH 4 buffer solutions with or without ricin and were dried as oriented films on glass slides. Drying clays on glass slides causes the clay platelets to lie flat on the glass surface. An oriented clay film makes it possible to measure interlayer expansion using x-ray diffraction. The montmorillonite with only pH 4 buffer yielded a 12 Å interlayer spacing characteristic of a K⁺-saturated montmorillonite (Figure 5.10). The K⁺ was derived from the potassium hydrogen phthalate in the pH 4 buffer. With both pH 4 buffer and ricin added, 34.6 and 23.1 Å spacings were produced that indicate interlayer expansion of montmorillonite. In contrast, montmorillonite treated with pH 10 buffer and ricin (not shown, Figure 6a, Jaynes et al., 2005) showed no expansion. No expansion at pH 10 indicates that ricin did not adsorb to montmorillonite interlayers, but some ricin (143 g/kg) did adsorb to montmorillonite at pH 10 (Figure 5.8). Significant ricin adsorption without interlayer expansion suggests that ricin must adsorb to montmorillonite edge sites at pH 10. The interlayer expansion of montmorillonite by water absorption is illustrated in Figure 5.11. An air-dried, K⁺-saturated montmorillonite sample yields a 12 Å interlayer spacing. When water is added to the K⁺-montmorillonite, the interlayers expand and physically separate. In a dilute montmorillonite suspension, the distance between interlayers

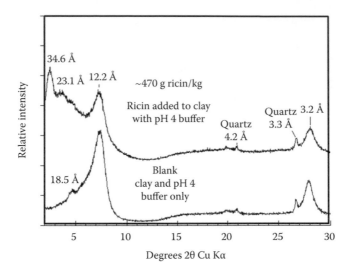

Figure 5.10 Ricin adsorption to montmorillonite from pH 4 buffer solution (potassium hydrogen phthalate) and interlayer expansion of montmorillonite.

can be indefinitely large. The large separation between montmorillonite layers allows large molecules, such as ricin, to move between layers and adsorb to interlayer surfaces.

5.2.7   *Ricin adsorption and desorption from soil clay minerals*

Adsorbed ricin might later be partially desorbed using wash solutions. Ricin was initially adsorbed to montmorillonite, illite, and kaolinite samples from pH 7 PBS solutions (Figure 5.12). The clay samples were then sequentially washed with PBS, pH 10 buffer, and once more with pH 10 buffer. Ricin concentrations in the wash solutions were measured to calculate the amounts of residual ricin still adsorbed to the clays. The PBS wash was not very effective in desorbing ricin, but the pH 10 washes desorbed greater amounts of ricin. Alkaline solutions, such as the pH 10 buffer, can effectively remove adsorbed ricin.

5.2.8   *Ricin sorption/desorption from textiles, fruits, and vegetables*

Ricin adsorption and desorption was examined for textiles (Figure 5.13). Ricin from pH 7 PBS solution was adsorbed to samples of wool, nylon, and cotton fabric. Initial ricin sorption by wool, cotton, and nylon were 4, 2.5, and 2.3 g/kg, which were about 100-fold less than montmorillonite.

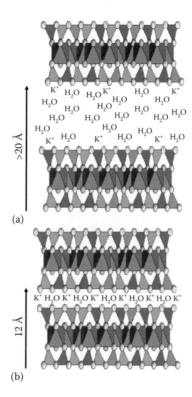

Figure 5.11 Illustration of K-montmorillonite interlayer expansion (a) suspended in water and (b) under air-dry conditions. The pH 4 buffer used in Figure 5.10 contained potassium hydrogen phthalate, which saturated the exchange sites with K^+ cations.

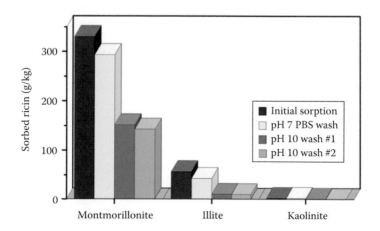

Figure 5.12 Ricin adsorption and desorption from common silicate clay minerals in soils.

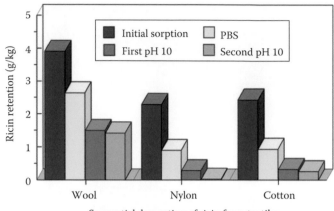

Sequential desorption of ricin from textiles

Figure 5.13 Ricin sorption to wool, nylon, and cotton textiles and sequential desorption with pH 7 phosphate buffered saline (PBS) and pH 10 buffer.

Ricin desorption by PBS was much less than desorption by pH 10 buffer. The use of an alkaline detergent in a washing machine might be as effective as pH 10 buffer in desorbing ricin. Wool is a protein and only about one-half of sorbed ricin was desorbed after one PBS and two pH 10 buffer washes. The wash treatments desorbed most of the ricin from cotton and nylon. Nearly all sorbed ricin was removed from the synthetic fabric, nylon, by the wash treatments. Ricin sorbed to the natural fabrics, wool and cotton, was more resistant to desorption. An Army Combat Uniform (ACU) was obtained and tested for the contact transfer of ricin from contaminated soil. The ACU fabric is a 50% cotton/50% nylon blend. Clothing is more prone to contamination at knee and elbow joints because significant pressure is usually applied to clothing in those areas and contact with contaminants is more likely. The greater applied pressure at knees and elbows can facilitate greater contaminant transfer from soils or other contacted surfaces. Checkai et al. (2011) developed a method to test the contact transfer of liquid chemical agents to clothing from contaminated soil. A similar procedure was used to measure contact transfer of aqueous ricin from contaminated soil to ACU fabric. A 1 kg weight was used to apply pressure to 93 mm diameter disks of ACU. The initial amount of ricin transferred to 93 mm ACU disks (Figure 5.14) was approximately 2 g/kg, which is comparable to cotton and nylon in Figure 5.13. A second pH 10 buffer wash likely would have reduced ACU-sorbed ricin in Figure 5.14 to levels intermediate between cotton and nylon (Figure 5.13). The alkaline detergent, greater water volume, and multiple water rinses used in a laundry washing machine would probably more effectively remove sorbed ricin than the pH 10 buffer washes.

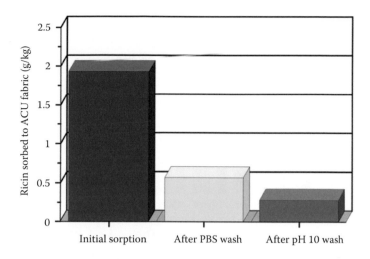

Figure 5.14 Contact transfer of ricin to Army Combat Uniform (ACU) textile from sand moistened with ricin solution. Desorption of ricin from ACU with pH 7 phosphate buffered saline solution (PBS) and pH 10 buffer.

Fruits and vegetables on grocery store shelves and salad bars might be intentionally contaminated with ricin. Grocery stores commonly use an aqueous spray to keep displayed fruits and vegetables fresh and prevent dehydration. The wash could be contaminated with ricin and adsorb to fruits and vegetables. Fruits and vegetables were dipped into a solution of ricin dissolved in pH 7 PBS and ricin amounts initially sorbed were measured (Figure 5.15). Broccoli, lettuce, carrots, and celery retained the most ricin. The more spherical fruits, blueberries, tomatoes, and grapes retained the least ricin. The amounts of ricin sorbed by fruits and vegetables (mg/kg units) were much less than fabrics and about 1000 times less than soil minerals (g/kg units). The fruits and vegetables were sequentially washed to desorb ricin with two PBS and one pH 10 buffer wash. The pH 7 PBS washes were not as effective in removing ricin as the pH 10 buffer. The effect of the different wash treatments suggest that washing with water (like PBS washes) would not be very effective and that washing with an alkaline detergent (like pH 10 buffer washes) would be needed to effectively remove ricin. The Figure 5.15 data indicate that fruits and vegetables contaminated by a grocery produce spray would not likely cause harm. Such an event could produce terror, but few, if any, casualties. A very large quantity of fruits and vegetables would have to be consumed to ingest a lethal oral dose of ricin. Washing fruits and vegetables before consumption would greatly reduce any risk.

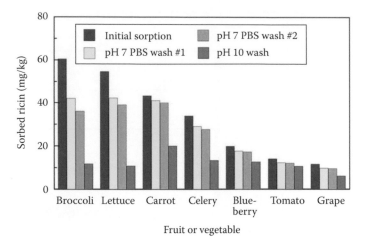

Figure 5.15 Ricin sorption and sequential desorption from fruits and vegetables. Note that the sorbed ricin units, mg/kg, are 1000 times less than the g/kg units used for clay minerals.

5.2.9   Ricin movement and concentration in soil dust and effect of surfactants

Ricin inhaled into the lungs is about 1000 times more toxic than orally ingested ricin. A dust generator/dust fraction collector assembly was built to examine the transport of ricin particles in soil dust (Figure 5.16a). The dust generator design was modified from the much larger USDA-ARS dust generator (Zobeck et al., 1997). Soil dust generated by wind or by passing vehicles at a ricin-contaminated site might carry respirable ricin particles to passing military personnel or civilians. The rotating dust

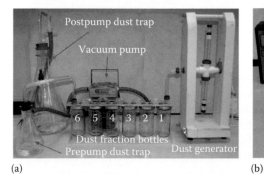
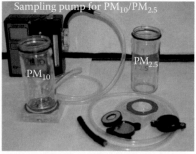

(a)   (b)

Figure 5.16 Dust generator/dust fraction collector assembly (a) with dust fraction particle size decreasing from bottle #1 to bottle #6. The PM_{10} and $PM_{2.5}$ dust samplers (b) were placed at the bottle #4 position in the dust fraction collector.

generator first suspends soil particles in the air and a vacuum pump then moves dust particles through the dust fraction collector bottles #1, #2, #3, #4, #5, and #6. The particle size of the dust fractions decreases from bottle #1 to bottle #6. The largest sand particles remain as residual in the dust generator. Water is added to the bottom of bottle #5 and #6 to prevent the smallest ricin/soil dust particles from escaping from the dust fraction collector. Past the dust fraction collector bottles, a prepump Erlenmeyer water dust trap and a postpump Erlenmeyer water dust trap were used to further ensure that no ricin particles enter the laboratory air. As a further safety measure, the dust generator/dust collector assembly was operated inside a fume hood. Very small dust particles of <10 μm (PM_{10}) or <2.5 μm ($PM_{2.5}$) diameter can be inhaled into the lung and are the most dangerous. Samplers for PM_{10} and $PM_{2.5}$ particles were placed at the bottle #4 position in the dust fraction collector to measure the actual size of the transported dust particles (Figure 5.16b). The flow rate of the PM_{10} and $PM_{2.5}$ sampling pump is one-fifth the flow rate of the dust generator/dust collector assembly. Hence, the PM_{10} and $PM_{2.5}$ samplers determine dust particle size and only collect about one-fifth of the quantity of moving dust. Dried ricin powder was mixed with samples of sand and clay soils (Figure 5.17), samples were placed in dust generator, and dust fractions collected. Most of the sand particles (residual) were too large to move out of the dust generator (Figure 5.17a). Most of the ricin was collected in trap1 and trap2. At a ricin-contaminated site, the ricin left in the coarser fractions (i.e., trap1, trap2) would repeatedly act as a ricin source that could be resuspended in air many times in

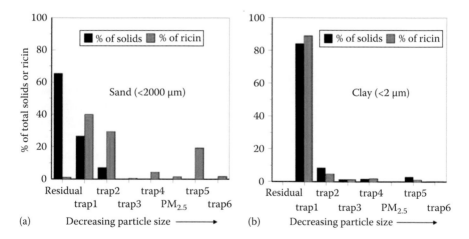

Figure 5.17 Movement and concentration of ricin in soil dust from (a) sand- and (b) clay-textured soil samples. Dust fractions were collected using a dust generator/fraction collector assembly. Ricin and soil particles collected in the $PM_{2.5}$ sampler were <2.5 μm in diameter.

subsequent wind gusts. Pure <2.5 μm particles of ricin were collected in the $PM_{2.5}$ sampler and even more respirable-size ricin particles were collected in trap5 and trap6. Ricin mixed with a sandy soil can be moved and respirable ricin particles can be concentrated in soil dust. In contrast, ricin was much less effectively moved or concentrated in dust from the clay soil (Figure 5.17b). The primary particles in a clay are <2 μm, but most primary particles form into larger silt-size (<50 μm) aggregates. Clay particles contain adsorbed water that acts to aggregate the particles together. About 90% of the clay soil and ricin particles were collected in trap1 and trap2 and very little moved as respirable-size particles. Negligible amounts of soil and ricin were collected in the $PM_{2.5}$ sampler. The proportion of clay soil material to ricin collected in trap5 was greater than clay soil/ricin sample before operation of the dust generator/dust collector. Hence, the clay soil trap5 dust was less dangerous than the clay soil/ricin sample before operation of the dust generator. Dust from a sandy soil contaminated with ricin would be very hazardous, but dust from a clayey soil contaminated with ricin would be much less hazardous.

Surfactants are often applied to road surfaces to control dust generated at construction sites. Samples of the commercial surfactants, polyacrylamide (PAM), Haul Road Dust Control (HRDC), Chemloc 101 (Chemloc), and Soiltac were purchased and applied to samples of Brownfield loamy fine sand soil contaminated with aqueous ricin from castor seed extract. Brownfield loamy fine sand soil (85% sand, 2% silt, and 13% clay) samples treated with castor seed extract and the commercial surfactants were air-dried and used in the dust generator/dust fraction collector assembly (Figure 5.16). The total weight of fine ricin dust in trap3, trap4, trap5, and trap6 was measured for each treatment and graphed (Figure 5.18). The Brownfield soil sample treated only with aqueous castor seed extract yielded ~0.85 mg ricin dust. This is much less fine ricin dust than was generated from soils mixed with dry ricin powder. Adsorption of dissolved ricin to soil particles greatly limits dust formation. Hence, rainfall would greatly reduce ricin dust from a contaminated soil. The Brownfield soil sample treated with PAM and castor extract formed much less ricin dust than the sample treated only with castor extract. The HRDC, Chemloc, and Soiltac surfactants were less effective than PAM (Zartman et al., 2005).

5.2.10   Rotifer use to measure ricin toxicity

Marine rotifers (*Brachionus plicatilis*) are small aquatic animals that are often used in toxicology testing (Snell, 2005). In toxicology testing, toxins or poisons are added to the aqueous media of rotifers. Rotifer populations were grown and maintained in an aerated bucket maintained at a temperature of ~25°C under moderate lighting in simulated seawater

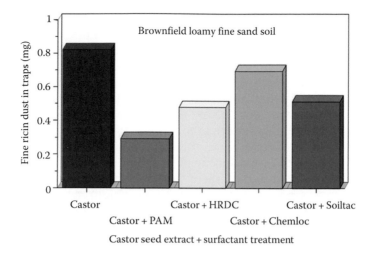

Figure 5.18 Dust control surfactant effects in limiting the generation of fine ricin dust particles and transport of ricin in soil dust.

(Hoff and Snell, 2008). Microalgae (Nannochloropsis) were used to feed the rotifers. Rotifers will consume particles of food or debris of <5 μm in diameter. Carmine consists of small red particles that can be ingested by rotifers. Under a microscope, ingested red carmine particles are easily identified within the gut of healthy rotifers (Figure 5.19a). Only healthy, living rotifers can ingest carmine and carmine can be added near the end of experiments to distinguish living from dead rotifers. Simulated

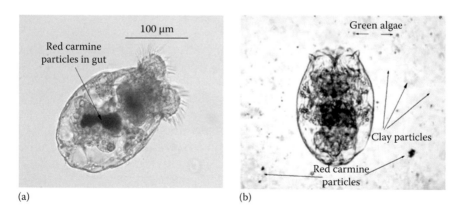

(a)   (b)

Figure 5.19 Marine rotifers (*Brachionus plicatilis*) used to examine ricin toxicity. Healthy rotifer (a) consumed red carmine particles. Montmorillonite addition (b) protected rotifer from lethal ricin dose.

seawater with and without ricin from castor seed extract was added to culture plate wells containing 10–100 rotifers. Preliminary experiments determined that an 18–24 hour incubation time at 25°C was needed to insure enough time for ricin toxicity to develop. Ricin from fresh castor seed extracts consistently killed rotifers, but ricin purified using dialysis and $(NH_4)_2SO_4$ precipitation was not consistently toxic. It is not clear why the purified ricin was not reliably toxic to rotifers. The ricin purification method might denature ricin to ricin toxoid. Ricin toxoid is a non-toxic or weakly toxic form of ricin that reacts with antibodies like ricin (Pradhan et al., 2008). Immunochemical measurement techniques, such as enzyme-linked immunosorbent assay (ELISA), cannot distinguish ricin from ricin toxoid. Alternatively, rotifers might need to ingest particles of castor seeds containing ricin to effectively absorb the toxin. In adsorption experiments, montmorillonite effectively adsorbs ricin and might be used to prevent toxicity to rotifers. Rotifers were added to culture plate wells containing simulated seawater and a lethal ricin concentration (~400 µg/mL) derived from a fresh castor seed extract. After an 18–24-hour incubation, 95%–100% of the rotifers were dead. In culture plate wells with 1 mg/mL montmorillonite in addition to the lethal ricin concentration, 95%–100% of rotifers were healthy and alive after 18–24 hours (Figure 5.19b). Red carmine, algae, and montmorillonite particles are visible within the rotifer gut and outside in the background (Figure 5.19b). Montmorillonite effectively adsorbed ricin and prevented toxicity to rotifers. This suggests that montmorillonite could be used as an antidote to oral ricin poisoning.

5.2.11   Ricin and activated carbon

Activated carbon is commonly recommended as an antidote to oral ricin poisoning, but it is a poor ricin sorbent based on adsorption isotherms (Figure 5.20). Activated carbon is very effective in removing nonpolar compounds, such as gasoline and pesticides, from water, but activated carbon has a problem with preloading (Manahan, 2004). In preloading, dissolved natural organic matter in wastewater can load up activated carbon surfaces and hinder pesticide sorption. Preloading can also be described as competitive adsorption where many different compounds compete for the same adsorption sites. Calcium humate (i.e., soil organic matter) is a polar material and a much better ricin sorbent than decolorizing activated carbon and cocoanut activated carbon was even less effective (Figure 5.20). Ricin and other proteins are polar compounds that do not readily adsorb to nonpolar activated carbon surfaces. Montmorillonite (or bentonite) is used as a food additive, and food-grade bentonite would be a much better antidote to oral ricin poisoning than activated carbon.

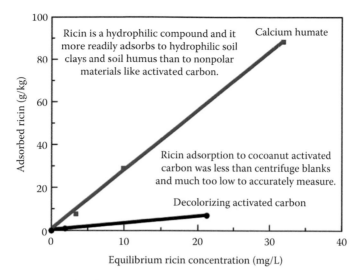

Figure 5.20 Activated carbon is a poor sorbent for ricin, but it is widely recommended as an antidote to oral ricin ingestion. Silicate clays, such as montmorillonite, and soil organic matter (e.g., calcium humate) are much more effective ricin sorbents than activated carbon.

5.3 Palliative measures to limit ricin contamination/toxicity

Ricin intoxication usually occurs through ingestion or inhalation. Conventional treatment for ricin ingested is to treat the patient with activated charcoal (Franz and Jaaks, 1997; Despott and Cachia, 2004; CDC, 2014). Since ricin is such a large polar molecule, we know that charcoal is not an effective way to treat ricin ingestion (USAMARIID, 2011). Our work (Figures 5.2, 5.3, and 5.20) has shown that expanding 2:1 clays such as montmorillonite would be much more effective than charcoal. Ricin inhalation is the most toxic form of exposure. Ricin is too large to pass through the skin and oral toxicity is 1000 times less than inhaled ricin. When it is suspected or known that ricin powder has been dispersed inside buildings, increasing the moisture content of the air to 100% humidity using a humidifier would be the most effective first step for response. Personnel in full protective gear could setup humidifiers and return after the building has been humidified with less restrictive protective clothing. Cooling the room would enhance condensation, but air drafts from an air conditioner might suspend ricin particles in the air. Air conditioners might be used after the room has been humidified. Ricin will absorb moisture from the air and increase condensation of water to contaminated surfaces. Condensed water on interior surfaces would act to dissolve, aggregate, and attach ricin to surfaces. This would largely eliminate the risk of inhaling ricin dust. Potential ricin-contaminated surfaces could then be safely wiped with bleach solutions to remove any ricin.

Steps to safely decontaminate dispersed ricin powder:

1. Increase relative humidity or apply water to eliminate ricin dust.
2. After water application or humidification, wipe contaminated surfaces with a bleach solution.
3. A montmorillonite gel applied to wipes could adsorb ricin and mitigate toxicity.

5.4   Conclusions

Ricin sorbs to a variety of materials, but smectite minerals, such as montmorillonite, sorb the most ricin. Ricin sorption is pH dependent with the greatest sorption to soil clays in acidic solutions. Ricin adsorption isotherms to montmorillonite have a Langmuir form, which suggests that ricin adsorbs to surfaces and more is adsorbed to high-surface area materials. Ricin adsorption occurs rapidly to montmorillonite and high ionic strength suppresses adsorption. Ricin adsorption expands the interlayers and shifts the basal spacing of montmorillonite. Very little ricin sorbs to activated carbon, which suggests that montmorillonite rather than activated carbon should be recommended as an antidote to oral ricin ingestion. Small amounts of ricin are sorbed by fruits and vegetables, but the consumption of a large quantity of contaminated fruits and vegetables would be required for a toxic oral dose. Adsorption isotherms and breakthrough curves indicate that ricin sorption to clays greatly limits ricin movement in soils and the potential for groundwater or surface water contamination is low except for very sandy soils. Inhaled ricin is the most toxic form and wind generated dust in soils can produce respirable-size (<10 μm, <2.5 μm) ricin particles. Ricin in the dust generated from dry ricin powder mixed with soils can be greatly concentrated in respirable-size dust particles, particularly for sandy soils. Dust control agents applied to ricin-contaminated soils can significantly reduce the formation of respirable ricin particles.

References

Arizona Department of Health Services. 2004. RICIN Bioterrorism agent profiles for health care workers, pp. 5.38–5.41. www.azdhs.gov/phs/emergency-preparedness/documents/zebra-manual/zm-s5-ricin.pdf (accessed November 1, 2015).

Atlas, R.M. 1999. Combating the threat of biowarfare and bioterrorism. *BioScience* 4:465–477.

Audi, J., Belson, M., Patel, M., Schier, J., and Osterloh, J. 2005. Ricin poisoning: A comprehensive review. *JAMA* 294(18):2342–2351.

Baker, J.C. et al. 2004. *Mapping the Risks: Assessing the Homeland Security Implications of Publicly Available Geospatial Information.* Rand Corporation, Santa Monica, CA, 40pp.

Barnes, D.J., Baldwin, B.S., and Braasch, D.A. 2009. Degradation of ricin in castor meal by temperature and chemical treatment. *Ind. Crops Prod.* 29:509–515.

BBC. 2003. Terror police arrest ricin suspect. http://news.bbc.co.uk/1/hi/uk/2688301.stm (accessed November 1, 2015).

Brandenberger, L. and McGlynn, W. December 2003. Food safety and fresh produce. CAST Commentary, Ames, IA.

Buonocore, C., Alipour, M., Omri, A., Pucaj, K., Smith, M.G., and Suntres, Z.E. 2011. Treatment of ricin A-chain-induced hepatotoxicity with liposome-encapsulated N-acetylcysteine. *J. Drug Target.* 19(9):821–829.

CDC. 2003. Investigation of a ricin-containing envelop at a postal facility—South Carolina. *MMWR* 52(46):1129–1131.

CDC. 2014. Ricin emergency response card Web page. http://www.bt.cdc.gov/agent/ricin/erc9009-86-3pr.asp (accessed November 1, 2015).

Checkai, R.T., Haley, M.V., Phillips, C.T., and Simini, M. 2011. A standard method for soil-to-clothing contact transfer of soil-sorbed chemical agents. *Poster (120–3) Presented at 2011 Annual Meetings of Soil Science Society of America,* San Antonio, TX October 16–19, 2011.

Crompton, R. and Gall, D. 1980. Georgi Markov: Death in a pellet. *Med. Leg. J.* 48:51–62.

d'Avila-Levy, C.M., Araújo, F.M., Vermelho, A.B., Branquinha, M.H., Alviano, C.S., de Araújo Soares, R.M., and Souza dos Santos, A.L. 2004. Differential lectin recognition of glycoproteins in choanomastigote-shaped trypanosomatids: Taxonomic implications. *FEMS Microbiol. Lett.* 231:171–176.

d'Errico, F. et al. 2012. Early evidence of San material culture represented by organic artifacts from Border Cave, South Africa. *Proc. Natl. Acad. Sci. USA.* 1009:13214–13219.

de Oliveira, A.S., Oliveira, M.R.C., Campos, J.M.S., Lana, J.M.S., Machado, O.L.T., Retamal, C.A., Detmann, E., and Valadares Filho, S.C. 2010. *In vitro* ruminal degradation of ricin and its effects on microbial growth. *Anim. Feed Sci. Technol.* 157:41–54.

de Virgilio, M. and Degryse, B. 2014. Harnessing the destructive power of ricin to fight human cancer. In: *Ricin Toxin,* ed. J.W. Cherwonogradzky, pp. 208–237. Bentham Scientific Publishers, Oak Park, IL.

Despott, E. and Cachia, M.J. 2004. A case of accidental ricin poisoning. *Malta Med. J.* 16(4):39–41.

Ding, X. and Henrichs, S.M. 2002. Adsorption and desorption of proteins and polyamino acids by clay minerals and marine sediments. *Mar. Chem.* 77:225–237.

Franz, D.R. and Jaax, N.K. 1997. Ricin toxin. In *Medical Aspects of Chemical and Biological Warfare,* eds. F.R. Sidell, E.T. Takafuji, and D.R. Franz, pp. 631–642. Office of the Surgeon General US Army, Falls Church, VA.

Friedlander, A.M. 1997. Anthrax. In *Medical Aspects of Chemical and Biological Warfare,* eds. F.R. Sidell, E.T. Takafuji, and D.R. Franz, pp. 467–478. Office of the Surgeon General US Army, Falls Church, VA.

Hale, M.L. 2014. Ricin—From pharaohs to bioterrorist and beyond. In *Ricin Toxin*, ed. J.W. Cherwonogradzky, pp. 3–37. Bentham Scientific Publishers, Oak Park, IL.

Hennessy, T. 2000. Safety moves to the soil. *Progr. Groc.* 79:83–88.

Hillel, D. 1998. *Environmental Soil Physics*. Academic Press, New York.

Hoff, F.H. and Snell, T.W. 2008. Rotifer culture, Chapter 5. In *Plankton Culture Manual*, 6th edn., 3rd printing, pp. 65–100. Florida Aqua Farms, Inc., Dade City, FL.

Jaynes, W.F., Zartman, R.E., Green, C.J., San Francisco, M.J., and Zak, J.C. 2005. Castor toxin adsorbed to clay minerals. *Clays Clay Miner.* 53(3):267–276.

Jury, W.A., Gardner, W.R., and Gardner, W.H. 1991. *Soil Physics*, 5th edn. John Wiley & Sons, Inc., New York, 328pp.

Kendall, R.J., Presley, S.M., Austin, G.P., and Smith, P.N. (eds.) 2008. *Advances in Biological and Chemical Terrorism Countermeasures*. CRC Press, Boca Raton, FL, p. 280.

Leggoe, J.W., Chang C., Cox, S.B., Presley, M., Zartman, R.E., and Gill, T. 2008. Predicting and characterizing threat transport. In *Advances in Biological and Chemical Terrorism Countermeasures*, eds. R.J. Kendall, S.M. Presley, G.P. Austin, and P.N. Smith, pp. 203–227. CRC Press, Boca Raton, FL.

Mackinnon, P.J. and Alderton, M.R. 2000. An investigation of the degradation of the plant toxin, ricin, by sodium hypochlorite. *Toxicon* 38:287–291.

Manahan, S.E. 2004. *Environmental Chemistry*, 8th edn. CRC Press, Boca Raton, FL.

Martin, J.H., Leonard, W.H., and Stamp, D.L. 1976. *Principles of Field Crop Production*. Macmillan Publishing Co., Inc., New York.

Merck. 2001. The Merck Index. *An Encyclopedia of Chemicals, Drugs, and Biologicals*, 13th edn. Merck and Co., Inc., Whitehouse Station, NJ.

Montfort, W., Villafranca, J.E., Monzingo, A.F., Ernst, S.R., Katzin, B., Rutenber, E., Xuong, N., Hamlin, R., and Robertus J.D. 1987. The three-dimensional structure of ricin at 2.8 Å. *J. Biol. Chem.* 262:5398–5403.

Ogunniyi, D.S. 2006. Castor oil: A vital industrial raw material. *Bioresour. Technol.* 97:1086–1091.

Owen, D. 2000. *Hidden Evidence*. Firefly Books Ltd., Ottawa, Ontario, Canada, pp. 126–127.

Perez-Castells, R., Alvarez, A., Gavilanes, J., Lizarbe, M.A., Martinez Del Pozo, A., Olmo, N., and Santaren, J. 1985. Adsorption of collagen by sepiolite. In *Proceedings of International Clay Conference*, Denver, CO, pp. 359–362.

Pradhan, S., Kumar, O., Jatav, P.C., and Singh, S. 2008. Detection of ricin by comparative indirect ELISA using fluorescence probe in blood and red blood cells. *J. Med. CBR Def.* 7, pp. 1–17, January 10, 2009.

Presley, S.M., Austin, G.A., Smith, P.N., and Kendall, R.J. 2008. Threats and Vulnerabilities Associated with Biological and Chemical Terrorism. In *Advances in Biological and Chemical Terrorism Countermeasures*, eds. R.J. Kendall, S.M. Presley, G.P. Austin, and P.N. Smith, pp. 13–28. CRC Press, Boca Raton, FL.

Public Health Security and Bioterrorism Preparedness and Response Act of 2002. (Bioterrorism Act)[Page 116 STAT. 594]Public Law 107–188.

Risen, J. and van Natta, D. January 25, 2003. *Bases the Target in Ricin Poison Plot Theory*. Sydney Morning Herald, Sydney, New South Wales, Australia. www.smh.com.au/articles/2003/01/24/1042911548292.html.

Schep, L.J., Temple, W.A., Butt, G.A., and Beasley, M.D. 2009. Ricin as a weapon of mass terror—Separating fact from fiction. *Environ. Int.* 35:1267–1271.

Schulze, D.G. 1989. An introduction to soil mineralogy. In *Minerals in Soil Environments*, 2nd edn., eds. J.B. Dixon and S.B. Weed, pp. 1–34. SSSA, Madison, WI.

Sidell, F.R., Takafuji, E.T., and Franz, D.R. (eds.) 1997. *Medical Aspects of Chemical and Biological Warfare*. Office of the Surgeon General US Army, Falls Church, VA, pp. 467–478.

Skaggs, T.H. and Leij, F.J. 2002. Solute transport: Theoretical background. In *Methods of Soil Analysis: Book 5 Part 4 Physical Methods*, eds. J. Dane and G.C. Topp, pp. 1353–1380. Soil Science Society of America, Madison, WI.

Snell, T.W. 2005. Rotifer ingestion test for rapid assessment of toxicity. In *Small-Scale Freshwater Environment Toxicity Test Methods*, eds. C. Blaise and J.F. Ferard. Springer, Dordrecht, the Netherlands.

Stryer, L. 1975. Introduction to protein structure and function. In: *Biochemistry*, pp. 11–45. W.H. Freeman and Company, San Francisco, CA.

Torok, T.J. et al. 1997. A large community outbreak of Salmonellosis caused by intentional contamination of restaurant salad bars. *JAMA* 278:389–395.

Tucker, J.B. and Pate, J. 2000. The Minnesota Patriots Council (1991). In *Assessing Terrorist Use of Chemical and Biological Weapons*, ed. J.B. Tucker, pp. 159–183. Harvard University, Cambridge, MA.

USAMRIID. 2011. *USAMRIID's Medical Management of Biological Casualties Handbook*, 7th edn. Fort Detrick, Frederick, MD. http://www.usamriid.army.mil/education/bluebookpdf/USAMRIID%20BlueBook%207th%20Edition%20-%20Sep%202011.pdf

U.S. Food and Drug Administration. October 7, 2003. Risk assessment for food terrorism and other food safety concerns. CFSAN/Office of Regulations and Policy, Silver Spring, MD. http://seafood.oregonstate.edu/.pdf%20Links/Risk%20Assessment%20for%20Food%20Terrorism%20and%20Other%20Food%20Safety%20Concerns.pdf (accessed November 1, 2015).

U.S. Food and Drug Administration. 2011. The food safety law and the rulemaking process: Putting FSMA to work. www.fda.gov/food/guidanceregulation/fsma/ucm277706.htm (accessed November 1, 2015).

Vitetta, E.S., Smallshaw, J.E., Coleman, E., Jafri, H., Foster, C., Munford, R., and Schindler, JA. 2006. Pilot clinical trial of a recombinant ricin vaccine in normal humans. *Proc. Natl. Acad. Sci. USA*. 103:2268–2273.

Wannemacher, R.W., Creasia D.A., Hines H.B., Thompson, W.L., and Dinterman, R.E. 1990. Toxicity, stability and inactivation of ricin. *Toxicologist* 10:166.

Wiggleworth-Cooksey, B. and Cooksey, K.E. 2005. Use of fluorphore-conjugated lectins to study cell-cell interactions in model marine biofilms. *Appl. Environ. Microbiol.* 71:428–435.

Zartman, R.E., Chang, C., Cobb, G.P., Fralick, J.A., and Presley, S.M. 2008. Assessment strategies for environmental protection from chemical and biological threats. In *Advances in Biological and Chemical Terrorism Countermeasures*, eds. R.J. Kendall, S.M. Presley, G.P. Austin, and P.N. Smith, pp. 203–227. CRC Press, Boca Raton, FL.

Zartman, R.E., Green, C.J., San Francisco, M.J., Zak, J., and Jaynes, W.F. November 2003. Food sorption of ricin and anthrax simulants. In *Joint Services Scientific Conference on Chemical and Biological Defense Research*, Towson, MD.

Zartman, R.E., Green, C., San Francisco, M., Zak, J., Jaynes, W., and Boroda, E. November 2002. Mitigation of ricin contamination in soils: Sorption and degradation. In *Joint Services Scientific Conference on Chemical and Biological Defense Research*, Hunt Valley, MD.

Zartman, R.E. and Jaynes, W.F. 2014. Ricin: Sorption by soils, minerals, textiles, and food; soil infiltration and dust transport. In *Ricin Toxin*, ed. J.W. Cherwonogrodzky, pp. 86–97. Bentham Scientific Publishers, Oak Park, IL.

Zartman, R.E., Jaynes, W.F., Green, C.J., San Francisco, M.J., and Zak, J.C. 2005. *Dust Transport of Castor Toxin*. Salt Lake City, UT.

Zentz, C., Frénoy, J.P., and Bourrillon, R. 1978. Binding of galactose and lactose to ricin equilibrium studies. *Biochim. Biophys. Acta* 536:18–26.

Zilinskas, R.A. 1997. Iraq's biological weapons: The past as future? *JAMA* 278:418–424.

Zobeck, T.M., Gill, T.E., Stout, J.E., Zhang, M.L., Kennedy, A.C., and Gregory, J.M. 1997. Analysis of laboratory generated dust suspensions derived from soils and roads. ASAE Paper No. 972030.

chapter six

Display phage therapy
Development of a probiotic biotherapeutic for countermeasures against cholera toxin

Joe A. Fralick and Mathew Kay

Contents

6.1   Introduction

Cholera is an ancient disease that is caused by the ingestion of aerobic, comma-shaped gram-negative bacterium, *Vibrio cholerae*. It is caused by a potent enterotoxin, cholera toxin (CT), that acts on intestinal epithelial cells, provoking the loss of water and electrolytes, which may lead to electrolyte imbalance, hypovolemic shock, and death. It is endemic in Asia and Africa, with over five million cases each year (Kaper et al., 1994; Faruque et al., 1998). It has been reported that in 1994, 10% of the cholera patients at Rwandan camps died during the cholera outbreak, with 1 day recording a case fatality rate of 48% (Lencer, 2001). Hence, fatality rates from cholera can be fairly high, and there is a growing concern over the potential use of *V. cholerae* as a bio-threat agent for biological warfare and terrorism. During World War II, the Japanese biological weapons program, Unit 731, experimented with multiple pathogens as potential bioweapons, including *V. cholerae*. It has also been reported that in 1941, the Japanese contaminated more than 1000 Chinese wells with choler and typhus, resulting in 10,000 cases of cholera. South Africa's biological weapons program, "Project Coast," developed cholera as a biological agent, which is used, during South Africa's civil war, along with other bacterial agents such as anthrax, to contaminate water in rebel-held areas. Furthermore, Iraq's biological weapons program included cholera as one of its biological agents, as has North Korea (Riedel, 2004) (http://www.globalsecurity.org/wmd/intro/bio_cholera.htm).

CT is a member of the A-B-type ADP-ribosylating toxin that exploits retrograde transport as a means to gain entry into the cytosol of host cells (Kaper et al., 1994; Faruque et al., 1998). Ricin toxin (RT) and shiga toxin (Stx) are also members of this family. CT is an oligomeric protein complex consisting of six protein subunits: a single copy of the A subunit (enzymatic) and five copies of the B subunit (receptor binding), denoted as AB_5 (Moss and Vaughn, 1988). The five B subunits are arranged to form a pentameric ring with the A subunit occupying the central channel of the donut-like structure (Mekalanos et al., 1979; Moss and Vaughn, 1988). Intact A subunit is not enzymatically active but must be nicked to produce fragments CTA1 and CTA2, which are held together via a disulfide bond. This nicking apparently occurs after the toxin is secreted from the cell. The A1 portion of the chain (CTA1) is a globular enzyme that ADP-ribosylates G proteins, while the A2 chain (CTA2) forms an extended alpha helix that sits snugly in the central pore of the B subunit ring (Lencer, 2001). To cause disease, CT enters the intestinal epithelial cell as a stably folded protein by occupying a lipid-based membrane receptor, ganglioside G (M1). It is thought that this receptor sorts the toxin into lipid rafts and a trafficking pathway to the endoplasmic reticulum, where the toxin unfolds and transfers its enzymatic subunit to the cytosol (Lencer et al., 1995, 1999; Wolf et al., 1998; Plemper and Wolf, 1999; White et al., 1999; Lencer, 2001). Once in the cytosol, CTA1 is able to stimulate adenylate cyclase activity by catalyzing the ADP-ribosylation of the G_{sa} subunit of the GTP-binding regulatory protein (Moss and Vaughn, 1988). The consequence of this and perhaps other effects, such as increased synthesis of postagalandins by the intoxicated cell, is the excessive accumulation of salt and water in the intestinal lumen and the copious "rice water" diarrhea characteristic of cholera. Most of the deaths from cholera result from excessive fluid (up to 20 L of water daily) and electrolyte losses, causing dehydration and acidosis. Thus, the majority of these deaths are avoidable providing that fluids and electrolytes are replaced promptly. However, even under the best circumstances, cholera is an incapacitation disease, requiring weeks of recovery. A pharmacological agent that could suppress the severe diarrhea or inactivate CT would be advantageous in treating this disease. Unfortunately there are no current antidotes for CT. However, we have developed a biological countermeasure to CT, a bacterial virus (i.e., bacteriophage or phage) that can bind to this toxin with high affinity and neutralize it (Fralick et al., 2008).

Probiotics are microorganisms that, upon ingestion, can exert benefits to its host. Probiotic therapy was once considered "folk" medicine. However, there is an emerging interest in the use of probiotics in human disease. Some examples of probiotic therapy include remission maintenance therapy for ulcerative colitis (Venturi et al., 1999); *Lactobacillus plantarum* for irritable bowel syndrome (Nobaek et al., 2000); *Lactobacillus* or *Saccharomyces boulardii*, a nonpathogenic yeast for Crohn's disease (Gupta et al., 2000; Guslandi et al., 2000); and *Bifidobacterium bifidum* for acute diarrhea (Saavedra et al., 1994). Probiotic therapy can provide elegant alternatives to chemical therapeutics. Some of the potential applications include modulation of the intestinal immune system, sequestration of toxins, competition and diminution of pathogens, immunization against intestinal pathogens, production of enzymes for detoxification and the complementation of enzyme deficiencies, and production of cytokines for immune intervention (for review, see Steidler, 2003). In this study, we employ probiotics to deliver a biological, CT-neutralizing bacterial phage that can multiply in normal flora *E. coli*.

Display phages are bacterial viruses that present random peptide sequences on their surface capsid protein(s), usually for the study of peptide–protein, protein–protein, and protein–DNA interactions. The most common phages employed for such studies are filamentous phage (fd and M13) and to a lesser extent T4, T7, and lambda. The display phage employed in this study is M13, a filamentous bacteriophage that belongs to a group of single-stranded DNA phage known as *Inovirus* (see Webster,

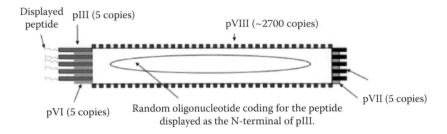

Figure 6.1 M13 display phage. Cartoon of an M13 filamentous bacteriophage depicting the five capsid proteins (pIII, pVI, pVII, pVIII, pIX), the single-stranded DNA genome, and the random oligonucleotide, cloned into the 5′ end of gIII, coding for random peptides displayed at the N-terminal of pIII.

2001, for a review on filamentous phage). It was obtained from the dodecapeptide phage display library kit (PhD 12) from New England Biolabs, displaying a 12-mer peptide fused to the N-terminal of the minor capsid protein, pIII, that binds to the B subunit of CT with high affinity and neutralizes its activity (Fralick et al., 2008).

Filamentous phages are able to infect a variety of gram-negative bacteria. They have a single-stranded circular DNA genome that is packaged in a long cylinder (filamentous) capsid made up of five genetically distinct proteins (pV, VI, VII, VIII, and IX), see Figure 6.1. The best characterized members of this group are M13, fd, and fl, which can infect *E. coli* cells harboring a conjugative F-plasmid. Because of their similarity and dependence upon the F plasmid for infection they are often referred to collectively as the Ff or "male-specific" phage (Webster, 2001). Their genomes have been sequenced and their life cycle and assembly has been studied extensively (Van Wezenbeek et al., 1980; Webster, 2001). They are unique in that they do not have a lytic cycle and hence do not kill their host (Webster, 2001). However, they are continuously secreted into the immediate environment. Their production is tolerated quite well and the infected bacteria (lysogens) continue to grow and divide albeit with a generation time approximately 50% longer than that for uninfected bacteria. Approximately 1000 progeny phage are produced during the first generation following infection, after which the host produces around 200 phage/cell/doubling time. This continues for many generations with the curing rate being quite low resulting in very high phage titers (up to 10^{13}/mL).

M13 phage uses the tip of the F conjugative pilus as a receptor for infection. Proteins required for the assembly of the F pilus are encoded by genes in the *tra* operon on the F+ or F′ (F-prime) conjugative plasmids (Frost et al., 1994; Firth et al., 1996). Hence only bacterial cells carrying the F plasmid can be infected by M13 and related phage. The F pilus is also required for the conjugal transfer for the F plasmid DNA from a donor cell (F^+/F' bacterium) into a recipient (F^- bacterium) lacking the plasmid. The result of this infective process is the presence of the plasmid in both the donor and recipient bacteria, eventually converting the entire population of F^- bacteria into F^+/F' bacteria.

The experimental strategy of this project is to deliver genetically modified probiotic *E. coli* strains to the gut of a mouse that will deliver F-factors (for the synthesis of M13 receptors) via conjugation and an M13 CT neutralizing phage (CT7) for the infection (lysogenization) of the normal flora *E. coli* harboring the F-factor. It is our working hypothesis that the CT7 producing normal flora *E. coli* will produce enough CT7 to neutralize CT and hence act as an antidote for cholera.

6.2   Results and discussion

6.2.1   Retention studies

For our initial studies, we examined the ability of a genetically modified mouse *E. coli* to establish itself with the normal flora of mice. To conduct these studies, we isolated an *E. coli* from the intestine of a mouse (MEC) and selected for a rifampicin-resistant (RifR) derivative (MEC1). We conjugally transferred an F'-factor containing a kanamycin-resistant (Km) marker (F'702) to this strain (MEC2) and infected it with CT7 phage (MEC3). We conducted several experiments in which we fed this probiotic strain to mice for differing time intervals. Following the feeding, we placed the mice in cages with new bedding and sampled mouse feces at 6-hour intervals and followed rifampicin (cells) and kanamycin (F'-factor) resistance. We found that the RifR/KanR bacteria were gone within 18–24 hours and that all of the KanR colonies tested were also RifR and produced CT7 phage, as determined by blue plaques on a lawn of ER2738 growing on an X-gal plate (see methods and materials). These results indicate that MEC3 did not establish itself in the normal flora of the mice we treated nor did it transfer the F-factor to normal flora *E. coli*. This could have been due to the *E. coli* isolate we choose or to the modifications employed.

6.2.2   Selection of F-prime factors and donor/recipient partners for delivering an F-factor and CT7 phage to the gut of a mouse

An alternative approach for the delivery of CT7 phage to the gut of a mouse is to convert the normal flora *E. coli* into CT7-producing strains (lysogens). To do this, we must be able to conjugally transfer an F-factor to the normal flora *E. coli* and then infect them with CT7 phage. The transfer of plasmids in the intestine of animals has been examined since the 1960s, and the transfer of drug-resistant factors (R-factors) in mice between enteric bacterial strains has been demonstrated (Kasuya, 1964; Roberts and Falkow, 1979; Licht et al., 1999; Garcia-Quintanilla et al., 2008). However, conjugal transfer to normal flora within the intestine has not been examined and will likely be dependent upon the conjugative plasmid and donor/recipient strains involved. In the following studies, we have examined these properties and tested them in a mouse model.

6.2.3   Influence of F-factors on transfer

To determine if the failure to transfer the F-factor by our mouse strain was due to the F-factor or the donor/recipient strain, we examined different F-factors derived from a collection of Hfr strains used for chromosome mapping, carrying either tetracycline-resistant (TetR) or kanamycin-resistant (Km) markers. Our collection included an F-factor in which the *tra* operon was constitutively expressed (obtained from the Yale collection, CGSC 4401), which we tagged with a mini-Tn505 (Km) insert (F-713) as well as an TetR F-factor obtained from the commercially available ER2738 strain used to grow the M13 display phage (F-2738). These F-factors were harbored in a recA *E. coli* K12 strain (LBB411) and mated to MEC1 (RifR). Matings were as described in the methods section, selecting for transconjugants on kanamycin or tetracycline + rifampicin plates for the presence of the F'-factor (TetR or KanR) and against the donor strain (rifampicin). The results are given in Table 6.1. It can be seen from these results that only three of the eight F-factors (F-706, F-713, and F-2738) tested were transferred, albeit with low efficiency, to the mouse *E. coli* strain (MEC1).

Table 6.1 Transfer efficiency of different F-primes to mouse *E. coli*

F-factor	Recipient	Efficiency of transfer[a]
F'-702	Mouse *E. coli*	$<10^{-8}$
F'-704	Mouse *E. coli*	$<10^{-8}$
F'-706	Mouse *E. coli*	2.5×10^{-6}
F'-708	Mouse *E. coli*	$<10^{-8}$
F'-712	Mouse *E. coli*	$<10^{-8}$
F-713	Mouse *E. coli*	9.21×10^{-7}
F'-2738	Mouse *E. coli*	7.27×10^{-6}
F'-3373	Mouse *E. coli*	$<10^{-8}$

[a]   Efficiency of transfer = transconjugants/donors × 100.

Table 6.2 Transfer efficiency of different recipients

F-factor	Recipient	Efficiency of transfer[a]
F'-706	Mouse *E. coli*[b]	2.5×10^{-6}
F'-706	Hamster *E. coli*[c]	4.7×10^{-2}
F'-706	*E. coli* K12[d]	6.85×10^{-1}
F'-2738	Mouse *E. coli*	7.27×10^{-6}
F'-2738	Hamster *E. coli*	7.14
F'-2738	*E. coli* K12	1.23×10^{-1}
F-713	Mouse *E. coli*	9.21×10^{-7}
F-713	Hamster *E. coli*	$1.23/5.72 \times 10^{-1}$
F-713	*E. coli* K12	5.5×10^{-2}

[a] Efficiency of transfer = transconjugants/donors × 100.
[b] An RifR derivative of a mouse *E. coli*, isolated from a mouse intestine (MEC1).
[c] An RifR derivative of a hamster *E. coli*, isolated from a hamster intestine.
[d] *E. coli* K12 is a lab strain of *E. coli* (LBB 1274).

6.2.4 *Influence of recipient on transfer efficiency of F-factors*

To examine the influence of the recipient on the efficiency of F-factor transfer, we examined the ability of the three F'-factors that had been transferred successfully to the mouse *E. coli* strain (F'-706, F'-713, and F'-2738), to be transferred to three different recipients: an *E. coli* strain isolated from a mouse, MEC1 (mouse *E. coli*), a rifampicin-resistant derivative of an *E. coli* isolated from a hamster (hamster *E. coli*), and a recA, spectinomycin-resistant (StpR) *E. coli* K12 lab strain, LBB1274. The results are given in Table 6.2. It can be seen that there are large differences in the transfer efficiency of the three different F-factors depending upon the recipient used. In general, the efficiency is as follows: K12 *E. coli* > Hamster *E. coli* > Mouse *E. coli*. There are as much as five orders of magnitude differences in the transfer efficiency between mouse and K12 *E. coli*. This could be the result of the restriction/modification (r/m) systems of the different *E. coli* strains employed.

6.2.5 *Influence of donor strain and CT7 phage on transfer of efficiency of F-factors*

To examine the influence of the donor strain and lysogeny by CT7 phage on the transfer of the F-factor to mouse *E. coli*, we transferred F-713 to two different laboratory *E. coli* K12 strains: LBB1206, a r⁻/m⁺ strain and LBB2208 a r⁻/m⁻ strain with (lysogenization) and without the CT7 phage. We conducted the matings in liquid media and on filters (to mimic the intestinal surface) and used mouse strain MEC1 as the recipient. The results are given in Table 6.3. It can be seen that these *E. coli* K12 donor

Table 6.3 Effect of donor strain, mating conditions, and M13F (CT7)
on transfer efficiency

Donor strain	Recipient	Efficiency of transfer[a]
Liquids[b]		
LBB2208/F-713	Mouse *E. coli*	2.3×10^{-2}
LBB2208/F-713/CT7K[c]	Mouse *E. coli*	6.9×10^{-3}
LBB1206/F-713	Mouse *E. coli*	3.05×10^{-1}
LBB1206/F-713/CT7K	Mouse *E. coli*	1.26×10^{-3}
Membrane filters[d]		
LBB2208/F-713	Mouse *E. coli*	4.6×10^{-1}
LBB2208/F-713	Mouse *E. coli*	7.19×10^{-2}
LBB1206/F-713	Mouse *E. coli*	21.5
LBB1206/F-713	Mouse *E. coli*	1.74×10^{-1}

[a] Efficiency of transfer = transconjugants/donors × 100.
[b] Matings were conducted in liquid (broth) at 37°C.
[c] Donor strain carries CT7K phage.
[d] Matings were conducted on sterile 0.25 m filters placed on an agar plate at 37°C.

strains transfer F'-713 much more efficiently than did the donor *E. coli* strain in the previous mating experiment. It can also be seen that the presence (lysogenization) of the M13 phage diminishes this transfer by one to two orders of magnitude; that LBB1206 was the better of the two donor strains; and that matings on membranes were more efficient than in liquids. These results suggest, as might be expected, that the r/m status of the donor strain plays an important role in transferring an F-factor to normal flora *E. coli*. It has also been recently reported that filamentous bacteriophages inhibit conjugal transfer through interference via phage coat protein pIII (Lin, 2011; Wan and Goddard, 2012).

6.2.6   *In vivo transfer of F-713 to the normal intestinal flora of mice*

To examine the ability of LBB1206 strain carrying F-713 to transfer its F-factor to the normal flora of mice, we fed eight mice LBB1206/F-713 for 2 days. The mice were moved to cages with fresh bedding, fecal pellets were collected each day after the feeding, and the number of KanR (F-713) or KanR/StrR (donor) colonies in the fecal pellets was determined. In Figure 6.2, we have plotted the ratio of the average of the KanR/KanR, StrR colonies with respect to time following feeding. It can be seen from these results that the ratio of KanR (F-factor)/KanR, StrR (donor *E. coli*) increases with time, indicating that the F-factor is being transferred to mouse normal flora *E. coli*. We have randomly selected KanR colonies

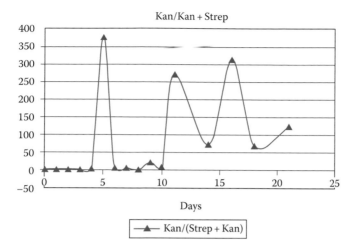

Figure 6.2 *In vivo* transfer of F-713 to normal intestinal flora of mice. Mice were fed LBB1206/F-713 (StrR/KanR) for 2 days. Fecal pellets were collected each day after the feeding, and the number of colonies that plated on kanamycin and kanamycin + streptomycin plates was determined. The ratio of the average of the kanamycin-resistant colonies divided by the kanamycin + streptomycin-resistant colonies is plotted with respect to the timing following feeding. In situations where the kanamycin + streptomycin-resistant colonies were zero, we substituted a value of one.

from these samples and tested them for streptomycin sensitivity and the ability to transfer KanR (F-plasmid) to a spectinomycin-resistant (SpcR) *E. coli* K12 strain (LBB1274). All of the KanR, streptomycin-sensitive cultures (i.e., mouse *E. coli*) could transfer the KanR marker, indicating that the F-plasmid was being transferred to the normal flora *E. coli* in the mouse intestine. These results also suggest that the F-factor can persist in the intestine of mice for 15–20 days.

6.2.7   *Mixed matings* in vitro

To monitor the presence of CT7 phage, we cloned a Km (KanR) marker into CT7 phage at the SfoI restriction site (i.e., at bp 6000 on the M13KE genetic map) resulting in CT7K bacteriophage. This construct was transfected into ER2738 and selected on X-gal plates containing tetracycline (for F'2738) and kanamycin (for CT7K phage). A single blue colony was selected and phage from that colony was used to produce CT7K phage (i.e., plaque purified).

The finding that the lysogenization of CT7 interferes with the conjugational transfer of an F-factor suggests that one should employ two different *E. coli* strains to deliver CT7 to the normal flora *E. coli*: one to transfer an

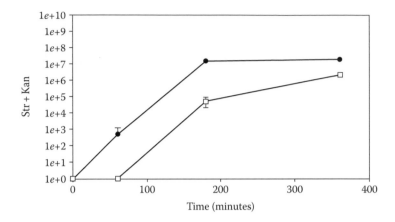

Figure 6.3 Mixed mating *in vitro*. A mixture (filled circles) of equal amounts of LBB1997 (F⁻. *rpsL*) plus LBB3576 (r⁻/m⁻)/F2738 (TetR) plus LBB3577 (LBB3576 lysogenized with CT7K) was added together at a density of 10^7 cfu/mL and incubated at 37°C, without shaking for 6 hours. A second mixture (open squares) consisting of equal amounts of LBB1997 plus 3577 (10^7 cfu/mL) was also incubated at 37°C without shaking for 6 hours. Samples were removed from each mixture at indicated times and plated on media containing streptomycin plus kanamycin.

F-factor and a second to deliver the CT7 phage. To test this approach, we compared a mixture of LBB1997, a streptomycin-resistant, F⁻, *E. coli* K12 strain, as the recipient, plus LBB3576, an r⁻/m⁻ *E. coli* K12 donor strain harboring F′2738 (TetR) plus LBB3576 lysogenized with CT7K phage (LBB3577) with a mixture of LBB1997 and LBB3577. The strains were added together at a density of 10^7 cfu/mL in LB, at 37°C for 6 hours without shaking. These mixtures were sampled at different times for LBB1997, which had acquired the F-factor and become infected by the CT7K phage by platting on streptomycin + kanamycin media. The results are given in Figure 6.3. It can be seen that using two different strains to deliver the F′-factor and CT7K was more efficient than using a single strain to deliver both.

6.2.8   Mixed matings in vivo

To examine the use of two different *E. coli* strains to deliver the CT7K phage to the normal *E. coli* flora of a mouse, we placed six mice on Kan water (1.33 mg/mL) for 2 days and then fed them two strains of *E. coli*: LBB3576 and LBB3580, a rifampicin-resistant derivative of LBB3577 for 2 days. The mice were moved to a cage with new bedding and feces were sampled at 1 day intervals. The results are given in Figure 6.4. From these results, it appears that LBB3580 is lost from the mice within 24–48 hours of feeding *E. coli* strains carrying the F′-factor (TetR), and the CT7K phage

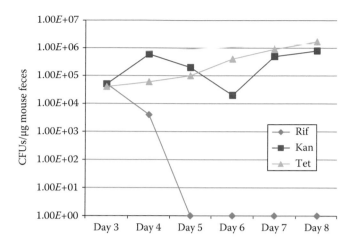

Figure 6.4 Mixed mating *in vivo*. Six mice were placed on water containing kanamycin (1.33 mg/mL) 2 days prior to beginning of experiment and then fed LBB3576 and LBB3580 for 2 days after which they were moved to a cage with clean bedding and maintained on kanamycin water. Samples were at day intervals beginning on day 3 (1 day following feeding) and plated on tetracycline-, rifampicin-, and kanamycin-containing plates.

(KanR) persisted throughout the experiment and show similar numbers and trends. All of the kanamycin (KanR) isolates tested were positive for carrying CT7K phage and were tetracycline resistant (TetR). We also checked the mice taken off kanamycin water for 3 weeks and found *E. coli* harboring both the TetR F'-factor and the KanR CT7K phage (data not shown). These results suggest that either the LBB3576 was able to colonize the mice and became infected with CT7K bacteriophage or that the F'-2738 was transferred to the normal flora *E. coli* after which they were infected with CT7K. Since LBB3580 was lost from the mice, it seems logical to expect that its parent, LBB3576, would be lost as well. In either case we have been able to demonstrate the delivery of CT7K phage to the gut of a mouse and its maintenance for 3 weeks in the absence of selection.

6.3 Conclusions

In a previous study, we were able to select a display phage that could bind to CT with high affinity and neutralize the toxin *in vivo* in the ilium of a mouse (Fralick et al., 2008). In this study, we have examined the properties of genetically engineered probiotic *E. coli* for the delivery of this toxin neutralizing the display phage to the intestinal flora of a mouse. As might have been expected, we have found that some F-factors are more efficiently transferred to mouse *E. coli* than are others and that the restriction/modification status of the donor as well as lysogenization by M13 phage plays an important role in the efficiency of F-factor transfer to mouse *E. coli*. We also found that employing two different *E. coli* strains, one to transfer the F-factor and one to deliver the phage, was much more efficient than using a single *E. coli* donor to deliver both. Furthermore, we found that under selective conditions we can maintain phage-producing *E. coli* in the gut of a mouse for greater than 7 days. Theoretically, this could be sufficient for the treatment of cholera since the disease progresses from the first liquid stool to shock in 4–12 hours to death following some 18+ hours later (without treatment).

Future studies will involve quantitating the number of CT7 phage that can be produced in the intestine of mice harboring CT7-producing *E. coli* (lysogens), determining what quantities of CT can be neutralized in such mice (i.e., ileal loop assays), determining if the production of CT7 bacteriophage in the gut of the mouse elicits an immune response, development of better *E. coli* strains for the delivery of F-factors and CT7 phage (Leatham-Jensen et al., 2012), genetically engineering the display phage to bind more CT (i.e., clone the CT binding peptide into gp8, which has 3000 copies/phage capsid), and determining if we can use other cloned genes, besides those encoding antibiotic resistance, for the selection and maintenance of CT7 or other M13 display phage in the mouse.

The use of biological agents has, in the past, been generally confined to military-led conflicts. However, there has been an increase in in-state-based terrorism, including the use of biological agents over the past few decades. Thus, it is becoming increasingly important to consider pre- and post-exposure medical countermeasure strategies for preventing and preparing for attacks by insurgents. In this study, we have examined one such strategy, the ability to probiotically deliver a CT-neutralizing display phage to the normal flora of the gut of a mouse as a potential prophylactic/therapeutic agent. As previously pointed out, this approach could theoretically be developed for any enteric toxin such as *Clostridium difficile* toxins, staphylococcal enterotoxin B, heat-stable *E. coli* enterotoxin, Campylobacter heat-labile cytotoxin, *Salmonella typhimurium* enterotoxin, and shiga-like cytotoxins produced by enteropathogenic *E. coli*.

6.4   *Methods and materials*

6.4.1   E. coli *strains*

The *E. coli* strains employed in this study are described in the text of this chapter and listed in Table 6.4. The K12 strains are laboratory strains and the mouse and hamster *E. coli* strains were isolated from mice or hamster intestines and certified to be *E. coli* by TTUHSC Pathology laboratory (Lubbock, TX).

Table 6.4 Bacterial strains used in this study

Strain	Relevant genotype	Source
MEC[a]	Wild-type	Mouse intestine
MEC1	rifR[b]	Mouse intestine
MEC2	MEC1/F'702	Mouse intestine
MEC3	MEC2/CT7 lysogen	Mouse intestine
ER2738	K12, lacZ/F'2738	New England Biolabs
LBB411	K12, *rec*A, *rps*L	Laboratory collection
LBB1206	K12, *rec*A, *hsd*R17	Laboratory collection
LBB2208	K12, Δ(mrr-hsdRMS-mcrBC), *rps*L	Laboratory collection
LBB1274	K12, *rsp*E, *rec*A	Laboratory collection
LBB1997	K12, *rps*L	Laboratory collection
LBB3576	K12, Δ(mrr-hsdRMS-mcrBC)/F'2738	Laboratory collection
LBB3577	LBB3576/CT7K lysogen	Laboratory collection
LBB3580	LBB3577, *rif*R	Laboratory collection

[a] An *E. coli* strain isolated from the intestine of a mouse.
[b] A rifampicin-resistant derivative of MEC.

6.4.2 Display phage

CT7 is from New England Biolabs PhD12 Phage Display Peptide library. It carries a *lacZ* allele cloned into its genome, which when expressed in a *lacZ* mutant strain, ER2738, produces blue plaques on Luria agar (LB) plates (Miller, 1972) containing the gratuitous *lac*I inducer, isopropyl β-D-thiogalactopyranoside (X-gal plates). It was selected for its binding to and neutralization of CT (Fralick et al., 2008). CT7K is CT7 into which we cloned the Km (KanR) gene from a pAT vector.

6.4.3 Mice treatment protocols

Mice were fed the probiotic *E. coli* strain by two different routes: (1) using a plastic pipette tip (50 μL of a 10^8/mL bacterial solution) and (2) withholding food pellets for 24 hours and then feeding the mice food pellets that had been soaked in cultures of the bacterial strains (~10^8/mL). In either case, the cages were changed following feeding, and fecal samples were collected at different time intervals and examined for the presence of the original *E. coli* strain employed, for the presence of the F-plasmid and for the presence of the M13 display phage based upon antibiotic resistance markers and blue plaques on a lawn of *E. coli* ER2738 growing on X-gal plates.

6.4.4   Processing of fecal pellets

Collected fecal pellets were weighed, crushed, and suspended in sterile saline. A portion of the suspensions were diluted serially with sterile saline and plated on selective (antibiotic) plates. The remaining suspension was frozen at −70°C in 20% glycerol. The presence of phage was determined by spotting the suspension on a lawn of ER2738 growing on X-gal plates.

6.4.5   F-factor mobilization assay

The donors were grown in LB plus appropriate antibiotics overnight at 37°C with shaking.

Cultures were diluted 1:200 in the appropriate media and grown to an OD_{600} of 0.5.

Donor and recipient cells were pelleted by centrifugation and the pellet suspended in an equal volume of phosphate-buffered saline (PBS). Donors and recipients were mixed at a 1:9 ratio (0.1 mL of donor, 0.9 mL of recipient) and incubated at 37°C without shaking.

After 2 minutes, the cells were vortexed vigorously for 10 seconds and placed into an ice bath. After 10 minutes serial dilutions were made into ice-cold PBS and 100 μL of each dilution plated on selective plates. 100 μL of the donors and 100 μL of the recipients (in PBS) were plated on the appropriate selective plate as a control. To determine the number of donors and recipients, serial dilutions of the donor and recipient cells were suspended in PBS and plated on appropriate selective plates. Mobilization efficiencies were calculated as the number of transconjugate colonies divided by the number of donor colonies.

Acknowledgments

We would like to acknowledge Mr. Ian Johnson for his excellent technical assistance.

References

Faruque, S.H., Albert, M.J., and Mekalans, J.J. 1998. Epidemiology, genetics, and ecology of toxigenic *Vibrio cholerae*. *Microbiol. Mol. Biol. Rev.* 62:1301–1314.

Firth, N., Ippen-Ihler, K., and Skurray, R. 1996. Structure and function of the F factor and mechanism of conjugation. In *Escherichia coli and Salmonella Cellular and Molecular Biology*, ed. F.C. Neidhardt, pp. 2377–2401. American Society of Microbiology, Washington, DC.

Fralick, J.A., Chadha-Mohanty, P., and Li, G. 2008. Phage display and its application for the detection and therapeutic intervention of biological threat agents. In *Advances in Biological and Chemical Terrorism Countermeasures*, eds. R.J. Kendall, S.M. Presley, G.A. Austin, and P.N. Smith, pp. 179–201. CRC Press, Taylor & Francis Group, Boca Raton, FL.

Frost, L.F., Ippen-Ihler, K., and Skurray, R.A. 1994. Analysis of the sequence and gene products of the transfer region of the F factor. *Microbiol Rev.* 58:162–210.

Garcia-Quintanilla, M., Ramos-Morales, F., and Casadesus, J. 2008. Conjugal transfer of the *Salmonella enterica* virulence plasmid in the mouse intestine. *J. Bacteriol.* 190:1922–1927.

Gupta, P. et al. 2000. Is lactobacillus GG helpful in children with Crohn's disease? Results of a preliminary, open-label study. *J. Pediatr. Gastroenterol. Nutr.* 31:453–457.

Guslandi, M. et al. 2000. *Saccharomyces boulardii* in maintenance treatment of Crohn's disease. *Dig. Dis. Sci.* 45:1462–1464.

Kaper, J.B., Fasano, A., and Trucksis, M. 1994. Toxins of *Vibrio cholerae.* In *Vibrio Cholerae and Cholera: Molecular to Global Perspectives*, eds. I.K. Wachsmuth, P.A. Blake, and Ø. Olsvik, pp. 145–176. American Society for Microbiology Press, Washington, DC.

Kasuya, M. 1964. Transfer of drug resistance between enteric bacteria induced in the mouse intestine. *J. Bacteriol.* 88:322–328.

Leatham-Jensen, M.P. et al. 2012. The streptomycin-treated mouse intestine selects *Escherichia coli* envZ missense mutants that interact with dense and diverse intestinal microbiota. *Infect. Immun.* 80:1716–1727.

Lencer, W.I. 2001. Microbes and microbial toxins: Paradigms for microbial-mucosal interactions V. cholera: Invasion of the intestinal epithelial barrier by a stably folded protein toxin. *Am. J. Physiol. Gastrointest. Liver Physiol.* 280:G781–G786.

Lencer, W.I., Hirst, T.R., and Holmes, R.K. 1999. Membrane traffic and the cellular uptake of cholera toxin. *Biochim. Biophys. Acta Mol. Cell. Res.* 1450:177–190.

Lencer, W.I., Moe, S., Rufo, P.A., and Madara, J.L. 1995. Transcytosis of cholera toxin subunits across model human intestinal epithelia. *Proc. Natl. Acad. Sci. USA* 92:10094–10098.

Licht, T.R., Christensen, B.B., Krogfelt, K.A., and Molin, S. 1999. Plasmid transfer in the animal intestine and other dynamic bacterial populations: The role of community structure and environment. *Microbiology* 145:2615–2622.

Lin, A. 2011. Inhibition of bacterial conjugation by phage M13 and its protein g3p: Quantitative analysis and model. *PLoS ONE* 6:e19991.

Mekalanos, J.J., Collier, R.J., and Romig, W.R. 1979. Enzymatic activity of cholera toxin. II Relationships to proteolytic processing, disulfide bond reduction, and subunit composition. *J. Biol. Chem.* 254:5855–5861.

Miller, J.H. 1972. *Experiments in Molecular Genetics.* Cold Spring Harbor Laboratory, Cold Spring Harbor, NY, pp. 431–436.

Moss, J. and Vaughn, M. 1988. CT and *E. coli* enterotoxins and their mechanisms of action. In *Handbook of Natural Toxins*, eds. M.C. Hardegree and A.T. Tu, vol. 4, pp. 39–87. Marcel Dekker, Inc., New York.

Nobaek, S. et al. 2000. Alteration of intestinal microflora is associated with reduction in abdominal bloating and pain in patients with irritable bowel syndrome. *Am. J. Gastroenterol.* 95:1231–1238.

Plemper, R.K. and Wolf, D.H. 1999. Retrograde protein translocation: Eradication of secretory proteins in health and disease. *Trends Biol. Sci.* 24:266–270.

Riedel, S. 2004. Biological warfare and bioterrorism: A historical review. *Proc. Baylor Univ. Med. Cent.* 17:400–406.

Roberts, M. and Falkow, S. 1979. In vivo conjugal transfer of R plasmids in *Neisseria gonorrhoeae. Infect. Immun.* 24:982–984.

Saavedra, J.M. et al. 1994. Feeding of *Bifidobacterium bifidum* and *Streptococcus thermophilus* to infants in hospital for prevention of diarrhea and shedding of rotavirus. *Lancet* 344:1046–1049.

Steidler, L. 2003. Genetically engineered probiotics. *Best Pract. Res. Clin. Gastroenterol.* 17:861–876.

Van Wezenbeek, P.M., Hulsebos, T.J., and Schoenmakers, J.G. 1980. Nucleotide sequence of the filamentous bacteriophage M13 DNA genome: Comparison with phage fd. *Gene* 11:129–148.

Venturi, A. et al. 1999. Impact on the composition of the fecal flora by a new probiotic preparation: Preliminary data on maintenance treatment of patients with ulcerative colitis. *Aliment. Pharmacol. Ther.* 13:1103–1108.

Wan, Z. and Goddard, N.L. 2012. Competition between conjugation and M13 phage infection in *Escherichia coli* in the absence of selection pressure: A kinetic study. *Genes/Genomes/Genetics* 2:1137–1144.

Webster, R. 2001. Filamentous phage biology. In *Phage Display—A Laboratory Manual*, eds. C.F. Barbas III, D.R. Burton, J.K. Scott, and G.J. Silverman, pp. 1.1–1.37. Cold Spring Harbor Laboratory Press, Cold Spring Harbor, NY.

White, J. et al. 1999. Rab6 coordinates a novel Golgi to ER retrograde transport pathway in live cells. *J. Cell Biol.* 147:743–760.

Wolf, A.A., Jobling, M.G., Wimer-Mackin, S., Madara, J.L., Holmes, R.K., and Lencer, W.I. 1998. Ganglioside structure dictates signal transduction by cholera toxin in polarized epithelia and association with caveolae-like membrane domains. *J. Cell Biol.* 141:917–927.

chapter seven

New perspectives on protective fibrous substrates

Uday Turaga, Vinitkumar Singh, Ronald J. Kendall, and Seshadri S. Ramkumar

Contents

7.1   Introduction

In this era of asymmetric threats, the field of textiles is constantly evolving to counter the various threats. The perception of textiles for aesthetics and basic protection no longer holds any significance. Some incremental developments in the field of textiles include technical textiles and functional clothing. Technical textiles are defined as textile fibers, materials, and support materials meeting technical rather than aesthetic criteria, even if, for certain markets like work wear or sports equipment, both types of criteria are met. Functional clothing could be considered as an advancement of technical textiles and is defined as clothing or clothing assemblies that are specifically engineered to deliver a predefined performance or functionality to the user, in addition to their normal functions. In other words, functional clothing offers some operational advantages to the user. Functional clothing can be divided into six categories: (1) protective functional, (2) medical functional, (3) sports functional, (4) vanity functional, (5) cross-functional assemblies, and (6) clothing for special needs (Gupta, 2011).

Depending on the intended use and from a design and performance point of view, functional clothing is required to have the following properties: (1) strength, (2) modulus, (3) antibacterial activity, (4) moisture management, (5) heat resistance, (6) electromagnetic radiation protection, and (7) water repellency (Majumdar et al., 2011).

This chapter aims to present an overview of the various aspects such as design and development of functional clothing to counter chemical and biological terrorism. Considerable emphasis has been placed on functional clothing for EMI shielding, ballistic protection, development of superhydrophobic textiles for protection, textiles for chem–bio defense, and the implications of nanotechnology in developing protective clothing.

7.2   EMI shielding

7.2.1   Mechanisms of EMI shielding

The three primary mechanisms of EMI shielding include reflection, absorption, and multiple reflections. Reflection necessitates the presence of mobile charge carriers like electrons that interact with the electromagnetic fields. Electrical conductors like metals can be used for this purpose. Absorption requires a combination of electric and magnetic dipoles to interact with the electromagnetic fields. Multiple reflections involve materials with high surface areas such as porous materials and fillings. Functional materials can be developed for effective EMI shielding by using metal coatings, electrically conducting polymers, and other composite structures (Chung, 2001).

The electromagnetic shielding capabilities of textile and other substrates are measured in terms of shielding effectiveness (SE). It is expressed in decibels (dB) and is a ratio of transmitted electromagnetic radiation in the presence and absence of a given fabric.

SE (dB) = 10 log ($P1/P2$), where $P1$ is the transmitted EM radiation in the presence of a fabric and $P2$ is the transmitted EM radiation in the absence of a fabric or the total incident EM radiation (Bonaldi et al., 2010).

Some commonly used test methods to assess the SE of textile materials are delineated in the following (Wieckowski and Janokiewicz, 2006):

ASTM D4935-10: Standard test method for measuring the electromagnetic shielding effectiveness of planar materials
IEEE-STD 299-2006: Standard method for measuring the effectiveness of electromagnetic shielding enclosures

Some of the important characteristics of textiles that determine their electromagnetic shielding capabilities include the type of material, number of fabric layers, yarn count, and the presence of mordants. Yarn count (linear density) was observed to have an inverse effect on electromagnetic shielding effectiveness where the number of fabric layers and the presence of mordants were observed to have a direct effect on electromagnetic shielding effectiveness (Das et al., 2009).

7.3   UV protection clothing

Sun-protective clothing: It is an item of personal apparel (including garments, hats, shoes, and fabric intended to be made into personal apparel) for which a claim of protective advantage against solar ultraviolet radiation is made (AS/NZS 4399, 1996).

UV-protective textile: It is any textile whose manufacturer or seller claims that it protects from sunlight, including harmful UV light, claims the reduction of risk of skin injury associated with UV exposure, or uses a rating system that quantifies the amount of sun protection afforded (ASTM D6603-00).

The effectiveness of textile substrates in protecting skin from UV radiation is measured in terms of Ultraviolet Protective Factor (UPF). UPF is defined as the ratio of extent of time required for the skin to show redness (erythema) with and without protection, under continuous exposure to solar radiation. In simpler terms, it can be described as the ration of risk with and without protection (Perenich, 1998). In textiles, UPF values are an indicator of how much does a textile substrate reduce the risks of UV exposure (Gies et al., 1998). The grading of textiles for their UV protection capabilities based on the Australian/New Zealand Standard, AS/NZS 4399 (1996), is presented in Table 7.1 (AS/NZS 4399, 1996).

Table 7.1 UPF grading of textiles

UPF range	UV radiation blocking (%)	UV radiation protection category
15–24	93.3–95.9	Good
25–39	96.0–97.4	Very good
40–50, 50+	97.5≤	Excellent

All fabrics offer varying levels of UV protection depending upon the UV reflection and absorption abilities of the fibers they are made of. Dyes and pigments often used in the finishing of textiles also possess UV absorption capabilities. Furthermore, textiles can be functionalized/ finished by various UV absorbing compounds and metal oxide nanoparticles to impart additional UV protection (Hatch and Osterwalder, 2006).

7.4   Ballistic protection

7.4.1   Mechanism of ballistic protection

Projectiles/fragments possess high kinetic energies aided by their mass and velocity. The absorption of energy at these ballistic speeds is an important consideration in the design and development of ballistic protection wear. Ballistic protection wear should often account for impact energy of projectiles and fragments generated due to the impact. The mechanisms by which ballistic protection wear minimize the impacts of projectiles/ fragments include (1) deformation of fabric layers upon impact, (2) punching/cutting of fabric yarns, and (3) reduction of impact energy by dissipating it from one fabric layer to the next. The factors that determine the energy absorption characteristics of ballistic protection wear include (1) properties of fabric such as fabric density, (2) fabric design (woven/ nonwoven), (3) mass of projectile and impact conditions, (4) projectile geometry, and (5) striking velocity (Agarwal, 2011).

7.4.2   Development of ballistic protection wear

The relative ballistic performance of materials could be estimated by Cunniff's equation (Cunniff, 1999):

$$U^* = (\sigma \, \epsilon/2 \, \rho)^* \, \text{sqrt} \, (E/\rho)$$

This equation considers some important material properties such as density (ρ), the ultimate tensile strength (σ), the strain at break (ϵ), and the tensile modulus (E) to give a parameter (U^*), which gives an idea on the relative ballistic performance of a given material. According to Cunniff's equation, an ideal antiballistic material should possess high modulus, high strength, high strain, and low density.

Table 7.2 Mechanical properties of high-performance fibers

	Strength (GPa)	Modulus (GPa)	Elongation at rupture (%)
Aramid	2.8–3.2	60–115	1.5–4.5
High-performance polyethylene	2.8–4.0	90–140	2.9–3.8
Liquid crystal polymer	2.8	65	3.3
Poly(*p*-phenylene-2,6-benzobisoxazole)	5.5	280	2.5
M5	4.0	330	1.2
Glass fibers	4.65	87	5.4

Technical textiles and functional clothing made of high-performance fibers with high tensile strength and large failure strain are ideal candidates for the development of ballistic protection wear as they can absorb impact energy at ballistic speeds (Cheeseman and Bogetti, 2003). A high degree of molecular orientation along fiber axis, high molecular weight, and high crystallinity are some of the important considerations in developing high-performance fibers for ballistic protection (Tam and Bhatnagar, 2008).

High-performance fibers play a crucial role in the development of light-weight armor for a range of applications that include (1) personal protection, (2) protection of vehicles such as helicopters, and (3) command shelters. The properties of a few high-performance fibers are delineated in Table 7.2 (Jacobs and Van Dingenen, 2001).

7.4.3   Ballistic protection shields

Ballistic armor plates and shields play a key role in protecting military and police personnel from high velocity and high-impact projectiles. Ramkumar (2005) have developed one such ballistic protection shield with enhanced next-to-skin properties and flexibility. It is a composite shield that involves the mechanical interconnection of a nonwoven next-to-skin layer, also referred to as a wear layer, to multiple layers of antiballistic materials. The use of nonwoven substrates as wear layer increases the comfort properties of the composite structure. More importantly, the mechanical interconnection of wear layer to antiballistic materials was accomplished by needle punching, thereby eliminating the use of adhesive bonds that compromise flexibility of the shield. Furthermore, needle punching facilitates the use of any fiber/blends of fibers as wear layer offers a good control on fiber orientation. Finally, leather was used as a strike layer due to its good abrasion-resistant properties. The use of leather as strike layer was found to increase the life of the composite shield. In another study, the technology of needle punching was employed by Price et al. (2006) to develop materials with enhanced energy-absorbing properties. These high-performance ballistic materials consist of at least one woven layer of ballistic grade fibers and at least one nonwoven layer of fabric. However, multiple woven layers of ballistic grade fibers are employed to enhance the performance characteristics. The nonwoven fiber layer is superposed on to the stack of woven ballistic fiber layers using needle punching till the nonwoven fiber layers get entangled in the interstices of the woven ballistic fibers. Such a process stabilizes the fabric layers that enable high ballistic performance at low thickness and areal densities. The technology was commercialized by Tex Tech Industries, Inc. (Figures 7.1 and 7.2).

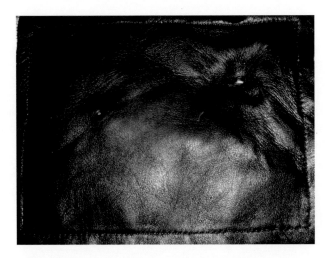

Figure 7.1 Bullet is trapped by the armor. (From Purushothaman, A. et al., *J. Eng. Fibers Fabr.*, 8(2), 97, 2013.)

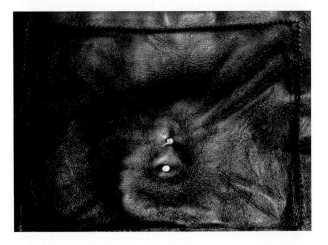

Figure 7.2 Leather dissipates the impact.

7.5   Development of superhydrophobic surfaces for protection

7.5.1   What is superhydrophobicity?

By definition, a static water contact angle larger than 150° and a low sliding angle, which is expressed as the difference between advancing and receding contact angles (contact angle hysteresis), confer superhydrophobicity to a given surface (Feng et al., 2002; Lee and Michielsen, 2007). A lotus leaf is a classic example of a super hydrophobic surface. When a water drop comes in contact with a lotus leaf, it takes a beaded configuration and rolls off the surface, collecting dirt along the way. This phenomenon is termed lotus effect (Cheng and Rodak, 2005). It was observed that a multilevel surface structure that involve micro- and nanoscale hierarchical structures (nanostructures on top of micropapillae) and a wax layer present on the surface confer superhydrophobicity to lotus leaves (Zhai et al., 2002; Cheng and Rodak, 2005). The kinetics of droplet movement and thermodynamics of wetting explain the significance of multiple scales of roughness in superhydrophobicity (Gao and McCarthy, 2006).

7.5.1.1   Superhydrophobicity and contact angle hysteresis

An important aspect that is often overlooked in discussing contact angle phenomena and superhydrophobicity is contact angle hysteresis. It is defined as the difference between advancing and receding contact angles at the leading and trailing edge of a moving droplet. It is important to understand contact angle hysteresis as contact angle greater than 150° alone does not justify droplet roll-off and self-cleaning properties of a lotus leaf. It was observed that water droplets roll-off the surface for a CA hysteresis of less than 10° and tend to stick to the surface for a hysteresis of more than 10°. Hence, it is imperative to understand the importance of CA hysteresis for the development of superhydrophobic surfaces (Balu et al., 2008).

7.5.1.2   Development of superhydrophobic surfaces

The two basic properties that govern the development of superhydrophobic surfaces are surface roughness and low surface energy. A combination of these two properties is required for the design of superhydrophobic surfaces and could be achieved in the following ways: (1) adding roughness to an inherently low surface energy material; (2) adding roughness to a hydrophilic surface followed by modification with a hydrophobic treatment; and (3) modification of a surface with low surface energy with the deposition of hydrophobic nanoparticles that adds roughness to it (Balu et al., 2008).

The significance of surface roughness in the development of super-hydrophobic surfaces has been well understood. However, any attempt to modify the roughness often affects the chemical nature of a surface. In the case of crystalline materials, roughening the surface exposes new lattice planes with different intrinsic surface energies. With amorphous materials, it results in a more open atomic surface structure (Yang et al., 2006).

A range of physical and chemical methods have been developed for the fabrication of rough surfaces. A few of those methods include (1) wax solidification, (2) lithography, (3) vapor deposition, (4) template method, (5) polymer reconformation, (6) sublimation, (7) electrohydrodynamics/electrospinning, (8) plasma technique, (9) sol-gel processing, (10) electrochemical methods, (11) bottom-up approach for the fabrication of nano-arrays, (12) hydrothermal synthesis, (13) layer-by-layer method, and (14) one-pot reaction (Zhang et al., 2008).

7.5.1.3   Plasma treatment to develop superhydrophobic surfaces

Plasma treatment is an environmentally friendly process that has been proven to functionalize the surface of materials without affecting their bulk properties. The type of plasma and the process gas involved determine the mechanism of action of plasma that involve the following: (1) fine cleaning, (2) surface activation, (3) etching, (4) cross-linking, and (5) chemical vapor deposition (Jinka et al., 2013, 2014; Marcandalli and Ricardi, 2007).

Plasma treatment was successfully employed to roughen the surface of cellulosic substrates, an important consideration to subsequently develop superhydrophobic surfaces. The significance of the etching effect of plasma in roughening the surface of cellulosic substrates such as cotton has been investigated by Balu et al. (2008). The authors have observed that plasma treatment selectively etches the amorphous domains and exposes the crystalline moieties in cellulose, which eventually roughens the surface of cellulosic substrates. More importantly, it was observed that the employment of processing gases such as Argon and Oxygen result in more etching (Caschera et al., 2013, 2014).

7.5.1.4   Microwave-assisted development of superhydrophobic textile surfaces

Hayn et al. (2011) have developed a novel microwave-assisted cross-linking of perfluoroalkoxy silanes (PFAS) for the development of highly hydrophobic and oleophobic textile surfaces. It is a multistep dip-and-cure process that involves dipping the substrates in a solution containing heptadecafluoro-1,1,2,2-tetrahydrodecyltrimethoxysilane (FS) and curing in the presence of microwaves. The employment of microwaves was found to enhance the covalent attachment of silanes to the textile substrates. The surface roughness, an important consideration in the development of superhydrophobic surfaces, was controlled by the use of neutral and base catalysts. It was observed that catalysis in the presence of water resulted in a smooth deposition of PFAS and catalysis in the presence of a base-induced micro- and nanoscale roughness to the surface of the fiber. In another study, Saraf et al. (2011) have developed superhydrophobic nylon nonwoven surfaces using microwave-assisted grafting of FS onto hydroentangled nylon substrates. According to the authors, the process of hydroentanglement increases the surface roughness of nylon fibers, thereby enabling the development of superhydrophobic nylon substrates. Silanes contain both organic and inorganic activity on the same molecule and the process of using microwave radiation to covalently attach silanes onto various substrates has been termed Reactive Surface Technology and has been commercialized by Alexium Ltd., Cambridge, U.K.

7.6   Protection from biological terrorism

7.6.1   Detection of biological agents

The efficient detection of biological agents could be accomplished by biological-agent warning sensors (BAWS). BAWS work on the principle of laser-induced fluorescence to differentiate suspicious particles from those that are found in nature. A pulsed UV laser operating at 266 nm is used to excite the suspicious aerosol particles and the emitted light is selectively filtered by another detection system to confirm the presence of biological entities (Primmerman, 2000). Another system for the real-time detection and identification of biological threat agents was developed by Heid et al. (1996). It is a fluorogenic probe-based PCR technique that uses an oligonucleotide probe with the sequence of interest. The probe is labeled with a fluorescent reporter and quencher dye molecules. When the probe hybridizes with a target, the fluorescent dyes emit characteristic emission spectra. Different probes with suitable dye molecules would enable the detection of a range of biological threats. Another multiplexed suspension array system for the simultaneous detection of multiple analytes was developed by Wang et al. (2009). In this system, the antibody–antigen reactions and the reactions between DNA and corresponding oligonucleotide probes are facilitated on fluorescent polystyrene microbeads. A range of biotinylated antibodies coupled to carboxylated fluorescent microspheres could be used to label the polystyrene microbeads. According to the authors, the suspension array system showed enhanced sensitivity and selectivity toward a range of biological agents with different physical and chemical properties and in complex mixtures.

7.6.2   Biocidal coatings

Michelsen et al. (2007) have proposed the development of light-activated antiviral materials from reactive dyes and dyes containing functional groups such as acridine yellow G, proflavin and acroflavin. According to the authors, these dyes generate singlet oxygen when exposed to light of a given spectrum and intensity and in the presence of oxygen. The generated singlet oxygen deactivates viruses upon contact. Such dyes could be used on fabrics to develop effective countermeasures in the following ways: (1) bonding, (2) coating, and (3) impregnation.

N-halamine biocidal polymers can also be used to develop biocidal coatings for use in textiles. N-halamine polymers contain either a nitrogen–chlorine or a nitrogen–bromine covalent chemical bond that is resistant to hydrolysis. N-halamine biocides are prepared by exposing the precursor polymer to free chlorine or free bromine that is lost over the course of activity of polymer. However, the activity could be regained by exposing the polymer to a fresh source of free halogens (Liang et al., 2006). Worley et al. (2003) have used N-halamine monomer copolymerized with acrylic polyol and isocyanate to develop biocidal polyurethane coatings. According to the authors, biocidal properties could be imparted to these coatings by exposing them to a source of free chlorine. Regeneration of biocidal properties could be accomplished in a similar fashion.

7.6.3   Plasma technology

The biocidal ability of glow discharge at atmospheric pressure (GDAP) and an enhanced corona discharge at atmospheric pressure (ECDAP) was studied by Laroussi et al. (2000). According to the author, the biocidal efficiency of GDAP depends on the type of media and microorganism, and whether it is a surface or volume sterilization. The efficiency of ECDAP depends on the intensity of plasma treatment, which in turn depends on the discharge power and exposure time. Plasma technology has also been used as a pretreatment to textiles for subsequent deposition of metals to impart various functionalities. Scholz et al. (2005) has used this approach to deposit metals like copper and silver using magnetron sputtering deposition technology.

7.7   Protection from chemical terrorism

It is important to understand the physical properties of chemical agents in order to develop efficient countermeasure strategies. The physical properties of a few selected chemical agents are depicted in Table 7.3 (Ganesan et al., 2010).

Table 7.3 Physical properties of chemical warfare agents

	Tabun (GA)	Sarin (GB)	Soman (GD)	VX	Sulfur mustard
Molecular weight (g/mol)	162.12	140.09	182.19	267	159.08
Vapor pressure (mm Hg at 25°C)	0.037	2.9	0.4	0.0007	0.11
Volatility (mg/m³ at 25°C)	610	22,000	3900	75	610

7.7.1   Detection of chemical agents

Wang et al. (2008) have developed a carbon nanotube/polythiophene chemiresistive sensor for detecting chemical warfare agents. Chemiresistors work on the principle of change in resistance in response to the binding of analytes. The authors have demonstrated that the carbon nanotube/ polythiophene chemiresistive sensor had an increased level of sensitivity and selectivity toward dimethyl methylphosphonate, a stimulant of sarin (Wang et al., 2008). Deng et al. (2009) have investigated the applicability of electrospun polyacrylonitrile (PAN) nanofibers for detection of 2,4,6-trinitrotoluene (TNT). The authors have coated PAN nanofibers with a TNT-sensitive conjugated polymer TPA-PBPV (poly[triphenylamine-alt-biphenylene vinylene]). The assembly has resulted in an increased sensitivity toward TNT compared to a regular (TPA-PBPV) film.

7.7.2   Perm-selective membranes

The next-generation chemical and biological protecting suits ought to have combinatorial measure capability against chemical and biological threats and reduced logistic burden. Permeable selective membranes depict a novel concept in CB protective clothing (Schreuder et al., 2003). Researchers at United States' Natick Soldier Center have developed permeable selective membrane to block chemical toxins without the use of the carbon adsorbent. These perm-selective membranes have superior mechanical properties, barrier properties, and moisture vapor transition rates. Perm-selective membranes have properties of impermeable as well as semipermeable materials. These membranes not only serve as barriers for hazardous chemical vapors but also facilitate moisture vapor transport to provide comfort. Mechanism governing the functioning of these perm-selective membranes is selective diffusion process, which is very different than protection provided via adsorption process of the carbon materials. This characteristic provides necessary comfort and protection against chemical toxins. Another feature of this selective permeable membrane consisting of microporous structure is higher specific surface area, which act as binding sites for biocides and other reactive compounds within the protective membrane (Wilusz and Truong).

7.7.3   Decontamination wipes

Despite the many technologies available to decontaminate chemical and biological wastes, it is convenient to wipe off bulk threat chemicals followed by appropriate decontamination methods. Dry nonparticulate decontamination products such as wipes could be an integral part of a low-cost personal decontamination system (LDPS) used for large-scale decontamination of chemical wastes (Lawrence Livermore National Laboratory, 2009). Research at Texas Tech University in this direction has led to the development of Fibertect® dry decontamination wipe. The wipe consists of three components: (1) an absorbent top layer, (2) an adsorbent porous activated carbon middle layer, and (3) a fibrous layer at the bottom for structural coherence and nonleaching capability (Ramkumar, 2009). Studies have showed that Fibertect adsorbs off-gassing mustard vapors more efficiently compared to particulate activated carbon and M291 reactive adsorbent substrate (Ramkumar et al., 2008). Fibertect was also found to be capable of adsorbing vapors from organophosphorous compounds like methyl parathion (Sata and Ramkumar, 2007, 2012; FirstLine Technology, 2014). Some of the important properties of Fibertect that facilitate its usage as a decontamination wipe include (1) its ability to wipe bulk toxic chemical agents; (2) its feasibility to be used on people, weapons, and sensitive equipment; (3) its ability to both absorb and adsorb toxic chemicals; (4) its indefinite shelf life; and (5) no issues of secondary contamination (FirstLine Technology). More importantly, recent studies by the United Stated Coast Guard have showed that Fibertect removes 80%–90% of contaminants likely to be encountered in a battle field (New Gear, 2011). Figure 7.3 shows Fibertect decontamination wipe in use.

With the recent crude oil spill in the Gulf of Mexico, which resulted in the major spill of about 4.9 million barrels of oil, new technologies, which do not add stress to the environment, are needed to clean-up and protect the environment (Singh et al., 2013). Recently, research carried out at Texas Tech University investigated the basic science behind the sorption phenomena in cotton fiber assembly using crude oil and regular motor oil for environmental protection (Singh et al., 2013; Singh and Ramkumar, 2014; Figure 7.4).

These authors reported that there are three major mechanisms that govern the sorption of crude oil onto raw cottons: (1) adsorption, (2) absorption, and (3) capillary action between the fibers. Interestingly, Singh et al. (2013) reported that a single gram of low-grade cotton was able to pick-up of about 35.83 g of crude oil. Furthermore, these authors have also reported on fundamental understanding and practical viability can be an environmentally friendly solution for oil spill and toxic chemical clean-ups. Results from these studies showed that low-grade cotton fiber in its nonwoven form could pick up oil as high as 50 times its own weight,

Figure 7.3 Fibetect® in use. (Photo courtesy of First Line Technology, LLC, Chantilly, VA.)

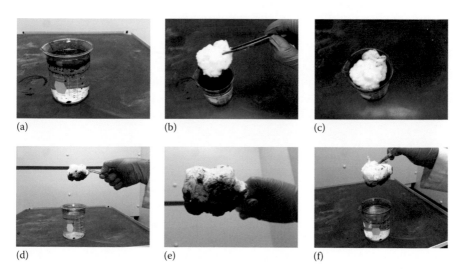

(a)   (b)   (c)

(d)   (e)   (f)

Figure 7.4 Raw cotton soaked in crude oil. (a) Oil in water, (b) cotton about to be put in a mixture of oil and water, (c) cotton floating on the surface of oil-water, (d) cotton removed from the mixture, (e) oil absorbed/adsorbed on to cotton and (f) set-up to demonstrate oil absorption by cotton. (From Singh, V. et al., *Ind. Eng. Chem. Res.*, 52(18), 6277, 2013; Singh, V. et al., *Ind. Eng. Chem. Res.*, 53(30), 11954, 2014.)

which is significantly higher than oil sorption capacity of many commercial oil sorbents reported in the literature (Singh et al., 2014). Additionally, these low-grade raw cotton fibers were also used to develop cotton-carbon nonwoven composite, which could be used for high-performance applications such as industrial chemical spill clean-up and oil absorption. Raw cotton–based cotton-carbon composite wipes can be used to absorb oil as well as adsorb toxic volatile vapors release from polycyclic aromatic hydrocarbons (Ramkumar and Singh, 2010; Singh et al., 2010; Singh and Ramkumar, 2010).

7.8   Role of nanotechnology in chem–bio defense

Nanotechnology and nanomaterials are finding an array of applications in the defense sector (Turaga et al., 2012) because of their unique properties such as high surface area-to-volume ratio, high porosity (Subbiah et al., 2005; Turaga et al., 2014), and filtration efficiencies (Lalagiri et al., 2013). In a broader perspective, nanotechnology could potentially serve the following function in the defense sector: (1) a significant reduction in the size of protective equipment and electronic systems in battle theatres; (2) development of systems with enhanced strength and heat-resistant properties for protection; and (3) design of protective overalls that track the health condition of wearer and respond accordingly (Altmann, 2004). From a textile point of view, the nanofunctionalization of textiles or the process of incorporating nanomaterials into textiles enables the development of nanotextiles with enhanced performance, functionality, and smartness (Ramkumar and Singh, 2011).

A few important properties of nanomaterials that have propelled their applicability in defense sector are summarized in Table 7.4 (Coyle et al., 2007).

Table 7.4 Properties of nanomaterials for use in defense applications

Type of nanomaterial	Properties
Carbon nanofibers	High tensile strength, electrical conductivity, and chemical resistance
Carbon black nanoparticles	Superior abrasion resistance, toughness, chemical resistance, and electrical conductivity
Clay nanoparticles	UV protection, flame retardancy, electrical, heat and chemical resistance, and anticorrosive properties
Metal oxide nanoparticles (ZnO, MgO, Al_2O_3, TiO_2, and silver)	Photocatalytic ability, electrical conductivity, UV absorption, neutralization of chemical and biological agents
Carbon nanotubes	Superior tensile properties, electrical and thermal conductivity

7.8.1   Carbon nanotube-based military protection wear

The unique properties of carbon nanotubes enable the development of protection wear with due emphasis to both the protection and comfort properties of the final product. Researchers at the Lawrence Livermore National Laboratory have been working on developing a carbon nanotube–based military uniform for chemical and biological protection. The design involves vertical alignment of carbon nanotubes spaced a few nanometers from each other to make the membrane highly breathable. It was observed that the pores in the membrane effectively blocked biological agents by virtue of their small size. To counter chemical threats, the researchers have functionalized the surface of carbon nanotubes with chemical threat–responsive functional groups. This functionalization enables the pores in carbon nanotubes to reversibly close in the presence of chemical agents thereby blocking them, while still being adequately breathable to provide comfort to the wearer (Lawrence Livermore National Laboratory, 2012).

Studies by Mylvaganam and Zhang have shown that the ballistic resistance capacity of a carbon nanotube is highest when a bullet strikes at its center. The study also revealed that the size of a carbon nanotube dictates its ability to withstand high kinetic energy impacts and that the protection offered by carbon nanotubes would be the same even if the bullet strikes multiple times at the same spot. Finally, the authors have estimated that a 600 μm body armor made of six 100 μm thick carbon nanotube yarns would potentially bounce of a 320 J muzzle energy bullet (Mylvaganam and Zhang, 2007). In another study, Mylvaganam (2008) has suggested that the elasticity of carbon nanotubes could be used to develop bulletproof vests that not only stop bullets but also prevent blunt force trauma.

7.8.2   Metal oxide nanoparticles

Vempati et al. patented a novel technology, which can be potentially used to replace the current toxic incineration method of destroying the chemical warfare agents (CWAs) stockpiles. Nanophase manganese oxide (NMO-V) and nanophase manganese oxide coating to clay (NMOC-V) acting as strong Lewis acids were successfully used to actively neutralize biological and chemical warfare agents (BCWAs). These materials can be directly used in its powder form as well as can be coated on different substrates such as fabrics, liners, and membranes to provide protection against BCWAs. Furthermore, NMO-V and NMOC-V are nontoxic and nonhazardous to humans and animals and can be safely used for developing protective suits for soldiers and civilian population to counter BCWAs.

7.9   Conclusions

The threats faced by defense and civilian communities are no longer conventional in nature. Due to the complex nature of these threats, they can be combined in a variety of fashions to increase their destructive potential. Emerging threats such as toxic industrial chemicals and oil spills present novel challenges in this regard. Ideal protective clothing provides wider protection capabilities, reduced logistic burdens, improved agility, and overall enhance the performance of the wearer. The development of such highly functional, multidimensional protective clothing system involves multiple disciplines and transdisciplinary research endeavors. Textile materials continue to be the foundation of such composite systems due to their comfort characteristics. However, the functionalization of textiles to tackle various threats requires a combinatorial and multidisciplinary approach that balances the comfort and protection characteristics.

References

Agarwal, B.J. 2011. High performance textiles for ballistic protection. *IEEE Def. Sci. Res. Conf. Expo (DSR)* 2:1–4.

Altmann, J. 2004. Military uses of nanotechnology: Perspectives and concerns. *Secur. Dialogue* 35(1):61–79.

American Society for Testing and Materials (ASTM International). 2004. Standard D 6603-12. In *Standard Guide for Labeling of UV-Protective Textiles*, eds. Bailey, S.J., Baldwin, N.C., McElrone, E.K. et al., vol. 7:03, pp. 1187–1191. ASTM International, West Conshohocken, PA.

Balu, B., Breedveld, V., and Hess, D.W. 2008. Fabrication of "roll-off" and "sticky" superhydrophobic cellulose surfaces via plasma processing. *Langmuir* 24(9): 4785–4790.

Bonaldi, R.R., Siores, E., and Shah, T. 2010. Electromagnetic shielding characterisation of several conductive fabrics for medical applications. *Text. Bioeng. Inform. Symp. Proc.* 1–3:536–543.

Caschera, D., Cortese, B., Mezzi, A., Brucale, M., Ingo, G.M., Gigli, G., and Padeletti, G. 2013. Ultra hydrophobic/superhydrophilic modified cotton textiles through functionalized diamond-like carbon coatings for self-cleaning applications. *Langmuir* 29(8):2775–2783.

Caschera, D., Mezzi, A., Cerri, L., de Caro, T., Riccucci, C., Ingo, G.M., Padeletti, G., Biasiucci, M., Gigli, G., and Cortese, B. 2014. Effects of plasma treatments for improving extreme wettability behavior of cotton fabrics. *Cellulose* 21(1):741–756.

Cheeseman, B.A. and Bogetti, T.A. 2003. Ballistic impact into fabric and compliant composite laminates. *Compos. Struct.* 61(1–2):161–173.

Cheng, Y.T. and Rodak, D.E. 2005. Is the lotus leaf superhydrophobic? *Appl. Phys. Lett.* 86(14):144101.

Chung, D.D.L. 2001. Electromagnetic interference shielding effectiveness of carbon materials. *Carbon* 39(2):279–285.

Coyle, S., Wu, Y.Z., Lau, K.T., De Rossi, D., Wallace, G., and Diamond, D. 2007. Smart nanotextiles: A review of materials and applications. *MRS Bull.* 32(5):434–442.

Cunniff, P.M. 1999. Dimensionless parameters for optimization of textile-based body armor systems. In *Proceedings of the 18th International Symposium on Ballistics*, San Antonio, TX, pp. 1303–1310.

Das, A., Kothari, V.K., Kothari, A., Kumar, A., and Tuli, S. 2009. Effect of various parameters on electromagnetic shielding effectiveness of textile fabrics. *Indian J. Fibre Text. Res.* 34:144–148.

Deng, C., Gong, P., He, Q., Cheng, J., He, C., Shi, L., Zhu, D., and Lin, T. 2009. Highly fluorescent TPA-PBPV nanofibers with amplified sensory response to TNT. *Chem. Phys. Lett.* 483:219–223.

Feng, L., Li, S., Li, Y., Li, H., Zhang, L., Zhai, J., Song, Y., Liu, B., Jiang, L., and Zhu, D. 2002. Super-hydrophobic surfaces: From natural to artificial. *Adv. Mater.* 14 (24):1857–1860.

FirstLine Technology. www.firstlinetech.com (accessed July 15, 2014).

Ganesan, K., Raza, S.K., and Vijayaraghavan, R. 2010. Chemical warfare agents. *J. Pharm. Bioallied Sci.* 2(3):166–178.

Gao, L.C. and McCarthy, T.J. 2006. The "lotus effect" explained: Two reasons why two length scales of topography are important. *Langmuir* 22(7):2966–2967.

Gies, P.H., Roy, C.R., Toomey, S., and McLennan, A. 1998. Protection against solar ultraviolet radiation. *Mutat. Res. Fundam. Mol. Mech. Mutagen.* 422(1): 15–22.

Gupta, D. 2011. Functional clothing-definition and classification. *Indian J. Fibre Text. Res.* 36(4):321–326.

Hatch, K.L. and Osterwalder, U. 2006. Garments as solar ultraviolet radiation screening materials. *Dermatol. Clin.* 24(1):85–100.

Hayn, R.A., Owens, J.R., Boyer, A.A., McDonald, R.S., and Lee, H.J. 2011. Preparation of highly hydrophobic and oleophobic textile surfaces using microwave-promoted silane coupling. *J. Mater. Sci.* 46(8):2503–2509.

Heid, C.A., Stevens, J., Livak, K.J., and Williams, P.M. 1996. Real time quantitative PCR. *Genome Res.* 6:986–994.

Jacobs, M.J.N. and Van Dingenen, J.L.J. 2001. Ballistic protection mechanisms in personal armour. *J. Mater. Sci.* 36(13):3137–3142.

Jinka, S., Behrens, R., Korzeniewski, C., Singh, V., Arunachalam, A., Parameswaran, S., Coimbatore, G., Kendall, R., Wolf, R., and Ramkumar, S. 2013. Atmospheric pressure plasma treatment and breathability of polypropylene nonwoven fabric. *J. Ind. Text.* 42(4):501–514.

Jinka, S., Turaga, U., Singh, V., Behrens, R., Gumeci, C., Korzeniewski, C., Anderson, T., Wolf, R., and Ramkumar, S. 2014. Atmospheric plasma effect on cotton nonwovens. *Ind. Eng. Chem. Res.* 53(32):12587–12593.

Lalagiri, M., Bhat, G., Singh, V., Parameswaran, S., Kendall, R., and Ramkumar, S. 2013. Filtration efficiency of submicrometer filters. *Ind. Eng. Chem. Res.* 52(46):16513–16518.

Laroussi, M., Alexeff, I., and Kang, W.L. 2000. Biological decontamination by non-thermal plasmas. *IEEE Trans. Plasma Sci.* 28(1):184–188.

Lawrence Livermore National Laboratory. March 2009. A better method for self-decontamination. *Sci. Technol. Rev.* 20–22. https://str.llnl.gov/Mar09/pdfs/03.09.04.pdf (accessed July 15, 2014).

Lawrence Livermore National Laboratory. 2012. New military apparel repels chemical and biological agents, Livermore, CA. Available from: https://www.llnl.gov/news/newsreleases/2012/Oct/NR-12-10-06.html (Accessed 15 July 2014).

Lee, H.J., and Michielsen, S. 2007. Preparation of a superhydrophobic rough surface. *J. Polym. Sci. Part B: Polym. Phy.* 45(3):253–261.

Liang, J., Owens, J.R., Huang, T.S., and Worley, S.D. 2006. Biocidal hydantoinylsiloxane polymers. IV. N-halamine siloxane-functionalized silica gel. *J. Appl. Polym. Sci.* 101(5):3448–3454.

Majumdar, A., Singh, S.P., and Ghosh, A. 2011. Modelling, optimization and decision making techniques in designing of functional clothing. *Indian J. Fibre Text. Res.* 36(4):398–409.

Marcandalli, B. and Riccardi, C. 2007. Plasma tratments of fibres and textiles. In *Plasma Technologies for Textiles*, ed. R. Shishoo, pp. 282–300. Woodhead Publishing Limited, Cambridge, U.K.

Michelsen, S., Churchward, G., Bozia, J., Stojilokivic, I., and Anic, S. Light activated antiviral materials and devices and methods for decontaminating virus infected environments. US2007/0238660 A1.

Mylvaganam, K. 2008. Carbon nanotubes build better protective body armor. *Adv. Mater. Process.* 166 (1): 24.

Mylvaganam, K. and Zhang, L.C. 2007. Ballistic resistance capacity of carbon nanotubes. *Nanotechnology* 18(47): 475701 (4pp).

New Gear. July 2011. *National Guard Magazine*, pp. 24–27.

Perenich, T.A. 1998. Textiles as preventive measures for skin cancer. *Colourage* 45:71–73.

Price, A.L., Erb, D.F., and Ritter, E.D. September 5, 2006. Enhanced energy absorbing materials. US Patent 7,101,818 B2.

Primmerman, C.A. 2000. Detection of biological agents. *Lincoln Lab. J.* 12:3–32.

Purushothaman, A., Coimbatore, G., and Ramkumar, S.S. 2013. Soft body armor for law enforcement applications. *J. Eng. Fibers Fabr.* 8(2):97–103.

Ramkumar, S.S. March 8, 2005. Ballistic protection composite shield and method of manufacturing. US Patent 6,862,971 B2.

Ramkumar, S.S. April 14, 2009. Process for making chemical protective wipes and such wipes. US Patent 7,516,525 B2.

Ramkumar, S.S., Love, A.H., Sata, U.R., Koester, C.J., Smith, W.J., Keating, G.A., Hobbs, L.W., Cox, S.B., Lagna, W.M., and Kendall, R.J. 2008. Next-generation nonparticulate dry nonwoven pad for chemical warfare agent decontamination. *Ind. Eng. Chem. Res.* 47:9889–9895.

Ramkumar, S. and Singh, V. 2010. Oil absorbing and vapor retaining nonwovens. Paper presented at the *NET Innovative Nonwovens Conference*, Raleigh, NC.

Ramkumar, S. and Singh, V. 2011. Nanofibers: New developments. *Nonwovens Ind.* 42:52–58.

Saraf, R., Lee, H.J., Michielsen, S., Owens, J., Willis, C., Stone, C., and Wilusz, E. 2011. Comparison of three methods for generating superhydrophobic, superoleophobic nylon nonwoven surfaces. *J. Mater. Sci.* 46(17):5751–5760.

Sata, U.R. and Ramkumar, S.S. 2007. New developments with nonwoven decontamination wipes. In *Proceedings of International Nonwovens Technical Conference*, Atlanta, GA, September 24–27, 2007.

Sata, U.R. and Ramkumar, S.S. 2012. Developments in decontamination technologies of military personnel and equipment. In *Defense-Related Intelligent Textiles and Clothing for Ballistic and NBC Protection: Technology at the Cutting Edge, NATO Science for Peace and Security Series-B: Physics and Biophysics*, eds. S. Jayaraman and P. Kiekens. SpringerLink Publishing Company, Springer, the Netherlands.

Scholz, J., Nocke, G., Hollstein, F., and Weissbach, A. 2005. Investigations on fabrics coated with precious metals using the magnetron sputter technique with regard to their anti-microbial properties. *Surf. Coat. Technol.* 192(2–3): 252–256.

Schreuder-Gibson, H.L., Truong, Q., Walker, J.E., Owens, J.R., Wander, J.D., and Jones, W.E. 2003. Chemical and biological protection and detection in fabrics for protective clothing. *MRS Bull.* 28:574–578.

Singh, V., Jinka, S., Hake, K., Parameswaran, S., Kendall, R.J., and Ramkumar, S. 2014. Novel natural sorbent for oil spill cleanup. *Ind. Eng. Chem. Res.* 53(30):11954–11961.

Singh, V., Kendall, R.J., Hake, K., and Ramkumar, S. 2013. Crude oil sorption by raw cotton. *Ind. Eng. Chem. Res.* 52(18):6277–6281.

Singh, V. and Ramkumar, S. 2010. Fibrous materials for oil spill applications. Paper presented at the *AATCC Symposium on Advances in Multi-Functional Materials & NTC Forum*, Greenville, SC.

Singh, V. and Ramkumar, S. 2014. Comments on "Hollow Carbon Fibers Derived from Natural Cotton as Effective Sorbents for Oil Spill Cleanup". *Ind. Eng. Chem. Res.* 53(8):3412.

Singh, V., Sata, U., Jinka, S., Muralidhar, L., Kapoor, A., and Ramkumar, S. 2010. Oil absorbing and vapor retaining fibrous mats. Paper presented at the *Fiber Society 2010 Fall Meeting and Technical Conference*, Salt Lake City, UT.

Standards Association of Australia. 1996. Australian/New Zealand Standard AS/NZS 4399, Sun Protective Clothing-Evaluation and Classification, Homebush, New South Wales, Australia/Wellington, New Zealand.

Subbiah, T., Bhat, G.S., Tock, R.W., Pararneswaran, S., and Ramkumar, S.S. 2005. Electrospinning of nanofibers. *J. Appl. Polym. Sci.* 96(2):557–569.

Tam, T., and Bhatnagar, A. 2008. High-performance ballistic fibers. In In Military textiles, eds. Wilusz, E., pp 207–241, Woodhead Publishing Limited, Cambridge, England.

Turaga, U., Singh, V., Behrens, R., Korzeniewski, C., Jinka, S., Smith, E., Kendall, R., and Ramkumar, S. 2014. Breathability of standalone poly(vinyl alcohol) nanofiber webs. *Ind. Eng. Chem. Res.* 53(17):6951–6958.

Turaga, U., Singh, V., Lalagiri, M., Kiekens, P., and Ramkumar, S. 2012. Nanomaterials for defense applications. In *Intelligent Textiles and Clothing for Ballistic and NBC Protection*, eds. P. Kiekens and S. Jayaraman, pp. 197–218. Springer, the Netherlands.

Vempati R.K., Biehl, E.R., Hegde, R.S., and Son, D.Y., 2011. Method for degrading chemical warfare agents using Mn (VII) oxide with-and-without solid support. US Patent 8,084,662 B2.

Wang, F., Gu, H., and Swager, T.M. 2008. Carbon nanotube/polythiophene chemiresistive sensors for chemical warfare agents. *J. Am. Chem. Soc.* 130:5392–5393.

Wang, J. et al. 2009. Simultaneous detection of five biothreat agents in powder samples by a multiplexed suspension array. *Immunopharmacol. Immunotoxicol.* 31:417–427.

Wieckowski, T.W. and Janukiewicz, J.M. 2006. Methods for evaluating the shielding effectiveness of textiles. *Fibres Text. East. Eur.* 14(5):18–22.

Wilusz, E. and Truong, Q.T. Development and evaluation of selectively permeable membranes for lightweight chemical biological protective clothing, Natick Soldier Center (NSC) Natick, MA. http://nsrdec.natick.army.mil/LIBRARY/00-09/R00-53.pdf (accessed August 14, 2014).

Worley, S.D., Li, F., Wu, R., Kim, J., Wei, C.I., Williams, J.F., Owens, J.R., Wander, J.D., Bargmeyer, A.M., and Shirtliff, M.E. 2003. A novel N-halamine monomer for preparing biocidal polyurethane coatings. *Surf. Coat. Int. Part B: Coat. Trans.* 86(4):273–277.

Yang, C., Tartaglino, U., and Persson, B.N.J. 2006. Influence of surface roughness on superhydrophobicity. *Phys. Rev. Lett.* 97(11):116103.

Zhai, J., Li, H.J., Li, Y.S., Li, S.H., and Jiang, L. 2002. Discovery of super amphiphobic properties of aligned carbon nanotube films. *Physics* 31:483–486.

Zhang, X., Shi, F., Niu, J., Jiang, Y., and Wang, Z. 2008. Superhydrophobic surfaces: From structural control to functional application. *J. Mater. Chem.* 18(6):621–633.

chapter eight

Conclusions and research needs for the future

Ronald J. Kendall, Galen P. Austin, Joe A. Fralick,
Steven M. Presley, Christopher J. Salice, Ernest E. Smith,
Seshadri S. Ramkumar, and Richard E. Zartman

Contents

8.1   Conclusions

As this book, *New Developments in Biological and Chemical Terrorism Countermeasures,* was being developed, the United States was under a heightened threat for terrorism, both in its homeland and globally. Since its formation in 1973, the National Intelligence Council (NIC) has served as a bridge between the intelligence and policy communities in the United States and a source of expertise in critical national security issues (NIC, 2007). The NIC is a summary compilation of the intelligence assessments and projections from 16 different intelligence-gathering agencies in the United States. As was the case when we wrote our book in 2008 (Kendall et al., 2008), "the U.S. homeland will face a persistent and evolving terrorist threat over the next 3 years. The main threat comes from Islamic terrorist groups and cells, especially Al Qaeda, driven by the undiminished intent to attack the homeland in a continued effort to adapt and improve their capabilities." Although we have seen chemical attacks in Syria and other countries, we have yet to see a direct and observable chemical or biological attack on the United States homeland. We, however, have seen other evidence of terrorism, such as the recent bombing at the Boston Marathon, which caused many deaths and injuries, but what was used was an explosive terrorist device vs. chemical or biological. However, the authors of the current book believe that the threat for biological and chemical attacks in the United States and other nations is real. We have observed that this threat will continue into the foreseeable future. Without question, 9/11 marked a defining point in global terrorist efforts and initiated the post-9/11 environment that has resulted in significantly increased counterterrorism efforts in the United States and globally, in particular the Western world.

The researchers who authored the current book have focused and continue to focus their efforts on novel research opportunities to meet the nation's biological and chemical threat countermeasures research and development needs as identified in a joint report by the Institute of Medicine and the National Research Council (Institute of Medicine, 1999), which included (1) preincident communications and intelligence; (2) personal protective equipment; (3) detection and measurement of chemical and biological agents; (4) recognized covert exposure; (5) mass casualty decontamination and triage procedures; (6) availability and safety of efficacy of drugs, vaccines, and other therapeutics; and (7) computer-related tools for training and operation.

To address the aforementioned research needs, research within the Admiral Elmo R. Zumwalt, Jr. National Program for Countermeasures to Biological and Chemical Threats, which began in 1998, has focused efforts upon four specific areas, including (1) modeling simulation and visualization; (2) agent detection, remediation, and therapeutic intervention strategies; (3) sensors and personal protective devices; and (4) environmental protection strategies.

Although the majority of the Zumwalt Program's research on countermeasures to biological and chemical threats has emanated from the U.S. Army, Department of Defense funding, the application relevance of our findings continues to be useful to homeland security, which is extremely important. In fact, our research team has concluded that better coordination is still needed with military-related research to protect and enhance warfighters and we encourage that those research findings be leveraged further for homeland security applications. Also, we strongly encourage an increased emphasis upon enhancement of research efforts to improve local response capabilities for biological and chemical incidents.

In the development of this book, the authors searched widely for information specifically related to advanced training in countermeasures to biological and chemical terrorism. Indeed, Texas Tech and relatively few other universities in the United States emphasize (in a graduate degree program in environmental toxicology) homeland security applications. With this knowledge in mind, we still encourage increased emphasis on graduate education, particularly research-based programs, in countermeasures to biological and chemical terrorism. This issue is not going away, as we have seen, and we believe that it will be with us for the foreseeable future.

We believe that better relationships have occurred between the U.S. federal laboratories and academic institutions, yet more needs to be done. More joint ventures and interactions are needed to achieve synergy between academic research institutions and U.S. federal laboratories. We need to continue to press ahead and increase interdisciplinary cooperation for this research enhancement. Indeed, with reduction in funding from federal agencies, which are less able to help researchers, particularly at the academic level, increased interaction with industry for commercialization and procurement of technologies to increase countermeasures to biological and chemical threats will be highly desirable. There are many new technologies being developed at this time where the U.S. federal government could be of great assistance in bringing commercialization support and help in transferring these to military use from the academic programs.

Even as we are developing efforts in 2015, much of the progress being made both in the United States and internationally has been slow, sporadic, and relatively uncoordinated. It is essential that there be better coordination among the Department of Defense, Department of Homeland Security, Department of Health and Human Services, Department of Energy, Department of Agriculture, Environmental Protection Agency, and the Food and Drug Administration, among others, with academia. This is particularly relevant in this tight budget era for federal funding due to budget deficits. Deficits decrease the ability to fund research for countermeasures to biological and chemical threats.

8.2 Future research needs and recommendations

The research team that developed *New Developments in Biological and Chemical Terrorism Countermeasures* still believes the July 2007 NIC press release that the threat of a biological, chemical, nuclear, or radiological attacks is real and continues to evolve. There should be continuing vigilance by the United States and other governments globally toward counterterrorism efforts. This will demand research and development that could provide new technologies to our first responders, leaders in homeland security, and military to thwart the efforts of terrorists to attack the United States. We believe that this continues to be essential and that there needs to be a concerted effort between detection of these threats and protection capabilities versus just responding. Cost-effective sensors with enhanced capabilities for detecting the presence of chemical and biological material as well as new and improved personal protective capabilities for our military and first responders still continue to be needed to ensure that we can assist casualties and potentially exposed individuals without risking the lives of health-care emergency responders. Indeed, the invention of "Fibertect," the nonwoven decontamination cloth invented at Texas

Tech with support from the U.S. Army, provides an effective decontamination system for chemical agents for human skin and sensitive equipment. This is one example of the leveraging of military-related technology into homeland security applications.

In the development of this book, the authors recognized that the rules of engagement with biological and chemical terrorism strategies are stacked against the civilian population when we are considering a war between state-sponsored organizations and terrorist organizations. In other words, we have observed that terrorists will use any means at any level of intensity to inflict casualties and terror on the people of the United States or any country who oppose their ideology. Therefore, we believe that new fields, such as nanotechnology, should be leveraged for new protective garments and highly mobile and applicable field deployable sensors in materials to assist us in assessing potential biological and chemical threats. This has become even more important as our world has changed considerably since the writing of our last book, *Advances in Biological and Chemical Terrorism Countermeasures*. For instance, we now have available for the world to use social media sites, such as Facebook, LinkedIn, and Twitter, among others. By virtue of the internet, terrorists can connect to coordinate targets and terrorist acts, including biological and chemical threats. The evolution of delivery systems that could be used for biological and chemical terrorist attacks has evolved tremendously. The current use of drone technology for anti-terrorism attacks in Asia has increased considerably. In the meantime, that technology could be reversed and used against us by virtue of being able to deliver biological and chemical weapons of mass destruction in very strategic ways to attack the people of the United States.

As we discussed in our previous book, we must stay ahead of the methodologies and technologies that terrorists may be able to access. For instance, genetically engineered organisms continue to be a significant potential threat of the future with, perhaps, modified strains of plague and smallpox that would, with genetic engineering, be even more difficult to fight if released into a susceptible population, such as the United States. Therefore, we continue to need and seek out new therapeutics that could address the common pathogenic threat agents, particularly from sub-lethal exposures. With the advancement of gene technologies, including genetically modified organisms, there are many new and innovative technologies being developed that could provide therapeutics quickly and could effectively target genetically engineered organisms that may be introduced by terrorists.

One of the most challenging obstacles faced by first responders and warfighters is determining the immediate and long-term extent of the region affected by the release of a chemical and/or biological toxin. Therefore, we need improved monitoring and surveillance that could be incorporated into databases that allow for short-term and long-term risk assessments to first responders as well as warfighters and/or the public in general. Providing training to personnel to understand the basic nature of dispersion processes and to understand the products provided by the modeling community is essential to enabling these personnel to react in an informed manner. Similarly, the National Research Council has recommended that table-top exercises need to be undertaken regularly to ensure that the modeling community understands that the operational needs of first responders and warfighters are met (NRC, 2003). Still, we recognize that limited information may be available that will immediately follow a release event; therefore, continuing research is needed to develop approaches by which live sensor data can be integrated to both characterize the source and improve the fidelity of dispersion predictions in real time as the release event evolves. As computational resources continue to develop, it is expected that the sophistication of meteorological and dispersion models will continue to increase to deliver progressively improving dispersion estimates. We also need to continue to improve and deliver progressively improved estimates.

For military and first responders who are assisting in homeland security efforts, we must improve our ability to protect them in their efforts to assist exposed individuals and casualties. This may be accomplished through improved barrier materials (such as "Fibertect") that could provide protective measures for our first responders and our military as needed, including those with self-detoxifying capabilities. In addition, combinational protective materials are needed that can be quickly applied and that have the ability to protect the wearer from both biological and chemical attacks.

We believe that the applications of research findings, particularly applications that enhance the readiness of our warfighters, can be leveraged to address threats of agrotech terrorism, emerging and resurgent diseases, border security, and security at our ports of entry, including air, land, and sea. We still argue and advocate that we must improve our ability to leverage our technologies and our knowledge to address the continuing threat of biological and chemical terrorist attacks.

We strongly encourage that there be a readily accessible central knowledge repository of emerging and existing biological and chemical threat agents. Although the ECBC Center at the U.S. Army provides such a repository for war-related issues, as far as the domestic homeland we are still yet to ascend to a level of capability of implementing such a response. Even with the realization that the United States remains the target of terrorist plans every day, it is still very difficult to access relevant information to increase research and development countermeasures on these threats. This becomes particularly important when we are not only considering single agents, but mixtures. Therefore, increased effort and scaling of research is necessary to not only address individual biological and chemical terrorist threat agents, but also the consideration in the future of mixtures exposures.

We believe that *New Developments in Biological and Chemical Terrorism Countermeasures* is timely and continues to be highly applicable in the post-9/11 world in which we live. We still believe that the threat of terrorist actions against us using biological and chemical agents is real, but not insurmountable. We need to develop the technologies and cooperation that are necessary to thwarting biological and chemical attacks. Indeed, this will be an issue facing everyone for many years to come, as we have learned. Therefore, we need to maintain the capabilities, resources, and resolve as a nation to take on and overcome this threat in the long run. We offer this book as a tool to assist us in bringing together the state of the knowledge and applying new strategies to address development of chemical and biological terrorist threats to the United States and to other countries.

References

Institute of Medicine and National Research Council. 1999. *Chemical and Biological Terrorism: Research and Development to Improve Civilian Medical Response.* National Academies Press, Washington, DC.

Kendall, R.J., Presley, S.M., Austin, G.P., and Smith, P.N. (eds.) 2008. *Advances in Biological and Chemical Terrorism Countermeasures.* Taylor & Francis/CRC Press, Boca Raton, FL, 280pp.

National Intelligence Council (NIC). July 17, 2007. National intelligence estimate the terrorist threat to the U.S. homeland, press release. National Intelligence Council, Washington, DC. http://www.dna.gov/press_release/20070717_release.pd (accessed July 17, 2007).

National Research Council (NRC). 2003. *Tracking and Predicting the Atmospheric Dispersion of Hazardous Materials Releases—Implications for Homeland Security.* National Academies Press, Washington, DC.

Glossary

Aerosol: A suspension of solid or liquid particles in a gas.

Analyte: A substance or chemical that is detected by an analytical procedure.

Antigen: A molecule that elicits an immune response (i.e., antibody production).

Arthropod vector: The phylum of arthropods includes insects, arachnids, and crustaceans. An arthropod vector is an arthropod, such as a mosquito, that transports pathogens from one host to another.

Biohazard detection systems (BDSs): The Anthrax detection system developed by the United States Postal Service®.

Biological threat agents: Microorganisms or toxins produced by living organisms that may be intentionally employed to cause morbidity or mortality in other living organisms and include bacteria, mycotoxins, rickettsia, toxins, and viruses.

Biological weapons: Microorganisms or toxins produced by living organisms that have been enhanced or modified to more effectively and efficiently cause morbidity or mortality in other living organisms and include bacteria, mycotoxins, rickettsia, toxins, and viruses.

Biosafety Level 4 lab: Required for work with dangerous and exotic agents that pose a high individual risk of aerosol-transmitted laboratory infections and life-threatening disease that is frequently fatal, for which there are no vaccines or treatments, or a related agent with unknown risk of transmission.

Bioterrorism: The calculated use of microorganisms or toxins produced by living organisms that may have been enhanced or modified to more effectively and efficiently cause disease, debilitate, or kill other living organisms in an attempt to intimidate or coerce a government, the civilian population, or any segment thereof, in furtherance of political, religious, or social objectives.

Biotoxins: Poisons that come from plants or animals, such as nicotine, ricin, and strychnine.

BioWatch program: Department of Homeland Security-implemented early warning system for detection of Category A and B agents.

Blister agents: Also known as vesicants, these are chemical weapon compounds that cause severe blistering of the skin and damage to the eyes, mucous membranes, respiratory tract, and internal organs. This class of chemical weapon agent includes the arsenicals/lewisites (L), phosgene oxime (CX), and sulfur mustards (HD, HN).

Blood agents: Also known as cyanogens, they include arsine (SA), cyanogen chloride (CK), and hydrogen chloride (AC) and are transported in the bloodstream through the body. Blood agents do not typically affect the blood but may interrupt the production of blood components and cause toxic effect at the cellular level.

Capsid: The protein or membrane coat that surrounds the genomic nucleic acid (DNA or RNA) of a virus. May be made up of multiple protein species.

Category A agents: Pathogens of the highest priority that have the potential to threaten national security. Examples include anthrax, botulism, plague, smallpox, tularemia, and viral hemorrhagic fevers (including Dengue, Ebola, and Marburg).

Category B agents: Pathogens and toxins of the second highest priority. Examples include Q fever, brucellosis, ricin toxin, typhus fever, mosquito-borne encephalitis viruses, such as West Nile virus and Saint Louis encephalitis, among others.

Category C agents: Agents of the third highest priority and includes emerging pathogens that have the potential to be manipulated for mass dissemination. Examples include Nipah and Hendra viruses, tickborne hemorrhagic fever viruses, yellow fever virus, tuberculosis, influenza virus, and rabies virus, among others.

Cation exchange capacity (CEC): Quantity of cations that an anionic colloid can hold or exchange and is expressed in terms of centimoles per kilogram (cmol/kg).

Caustics (acids): Chemicals that burn or corrode people's skin, eyes, and mucus membranes (lining of the nose, mouth, throat, and lungs) on contact. An example is hydrogen fluoride.

Chemical terrorism: The calculated use of hazardous and toxic compounds or substances that may have been enhanced or modified to more effectively and efficiently debilitate or kill humans in an attempt to intimidate or coerce a government, a civilian population, or any segment thereof, in furtherance of political, religious, or social objectives.

Chemical threat agents: Compounds or substances, either produced naturally or synthetically, that have been designed or modified to maximize exposure through delivery methodologies to cause significant morbidity or mortality in humans and other organisms. These compounds or substances are generally classified as blood agents, choking agents, nerve agents, psychotic agents, and vesicants.

Choking agents: Chemicals that are typically inhaled and cause tissue damage and inflict injury to the respiratory tract (especially the lungs), leading to pulmonary edema and respiratory failure. Such agents include chlorine (CL), chloropicrin (PS), diphosgene (DP), and phosgene (CG).

Clay: (a) A particle less than 0.002 mm in effective diameters, (b) a soil containing a large quantity (>40%) of clay-sized particles, (c) an inorganic particle generally as a layered aluminosilicate but may be fibrous or amorphous.

Concentration: The quantity of material per unit volume. Concentration may be defined in terms of mass per unit volume or the number of moles of material per unit volume.

Convention of chemical weapons: An organization whose goal is to eliminate an entire category of weapons of mass destruction by prohibiting the development, production, acquisition, stockpiling, retention, transfer, or use of chemical weapons by States Parties. States Parties, in turn, must take necessary steps to enforce that prohibition in respect of persons (natural or legal) within their jurisdiction.

Decontamination: Removal or neutralization of toxic agents.

ELISA: Enzyme-linked immunosorbent assay. A biochemical or immunological method by which an analyte is detected in a sample.

Endoplasmic reticulum: An intracellular organelle responsible for protein translation, folding and transport of proteins, and serves as a storage site for calcium.

Enhancement or weaponizing: Utilizing chemical, genetic, or other methods and technologies on biological pathogens, toxins, or chemical substances as a means to improve ease of delivery, longevity in the environment in which it is delivered, pathogenic or toxic effects upon the intended target population, or speed of action once within the intended target population.

Enzootic foci: Locations where a disease has become endemic in a nonhuman population.

Epizootic: Disease affecting many animals at once, similar to an epidemic in humans.

FiberTect®: A three-layer, inert, flexible, drapable, nonwoven composite substrate for absorbing and adsorbing chemical warfare agents (CWA), toxic industrial chemicals (TICs), and pesticides.

GIS: Geographic information system.

Glutamate: Primary excitatory amino acid transmitter in the CNS associated with synaptic development, fast synaptic transmission, memory, and excitotoxicity when present in excessive amounts.

Hypovolemic shock: A state of decreased blood (plasma) volume.

Incapacitating agents: Drugs that make people unable to think clearly or that cause an altered state of consciousness (possibly unconsciousness). These include fentanyls and other opioids.

Lipid rafts: A membrane domain that is enriched in cholesterol.

Liquid crystal (LC): Liquid crystals are substances that exhibit a phase of matter that has properties between those of a conventional liquid and those of a solid crystal. For instance, a liquid crystal (LC) may flow like a liquid but have the molecules in the liquid arranged or oriented in a crystal-like way. There are many different types of LC phases, which can be distinguished based on their different optical properties (such as birefringence).

Long-acting anticoagulants: Poisons, such as super warfarin, that prevent blood from clotting properly, which can lead to uncontrolled bleeding.

Lysogenization: The process by which a bacterium acquires a phage that becomes integrated into its genome.

Macrophages: Important cells of the immune system that are formed in response to an infection or accumulating damaged or dead cells. They are large, specialized cells that recognize, engulf, and destroy target cells.

Metals: Agents that consist of metallic poisons, such as arsenic, mercury, and thallium.

Montmorillonite: Any of a group of clay minerals and their chemical varieties that swell in water and possess high cation-exchange capacities.

Nerve agents: Also known as anticholinesterase agents, they are chemical compounds that inhibit the ability of cholinesterase to hydrolyze acetylcholine, which is essential to mediation of neurotransmitter function in nerve impulses. Nerve agents include VX (*O-ethyl S-(2-diisopropylaminoethyl) methylphosphonothioate*) and the G-series agents tabun (GA)-*dimethylphosphoramido-cyanidate*, sarin (GB)-*isopropl methylphosphonofluoridate*, and soman (GD)-*pinacolyl methyl phosphonofluoridate*.

Nonwoven: Unconventional fabrics wherein fibers are directly converted into fabrics using mechanical, chemical, and thermal methods.

Organic solvents: Agents that damage the tissues of living things by dissolving fats and oils. An example is benzene.

Pathogen: A biological agent that causes disease or illness to its host. The term is most often used for agents that disrupt the normal physiology of a multicellular animal or plant.

Peptide: Short, linear polymers of alpha amino acids formed by covalent bonds between the amino (NH_2) group of one amino acid and the carboxyl (COOH) group of another.

Phage: A virus that infects bacteria. The term can be singular or plural.

Phage display: A high-throughput technique to identify peptides that bind to a specific target molecule.

Plaque: Clear spots in a bacterial lawn caused by phage killing of bacteria as the bacterial lawn is forming.

Polymers: Substances whose molecules have high molar masses and are composed of a large number of repeating units.

Prion: An infectious agent composed of protein in a misfolded form.

Real-time ability: Ability to accept real-time data.

Riot control agents/tear gas: Highly irritating agents normally used by law enforcement for crowd control or by individuals for protection (mace).

Sand: (a) Particle between 2 and 0.05 mm in effective diameter, (b) a soil containing a large quantity (85%) of sand-sized particles.

Selectively permeable membranes: Barrier materials that can let moisture vapor pass through and prevent aerosolized agents and toxic vapors from passing through.

Soil: Unconsolidated, dynamic three-phase system comprised of solids, liquids, and gases found at the Earth's surface that serves as a medium for plant growth.

Soil texture: Percentage of sand-, silt-, and clay-sized particles contained in the soil.

Solid flux density: The mass flow rate of solute across a cross-section per unit area.

Superhydrophobicity: A surface layer that repels water.

Textiles: A type of cloth or woven fabric.

Toxic: Substance that causes adverse effects, morbidity, or mortality in living organisms, with either or both acute or chronic pathology; poisonous.

Toxic alcohols: Poisonous alcohols, such as ethylene glycol, that can damage the heart, kidneys, and the nervous system.

Toxicant: Toxic substances that are produced by or are a by-product of anthropogenic activities.

Toxins: Toxic substances that are produced as metabolic by-products of microorganisms, plants, and animals, and may be used to poison other living organisms.

Vapor pressure: The pressure exerted by a vapor that is in equilibrium with its liquid form.

Vector-borne diseases: Illnesses caused by pathogens and parasites in human populations. Vector-borne diseases rely upon organisms, named vectors, such as mosquitoes, ticks or sandflies, that have an active role in the transmission of a pathogen from one host to the other.

Velocity inflection: A point at which the second derivative of the velocity with respect to height changes sign.

Vomiting agents: Chemicals, such as adamsite (DM), that cause nausea and vomiting.

Weaponized aerosols: Aerosols in a form that optimizes the range of atmospheric transport or the potential for aerosols to deposit within the respiratory system in a manner that maximizes their effect on human targets.

Zoonoses: Diseases that normally exist and are maintained in cycles among wild animals and whose causative pathogen may be transmitted to humans that come into contact with infected animals, or in many instances ectoparasites associated with the infected animals.

Zoonotic: A disease that can be passed between animals and humans. Zoonotic diseases can be caused by viruses, bacteria, parasites, or fungi. These diseases are very common. It is estimated that more than 6 out of every 10 infectious diseases in humans are spread from animals.

Zootic: Pertaining to animals other than humans.

Index